D1463192

Men's
Health
Advisor
1996

Men's Health Advisor 1996

Essential *New* Information about Sex, Fitness *and* Other Male Stuff

Edited by **Michael Lafavore, Men'sHealth Magazine**

Rodale Press, Inc.
Emmaus, Pennsylvania

This book is being published simultaneously as *The Male Almanac*.

Copyright © 1996 by Rodale Press, Inc.

Cover photos copyright © 1996 by Mitch Mandel
Illustrations copyright © 1996 by Jeff Marinelli

Printed in the United States of America on acid-free ∞, recycled paper ♻

ISBN 0–87596–298–X   hardcover

Distributed in the book trade by St. Martin's Press

2   4   6   8   10   9   7   5   3   1   hardcover

——— OUR MISSION ———

We publish books that empower people's lives.

——— RODALE ✣ BOOKS ———

Men's Health Advisor 1996 Editorial Staff

Executive Editor, *Men's Health* Magazine: **Michael Lafavore**

Managing Editor, *Men's Health* Books: **Neil Wertheimer**

Editor: **Brian Chichester**

Book and Cover Designer: **Joe Golden**

Cover Photographer: **Mitch Mandel**

Photo Editor: **Susan Pollack**

Illustrator: **Jeff Marinelli**

Studio Manager: **Joe Golden**

Technical Artists: **Kristen Morgan Downey, William L. Allen**

Layout Designer: **Mary Brundage**

Research Chief, *Men's Health* Magazine: **Melissa Gotthardt**

Office Staff: **Roberta Mulliner, Julie Kehs, Bernadette Sauerwine, Mary Lou Stephen**

Office Manager, *Men's Health* Magazine: **Susan M. Campbell**

Rodale Health and Fitness Books

Vice-President and Editorial Director: **Debora T. Yost**

Art Director: **Jane Colby Knutila**

Research Manager: **Ann Gossy Yermish**

Copy Manager: **Lisa D. Andruscavage**

Contents

4. Disease Free

5. Women and Sex

6. The Looking-Good Guide

7. Man to Man

Introduction

What Men Really Want to Know

We get asked a lot about "the men's movement" at *Men's Health* magazine and books—what it is, why it is, how to join— as if by the nature of what we print, we must be proponents, even spokespeople.

We have a hard time answering these questions. Problem is, we're not sure a men's movement exists, despite all the media attention to the contrary.

Certainly there are more academics and deep thinkers writing today on the state of manhood than ever before. We also hear that annual conferences on male issues are increasingly well-attended. But does all this solidify into a single "movement"? Last I heard, no one is inviting us to take to the streets, or handing out "Join Us!" propaganda. Maybe a few thousand guys have gone to beat-drums-in-the-woods seminars over the past few years, but let's also remember there are more than 90 million adult men in America. Right or wrong, the vast majority of guys continue to deal with challenges in that supremely male way: on their own.

What we do acknowledge is that the world is increasingly busy and complicated and that more men than ever want better information on how to cope with it all. That's not a movement—that's survival.

We don't necessarily buy that malehood is in a state of crisis. Sure, stress levels among many men are rising as the workplace becomes more brutal and the demands of family and community grow stronger. But it isn't so easy being a woman or a kid today, either. Face it—life is a challenge for everyone in these hyperspeed times.

In the face of this, we take an entirely different opinion: that never before has the opportunity for good health, top fitness, great sex, adventurous eating, workplace accomplishment and a happy life been so available. It's true, too. We've come to know immense amounts about health, fitness and diet, and most important, how to achieve the most with the least amount of effort. All it takes is getting our hands on the right instructions.

And there's the rub. Dad's wisest sayings only go so far in this age of Internet, AIDS and corporate downsizing. What's changed is that men increasingly need to go to new sources to get the type of mentoring they need—smart, trustworthy, specific advice that guides you down paths that are only beginning to be pioneered.

Now in its fifth year, *Men's Health Advisor 1996* continues to be that source. From improving your sexual technique to becoming a better salesman, from perfect workout routines to picking the right clothing, this year's model offers tons of useful tips for real guys with little time but lots of vision.

Our writers operate from a common platform: that each of you is in charge of your own health; that not everything is bad for you, and even if it is bad for you, it still might be all right in small doses; that change doesn't come easily and that good health is not merely the absence of illness but a state of being that enriches all aspects of your life, from sexual prowess to workplace performance to fitness challenges.

This book gives you the best current available information on doing better, written 100 percent for active guys like you. We say, forget the men's movement—just get moving.

Michael Lafavore
Executive Editor, *Men's Health* Magazine

PART 1

Eating
Right

Where's the Beef?
(and Other Food Facts)

When you talk about men and food, there's more that meets the eye than just pizza and beer. Here are some facts about guys and grub, based on research recently released.

1. Advertisers label certain foods "male" or "female," based on eating habits of men and women. Male foods include meat, peanut butter, beer, raisins, steak sauce, grapefruit juice, sports drinks, salty snacks and large cookies. Female foods include mint ice cream, hot teas and frozen entrées.

2. Men fork over 66 percent more money when shopping with their kids.

3. On any given day, 18 million men are dieting.

4. Men make more fast-food purchases at convenience stores than women. The most-bought items are soda, coffee, deli sandwiches, breakfast foods and hot dogs.

5. Fifty percent of men use coupons while grocery shopping.

6. Sixty-seven percent of men experience food cravings five to nine times a month. The most common cravings are for steak, hamburger, lasagna and seafood.

7. Seventy-seven percent of married men don't help prepare dinner and 78 percent of married men don't help wash the dishes.

8. Men are more likely to request paper grocery bags than plastic.

9. Eighty-seven percent of all men say they eat low-calorie, sugar-free and/or low-fat foods and drinks at least once every two weeks.

10. Sixty-one percent of men who help buy and prepare food admit that they enjoy grocery shopping.

Minerals for Men

The Naked Truth about "Heavy Metal"

If you're a busy man with too many things on your mind and too little time on your hands, you're probably being cheated out of some precious metals. No, we're not talking silver and gold here—we're talking zinc and magnesium. We're talking minerals.

Just about everything a man's body is supposed to do—from making muscle to making love—requires minerals. Unfortunately, the more full and hectic your lifestyle, the more likely it is that you're not getting your share.

That's because, for most men, keeping track of one's diet often comes in behind a lot of other less important but more pressing things. And that occasionally means forgoing a healthy home-cooked meal and ordering dinner from a clown face instead.

Damning the Drive-Through Diet

Sure, they're convenient. But the trouble with fast foods is that they tend to be mineral-deficient. The richest mineral sources are, by and large, whole-grain products and fresh fruits and vegetables—with emphasis on the word "fresh." Foods that are refined and processed can suffer a significant reduction in their mineral content.

The precise way minerals help you has to do with their interplay with enzymes. Enzymes are proteins made by the body that help with everything from building tissue to fighting disease to speeding messages through networks of nerves. Each one has an important and highly specific job to do. But most enzymes are dormant by nature. They need the right minerals to act on them, switch them on and get them working.

We're not talking about mega-amounts: Consider that the recommended daily intake for all minerals adds up to less than 1 percent of the nutrients in a well-balanced diet. Small, but crucial.

"Without this minute amount, your body wouldn't correctly utilize the foods you eat," says Jeanne Freeland-Graves, Ph.D., professor of nutrition at the University of Texas at Austin.

So if you're too pressed for time to pay attention to your diet, take a multivitamin that contains all the minerals a man needs. It beats robbing your body of what it needs by chowing down on fast food for the rest of your life.

Ironing Out Iron Myths

About the best thing we can say about iron is that it won't kill you. A couple of years ago, researchers from Finland reported on a study that seemed to link iron to heart disease. They found that men with high levels of an iron-storing protein in their blood apparently had double the heart attack risk of men with lower levels. Their small study, which garnered worldwide attention, scared a lot of men who'd been taking iron supplements.

Does iron cause heart disease? The answer, according to further research, appears to be no.

"The evidence for iron as a risk factor is pretty meager," says Meir Stampfer, M.D., Dr.P.H., professor of epidemiology and nutrition at Harvard School of Public Health. In fact, says Dr. Stampfer, since the major dietary source of iron is meat, it could have been the men's intake of meat (and all the accompanying fat and cholesterol) that accounted for the increased rate of heart disease.

But while iron isn't necessarily bad for you, there's no compelling evidence that you need a lot of it unless you're iron-deficient to begin with, Dr. Stampfer says. The bottom line: If you choose to look into mineral supplements, look for brands labeled "For Men," or those that contain no iron.

The Minerals You Need

Here's a list of the minerals that every man needs. Remember, you don't need to OD on them, but you do need them.

Zinc. This important metal is intricately tied up with your potency, your fertility—even your sex drive. And the more sexually active you are, the more you need it. Every time you ejaculate, it costs you 420 micrograms of the stuff.

In fact, any kind of physical activity can be costly to your zinc supplies, since minute amounts also pass out of the body in sweat. Research has linked low zinc stores to decreases in semen volume and low blood levels of testosterone. Zinc is also vital for wound healing, immunity and the senses of smell and taste.

Another benefit for men: There's evidence that zinc sulfate supplements may be helpful in controlling benign prostate enlargement, a noncancerous swelling of the prostate that's common in men over 50 and afflicts 80 percent of men over 60.

One four-ounce helping of lean beef provides almost half the 15 milligrams of zinc you need daily. Other good sources are turkey, oysters (a single oyster gives you a full day's supply), cereals and beans.

Calcium. One in four men suffers from high blood pressure. Why? Part of the problem may be that we don't get enough calcium. The Framingham Heart Study, which tracked 432 men for 18 years, found that men who consumed the highest levels of this mineral had a 20 percent lower risk of developing high blood pressure than men who consumed the lowest levels.

Calcium is also a major building block of bone. If you can't remember the last time you drank a glass of milk, keep in mind that your bones have to pony up the difference when your body needs to use its store of calcium for other functions such as the maintenance of blood, muscles and nerves. A

persistent calcium deficit in your diet will leave bones weak and brittle. That condition, osteoporosis, is not just a women's problem; one-third of the hip fractures tied to this condition occur in men.

The Recommended Dietary Allowance of calcium for men is 800 milligrams daily. You'll get 300 milligrams in a single glass of milk. Other good sources are canned salmon or sardines and many garden greens.

Copper. Here's another warrior in the battle against heart disease, yet two out of three of us get less than the recommended minimum of 1.5 to 3 milligrams a day.

Serious copper deficiency, although rare, can raise cholesterol and blood pressure and lead to problems with maintaining heart rhythms. Also, like zinc, it plays an important role in the function of the immune system, making sure that T-cells and antibodies are working optimally. You get copper from nuts, peas and beans, fruits, oysters and shellfish.

Chromium. An estimated three million men are walking around with early signs of diabetes and don't even know it. Taking this mineral could protect them from full-blown diabetes by boosting their bodies' ability to regulate blood sugar levels. Keeping chromium stores up also seems to help the body manage stress.

Fruits, vegetables, fish and chicken will supply some of the body's needs. But a good diet alone isn't likely to get you adequate stores of chromium, says Richard Anderson, Ph.D., a biochemist with the U.S. Department of Agriculture Human Nutrition Research Center in Beltsville, Maryland. Dr. Anderson recommends taking a daily supplement to assure you the male-recommended dose of 50 to 200 micrograms. Two chromium-fortified tablets of brewer's yeast should do the trick.

Magnesium. Heading to the gym? You won't get much of a workout without magnesium, which plays a critical role in muscle activity. Research suggests that getting your fair share may double your strength gains from resistance training.

Another vital role magnesium plays is to protect against heart disease, which kills more than 350,000 men a year. The mineral appears to encourage artery dilation and inhibit blood clotting.

A good magnesium goal is 350 milligrams. You'll get more than one-third of this by eating a breakfast of two cups shredded wheat, a glass of skim milk and a banana. Cooked spinach contains over 150 milligrams a cup. The mineral is also found in seafood, nuts and meats.

Selenium. This disease-fighter has been linked to decreased risks for skin, lung and stomach cancers, which will kill more than 100,000 men this year. The mineral works closely with vitamin E to protect cells from damage by oxygen-containing molecules called free radicals.

"Selenium can replace vitamin E in some functions," says Dr. Freeland-Graves. The Recommended Dietary Allowance of selenium for men is a minuscule 70 micrograms per day, but even moderately low levels can cause anxiety and feelings of tiredness. Good sources include grains, fish and vegetables such as broccoli, cucumbers, onions, garlic, radishes and mushrooms.

—Carol Ann Shaheen

Meal Plans

A Guy's Guide to Cutting the Fat

Everybody knows too much fat in your diet is bad for you, so let's just skip the gruesome details (heart disease). We're not going to bore you with a whole list of reasons why you need to cut down on fat (diabetes). The last thing you need is another diatribe about the hazards of too many chili dogs (high blood pressure). Because, dammit, you want to look on the bright side of life (cancer). Right?

Right. Are we not men? Do we not crave calzones and T-bones and Dad's chili con carne recipe, fiery hot and loaded with ground chuck? We do! And we will eat these things and revel in the greasy and deliciously unhealthy flavors and march to those counters at those shopping malls and outlet stores and proudly declare, "I'd like the size 38 relaxed-fit stretch jeans, please."

All right, look. You eat too much fat. I eat too much fat. We're guys. It's what we do. And we have no intention of cutting out the best things in life just so we can live longer, but more miserably. Still, though, it'd be nice to fit into last fall's pants again. And sticking around long enough to party at your grandkid's fraternity is an admirable goal.

Flushing Fat without Fluster

The key to cutting fat is not wiping it out entirely, but sneaking it out in ways you'll hardly ever notice.

"Trim fat gradually, where you won't miss it," suggests Connie Diekman, R.D., a nutrition consultant and spokesperson for the American Dietetic Association. "If you like pizza and beer with your buddies on Friday nights, that's not where you want to cut."

It's the gradual, hard-to-notice adjustments in the diet that get results, she says. For example, knocking back from two pats of butter on your morning toast to one will save you 34 fat calories without a lot of heartache. In a week, you'll have saved nearly 250 fat calories. In 15 weeks, you'll have saved more than 3,500 calories of pure fat—which translates into a full pound of body weight.

Now, mushroom those savings by scraping a little fat from all of your meals. You'll feel more alert and more energetic in no time—not to mention lighter on your feet. How do you do this? Below we've compiled dozens of easy ways, with emphasis on "easy."

Breakfast: Rise and Eat Right

When you wake up in the morning with the appetite of a lumberjack and you're hankering for a man-size breakfast, here are some quick tips on breaking your fast right.

Think fruit first. Have some melon or grapefruit, then move to the less healthy stuff—you'll get your vitamins and fiber, and you'll eat less of what could ail you.

Don't be yellow when cooking eggs. It's the egg yolks that are bad, not the whites. If you want a three-egg omelet, use one whole egg and two egg whites. You won't taste any difference, and you'll be saving ten grams of fat and 426 milligrams of cholesterol. Use the same recipe for French toast.

Hash it out with hash browns. For healthy hash browns, pick up a pack of frozen hash-brown potato patties. Do not read the cooking instructions (trust us). Instead, do this: Brown them in a nonstick skillet coated with cooking spray. Use medium heat and give them about 12 minutes per side to make them crispy. Fat savings: about ten grams per serving over homemade hash browns fried in oil.

Copy the Canadians when makin' bacon. When you absolutely need bacon, have some Canadian bacon. You can eat twice as much for less than half the fat. Two medium slices (about 1½ ounces) has just 4 grams of fat, compared to 9.4 for three slices (¾ ounce) of regular bacon.

Forget frying the flapjacks. Pop a pancake in your toaster instead of frying it in a pan. Aunt Jemima Low-Fat Pancakes are frozen and ready for toasting. They have just ½ gram of fat per three-hotcake serving, instead of the 6 that come with the kind you make from batter.

Watch that stuffin' in your muffin. Bran muffins sound innocent, but many are astoundingly high in fat. Some contain up to 12 grams, almost as much as a hamburger. An exception to this rule: low-fat muffins, such as those made by Hostess.

JUST THE FACTS

Percentage decline in U.S. egg consumption since 1984: 32

Lighten up, Joe. Lighten your coffee with evaporated skim milk instead of half-and-half. It's creamy because it has less water, not more fat. Savings: 3.5 grams of fat and 14 calories.

Nixing Noontime Fat

Sandwiches are the architecture of the common man, but you need to start with a solid foundation. Don't let lunchtime be blubber time.

Hail the hierarchy. The hierarchy of health, in descending order: turkey and chicken; roast beef; ham; weird processed things like salami and olive loaf. For example, instead of an Italian submarine sandwich with cheese and mixed cold cuts like salami and bologna, choose a roast beef hero and you'll trim your fat intake by 30 percent.

Try a healthy tune-up for your tuna. Don't turn a perfectly good sandwich of water-packed tuna (two grams of fat per three-ounce serving) into a fatty disaster by mixing in a lot of mayonnaise. Instead, squeeze lemon juice and add pepper and hot-pepper sauce into your tuna. It tastes great—and it'll pack less fat.

Ask for "extra lean" or "reduced fat" ham at your deli counter. Enough of this type of ham for a manly sandwich will burden you with less than three grams of fat, compared with six grams for regular ham.

Try a micro-melt. For a less greasy grilled cheese sandwich, don't fry it. Start by toasting two slices of bread. When done, slip a slice of reduced-fat Cheddar cheese between them. Place the sandwich on a paper towel in the microwave. Cook on high for 25 seconds to melt the cheese. Fat savings: eight grams.

Taste the "grateness" of cheese. When it comes to cheese, get handy with a cheese grater. Grate a piece of Parmesan or other hard cheese on your sandwich and you'll save boffo fat calories over the standard sliced fare.

JUST THE FACTS

The most germ-infested spot in the house, believe it or not, is the surface of a used dishcloth or sponge.

Eat a no-meat monster sandwich, Italian-style. Make a meat-less hot Italian sub the next time you're hankering for a veal Parmesan sandwich. Brown some cubed eggplant pieces under a broiler with a little olive oil. Then mix with tomato sauce and capers. Place in a kaiser roll. Top with grated Parmesan. Fat savings: 18 grams.

Pour the fat away on a PB&J. For a lighter peanut butter sandwich, buy natural peanut butter, the kind where the oil rises to the top. Pour out the oil before you make a sandwich and you'll pour away the fat.

Avoid that Reuben-esque look. Sure, Reuben sandwiches are good. But all that cheese and fatty corned beef isn't good for you. Simulate a cheese Reuben by replacing corned beef with turkey ham and topping it off with low-fat mozzarella, mustard, spicy shredded cabbage and pickles. Slap all that on traditional rye bread and broil until the cheese melts. Fat savings: ten grams.

Suppertime Strategies

Far be it from us to deny you your carnivorous pleasures. When nothing will do but a serious piece of meat, simply hunt and gather wisely.

Look around for less fat. When it comes to red meat, choose leaner "round" cuts. A top-round steak contains 8.4 grams of fat per six-ounce serving, whereas a ribeye steak contains 20 grams.

Cut the fat. Always trim visible fat from meat before cooking. You'll recognize the fatty portions because they're white. For example, three ounces of untrimmed beef chuck arm has 21.9 grams of fat. Trimmed, the same cut has 7.4 grams.

Free yourself from the frying pan. Frying is the worst way to cook anything. That's because your food is simply sitting in butter or oil, having a gay old time absorbing all that pure liquid fat and delivering it straight to your belly. To cut back on the bad stuff, follow these simple rules.

- Use a cooking spray instead of oil or butter. You'll save on fat no matter what you're cooking.
- Don't bread your meats and fish. Bread crumbs tend to soak

up a large amount of cooking oil and fat.
- Heat the skillet before adding oil. Less fat will be absorbed by the food. Warm oil cooks more efficiently; cold oil tends to soak into meats and vegetables.
- Learn pseudo-sautéing. Instead of stir-frying, cook vegetables in a skillet or wok with their own natural moisture. Begin with the tiniest quantity of oil and add water—not more oil—as needed for additional moisture.

Stay out of the dark. When it comes to chicken, remember that white meat contains about one-third less fat than dark. If you can bear to pass up the skin, you'll save a lot of fat calories.

Have a rack attack. When you roast meat, use a rack. The fat drips off so the meat doesn't stew in it, reabsorbing all the bad stuff. If it's warm out, barbecue. Same deal.

Watch fat take flight from your Buffalo wings. Enjoy spicy, low-fat Buffalo wings, but instead of using chicken wings, make them with skinless chicken-breast tenders. Marinate overnight in a mixture of Louisiana hot sauce, olive oil, lots of garlic powder and red-wine vinegar. (Experiment with the amounts to suit your taste.) Then roast the chicken "wings" at 400° for 15 minutes.

Take the OJ additive. If you have a can of frozen orange juice concentrate, you have a great way to add flavor to stir-fried chicken or beef and vegetables without adding fat. Just a few spoonfuls will do (great if you add garlic, too).

Slice and savor low-fat french fries. Instead of deep-fried french fries, make low-fat oven fries. Slice baking potatoes into wedges, sprinkle with ground red pepper and roast in the oven until brown. Fat savings: 12 grams per serving.

Avoid fat while getting sauced. If you're making your own spaghetti sauce, look for the "seasoned stewed" varieties of canned tomatoes. They tend to be lower in oil than those labeled "pasta ready." That means they're lower in fat and better for you.

JUST THE FACTS

The average American eats 7.4 pounds of carrots in any given year.

Your Just Desserts

Sometimes it's wise to skip the dessert. Other times—for example, when your brother-in-law's buying—you have to take advantage of the dessert tray. At home or in a fancy bistro, here are some smart moves.

Stop viewing cookies in black and white. Put away the Oreos (213 calories and nine grams of fat for four) and try low-fat and no-fat cookies. It'll not only expand your cookie horizons, it'll help keep those tasty snacks from sticking to your stomach. Tasty choices: R. W. Frookie Fat-Free Apple Spice Cookies, Entenmann's Oatmeal Raisin Cookies, Nabisco SnackWell's Reduced-Fat Chocolate Sandwich Cookies and A Whale of a Snack fat-free fruit bars (fig, apple, blueberry and strawberry) from Fleetwood Snacks.

Get cultured with yogurt. Substitute nonfat frozen yogurt for ice cream and you'll save more than seven grams of fat per single-scoop cone. But make sure you look for "nonfat" on the label; some frozen yogurts have as much fat as ice cream.

Dig divine dessert for snack attacks. Instead of taking a huge gooey hunk of Black Forest cake, go for the dessert of the gods: angel food cake. Get a huge slice of angel food cake topped with sliced fresh strawberries or peaches and a scoop of frozen yogurt. Since angel food cake has no fat, you'll get the fat only from the yogurt. Not a bad deal for a satisfying dessert.

Surviving Snack Attacks

Cooking is a skill. Snacking is an art. Between beers, look for these healthier alternatives to the standard chips-and-sour-cream-dip regimen.

Do the twist. Pretzels are better than chips. So when you're looking for finger food between brews, pick the basket of pretzels.

Don't go with the glow. If it leaves an unnatural orange glow on your fingertips, you shouldn't be eating it.

Buy nuts in their shells. More time spent shelling means less time eating. Shelled nuts are too easy to swallow by the handful and they're higher in fat than those in the shell. Eat just two handfuls of shelled roasted peanuts and you've downed nearly 28 grams

of fat. Shell them your-
self and you can save 10
grams. Should you find
yourself in the vicinity of
an open fire, try roasted
chestnuts. They have barely any fat.

**Look for Louise's Fat-
Free Potato Chips.** Most
regular chips are fried in
shortening. These are baked—and not
bad, either. If you're in the mood for tortilla chips, make your own
low-fat variety. Buy some corn tortillas, cut them into wedges and
bake at 375° on a baking sheet until crisp. Fat savings: eight
grams per ten chips.

Send nacho fat south of the border. Nachos are *muy delicioso*,
but they can also make you *muy gordo*. So make yourself a heap
o' low-fat cheese nachos: Top a plate of those low-fat tortilla
chips with a mound of salsa. Then sprinkle with nonfat Cheddar
cheese and broil or microwave just long enough to soften the
cheese. Fat savings per serving over standard cheese nachos: nine
grams.

Make your own dips. Make your own dips using nonfat sour
cream or yogurt. Mix in an equal part of salsa—the hotter the
better. Jazz it up with lemon, dried herbs, whatever.

—Jeffrey Csatari

Eating Clear of Cancer

The Right Rations May Be Your Miracle Medicine

If there's one thing you can learn from the television news, it's this: Fear is a highly marketable commodity. Just look at how those overpaid haircuts cover health news, for example. "Slow death in your refrigerator! . . . Story at 11." Watch enough of this drivel and you'll wonder why they don't just drape a big Biohazard sign over the entrance to your local supermarket.

Well, get ready for some good news. There are thousands of foods that will protect you from disease and very few that, if eaten in moderation, will do you any harm. Studies suggest that your risks of disease aren't affected by what you do eat so much as by what you don't eat. Have a bowl of junk food once in a while—just don't forget the produce, grains and other good foods your body needs regularly.

These foods are particularly effective at cutting your risk for cancer. It's the second leading cause of death for American men, and it's not radon, secondhand smoke, cellular telephones or staring into our microwaves that causes most cases. It's our diets. Experts estimate that eating poorly is responsible for up to 70 percent of all cancers, says Gladys Block, Ph.D., professor of public-health nutrition at the University of California, Berkeley.

You know you need to exercise, stop smoking and get regular checkups, including a prostate exam every year after age 40. (And if you didn't know that, you do now.) You also know enough to cut your fat intake as much as possible: Less than 30 percent of your total calories should come from fat, and even that's kind of pushing it (20 percent is better). But beyond that, you can protect yourself from cancer with a few simple eating strategies that, quite frankly, are not much of a stretch. Here they are.

Vary the greens. Plenty of studies have shown that certain foods, such as broccoli, oranges and carrots, have particular cancer-fighting powers. The problem is, you won't be healthy if you subsist only on a diet of broccoli, oranges and carrots. Experts now say that different foods and nutrients work together as a team to combat cancer. Concentrate only on a few good foods and you'll miss the health benefits that lie hidden in everything from tomatoes to tangerines. So shoot for nine servings of different fruits and vegetables every day. Somewhere on that list, try to include:

- One serving of citrus fruits, like oranges or grapefruit. Lime margaritas don't count, but tangerines and tangelos do.
- One serving of a cruciferous vegetable. That means broccoli, cauliflower, brussels sprouts or cabbage, all of which contain chemicals with names such as indoles, iso-thiocyanates and monoterpenes, which are proven to fight cancer and cause serious injury when pronounced correctly. Also try bok choy, an Asian cabbage that cooks up with more flavor than its domestic cousin.
- One serving of dark green, leafy vegetables such as spinach or romaine lettuce. Avoid iceberg lettuce, which is nearly worthless nutritionally.
- One serving of something yellow or orange, including carrots, sweet potatoes or squash. Cheese puffs don't count.

You're probably thinking this sounds impossible in an average day. It's not. Have half a grapefruit and throw some berries on your cereal at breakfast, eat a big spinach salad with some carrots, peppers and tomatoes at lunch, and order broccoli or brussels sprouts

JUST THE FACTS

University of Nebraska researchers say that stir-fried beef retains more vitamins and nutrients than microwaved or broiled beef. Taste-testers also say it tastes the best.

with dinner. Now throw in an apple and a banana for a snack and you're home free.

Here are some other tips on keeping cancer at bay with what's in your kitchen cabinets.

Go with the grain. The three biggest cancer threats to men are lung, colon and prostate cancer. The first one you avoid by not lighting up. As for the other two, think whole-wheat bread.

When you eat whole grains such as wheat and oat bran, you're eating fiber—insoluble fiber, which means you can't digest it, which means it passes through your body like a land developer through the rain forest. The stuff not only scours your plumbing of all evil, thereby lowering your chances of colon cancer, but also may help rid your body of cancer-causing agents that threaten the prostate and pancreas.

We're talking a minimum of six daily servings of high-fiber cereal, breads or grain dishes. Have a bowl of oatmeal for breakfast with some whole-grain toast, a sandwich on whole-wheat bread with some beef barley soup for lunch and a side of brown rice with dinner. You're covered.

Jump for soy. Soybeans and soy-based foods such as tofu,

Top Ten Cancer-Fighting Foods

Science has shown that eating lots of fruits and vegetables can help you avoid disease. But you may want to know which ones work best. Here, according to Patrick Quillin, R.D., Ph.D., vice-president for nutrition at Cancer Treatment Institutes of America and author of *Beating Cancer with Nutrition,* are the top cancer-fighting foods and the chemicals in them that make them so tough.

Food	Active Ingredients
1. Broccoli	Sulforaphane, beta-carotene, indole-carbinol
2. Tomatoes	Lycopene
3. Spinach	Glutathione
4. Oranges	Bioflavonoids, vitamin C
5. Garlic	Allicin
6. Apples	Elagic acid, fiber
7. Soybeans	Genistein
8. Carrots	Beta-carotene, fiber
9. Hot red peppers	Capsaicin
10. Green tea	Catechin

tempeh and soy milk contain a chemical known as genistein. In test-tube studies, this chemical stymies the growth of precancerous cells in the prostate. Consider the fact that rates of prostate cancer are considerably lower in cultures that include soy dishes in their diets. Then consider the fact that soy may also help reduce your cholesterol levels. Then consider whether or not real men eat tofu.

But, seriously, you're not going to sit down and eat a chunk of tofu for dinner. (Well, maybe you are, but we're not.) Here are a few painless ways to add soy to your diet a couple of times a week.

- Try soy milk. It has a vaguely nutty flavor, and with breakfast cereal, that might be a good thing. For snacks, try flavored soy milks. Edensoy Vanilla is one brand that performed well in a taste test for us.
- Try a smoothie. Pour three cups unflavored soy milk into a blender with a ripe banana and one cup frozen strawberries. Mix, then drink.
- Hide the tofu. Slice it into salads, canned tuna or stir-fry dishes or add it to your favorite lasagna recipe. Just about any time you make a chicken dish, replace half the chicken with tofu and you'll hardly notice the difference.
- Learn to bake. Soy flour can give you the same cancer-fighting benefits as other soy products, but it looks, tastes and acts like regular flour.

Two caveats: Stick to low-fat (1 percent fat) tofu, soy milk and soy flour. Regular versions of these products get anywhere from 30 to more than 50 percent of their calories from fat. And no, the health benefits of soy don't apply to soy sauce.

Bait your plate. You've been hyped to death about how omega-3 fatty acids—the kind of fats found in certain seafoods—can protect you from heart disease. Overlooked in all the happy heart news is some real evidence that seafood may play other positive roles as well. For example, seafood is a great source of selenium, a mineral that may help protect men from prostate and pancreatic cancers. Some of the best sources of these nutrients are herring, salmon, sardines, mackerel, swordfish, whitefish and Pacific oysters. *Bon appétit!*

—Jeff Stevenson

PART 2

Youthful
Living

TOP TEN

USA's Richest Young Men

Here are the youngest on a recent list from Forbes *magazine of the nation's 400 richest people.*

1. Bill Gates—early forties/$9.4 billion
Dropped out of Harvard at 19 to co-found Microsoft, the world's largest computer software company.

2. Jim C. Walton—late forties/$4.34 billion
One of the heirs to the riches of his discount king dad, Sam Walton, founder of Wal-Mart and Sam's Club stores.

3. John T. Walton—late forties/$4.34 billion
Vietnam vet who inherited much of his money from his father's reigning discount businesses, Wal-Mart and Sam's Club stores.

4. Paul G. Allen—early forties/$3.9 billion
Teamed up with computer guru Gates to write the Basic computer language for PCs, and again to start Microsoft in 1975.

5. Robert Muse Bass—late forties/$2 billion
Gained much of his cash from an oil tycoon uncle. Made high-profile deals in the media, banking and real estate markets.

6. Stephen Anthony Ballmer—late thirties/$1.8 billion
Raised by a hard-working Swiss immigrant father. Met Bill Gates at Harvard and later joined him at Microsoft.

7. Lee Marshall Bass—late thirties/$1.8 billion
Inherited oil holdings from Uncle Sid Richardson, an oil tycoon who died before Bass's birth.

8. Riley P. Bechtel—midforties/ $1.4 billion
CEO of his dad's worldwide construction company.

9. Bennett Dorrance—late forties/$1.2 billion
Grandfather created the process for making condensed soup. Won a fight to maintain family control of the Campbell Soup Company.

10. Winthrop Paul Rockefeller—late forties/$1 billion
Great-grandson of John D. Rockefeller.

What's Your True Age?

Find Out with This Total-Body Test

The first time always hurts. And it always hurts bad. It happens to most of us in our midtwenties—though for the lucky ones, it may come a few years later. But eventually, it happens.

It usually goes something like this: A young woman walks your way along a busy street, her stride full of youthful confidence, her face flushed with future possibilities. She slows as you approach, turns her baby blues upward to meet yours, parts those lips that speak of prom nights and first kisses . . . and strikes you dead—with one word.

"Excuse me, sir."

Sir. Is there any more heartbreaking word for a man to hear in such a situation? It sums up its message so succinctly: You have passed into another age, and there's no going back. The female equivalent, of course, is "ma'am," and if you don't think looks can kill, try addressing any 32-year-old woman with the word and see if the daggers don't shoot straight out of her eyes.

There's good reason for such defensiveness. On the one hand, we realize that there are predictable physical declines that occur over time and that they usually kick in at roughly the same point for all of us. At the same time, we instinctively grasp the biological maxim that people can age at vastly different rates. In other words, there's an aging curve, and you can be either ahead of or behind it. The question, as the great Satchel Paige once put it, is, "How old would you be if you didn't know how old you was?"

Let's find out. Use this compendium of simple tests to take a reading of how well you've aged. Bear in mind that age is an accumulation of changes. If you consistently score above average, you're obviously a fine specimen and we should be taking lessons from you instead of the other way around. If you consistently score below average, you probably need help youth-wise and will want to pay special attention to the prevention and fix-up pointers we've included.

Vision

As Bill Clinton has learned, even a young president can lack "the vision thing." Virtually all of us will have trouble focusing on objects close up by our midsixties or -seventies, the result of a condition known as presbyopia (not to be confused with "Presleyopia," which is an inability to see Elvis when everybody else claims he's still around).

With age, the lens becomes less pliable, so it can't make vision-correcting shape changes as easily. This starts as early as the teens but typically doesn't become noticeable until the forties, according to Martin Birnbaum, O.D., a professor at the State University of New York College of Optometry in New York City.

The Test: Fine-print reading. Hold the stock page from the financial section of a newspaper at arm's length and slowly move it closer to your face. Note how far the paper is from your eyes when the numbers begin to blur. Depending what decade you're in, you should be able to read the fine print all the way from arm's length in to a distance of:

> *Twenties:* 6 to 7 inches
> *Thirties:* 10 inches
> *Forties:* 13 inches
> *Fifties and beyond:* More than 13 inches

"Those in their fifties and beyond will have difficulty focusing on anything closer than arm's length," Dr. Birnbaum explains.

What to Do: From a practical standpoint, presbyopia isn't a problem until it bothers you. Still, Dr. Birnbaum suggests that dealing with it early can help your eyes generally work more efficiently, possibly warding off declines in distance vision.

Presbyopia can't be reversed, but it can be compensated for. You'll need to go to an optometrist or ophthalmologist and get a prescription for bifocals. And, no, they needn't make you look like your grandfather. The new generation of bifocals don't have a fogyish straight edge across the middle of the lens. Instead, they change thickness gradually from top to bottom, so no one can tell that the glasses you're wearing are actually bifocals. Initial versions of these lenses often distorted vision at the sides, but that problem has largely been eliminated. Ask your optometrist for one of the new designs, such as the Varilux Comfort lens.

Upper-Body Strength

Between ages 30 and 80, muscle power in men declines by 30 to 40 percent, according to Leonard Hayflick, Ph.D., author of *How and Why We Age.* But experts say that happens only if you take this news lying down. The fact is, if you keep muscles working, they'll retain their youthful strength well into your later years. With strength comes related benefits, such as greater bone density, more efficient fat-burning metabolism and better posture.

The Test: Chair-lifts. Sit on the edge of an armless chair or bench with your legs straight out so that your heels are on the floor and your toes are pointing up. Place both hands on the sides of the chair seat and inch forward off the chair so that you're supported by your heels and hands. Now lower yourself until your butt touches the floor. Hold for one second, then push back up. "It's a more accurate test than something like push-ups, because you can't cheat on it," says *Men's Health* magazine strength-training adviser Wayne Westcott, Ph.D., who is also the YMCA's national strength-training consultant. A man of moderate strength should be able to do ten of these in his twenties, with power falling off about 10 percent per decade. The curve with age:

> *Thirties:* Nine lifts
> *Forties:* Eight lifts
> *Fifties:* Seven lifts
> *Sixties and beyond:* Six lifts

What to Do: Weight exercises like bench and military presses, as well as simple push-ups, will keep your upper-body muscles up to par. But the single best exercise is the test's chair-lift move, which simultaneously works the chest, triceps, shoulders and midback. Do as many repetitions as you can comfortably, taking two seconds to lower and two seconds to raise up again, with a one-second pause in between. Do two sets.

Lower-Body Strength

The same declines men see in their arms, shoulders and chest can occur in the lower body as well. That, in the long run, leads to creaky knees and painful falls.

The Test: One-minute squats. To say the major muscles of the lower body are in decent shape, you should have both power and endurance. The object of this move isn't to exert bursts of strength in multiple short moves but to do a slow burn with one long move.

Stand with your feet shoulder-width apart. Keeping your feet flat on the floor, very slowly bend your knees to lower your body toward the floor, taking 30 seconds to reach a point at which your hips are just below parallel with your knees. Take another 30 seconds to raise yourself back to starting position. A guy in his twenties should have enough strength and staying power to go the full minute. With age, it's normal to have to cheat, knocking 5 to 8 seconds off this time. And don't try this test if you have a history of serious knee problems, or you might be asking for trouble.

Thirties: 52 to 55 seconds
Forties: 44 to 50 seconds
Fifties: 38 to 45 seconds
Sixties and beyond: 40 seconds or less

What to Do: For lower-body strength, squats also hit multiple muscles: the thighs, hamstrings and buttocks. As an exercise, shorten the down portion to 12 seconds and the up portion to 10 seconds. To prevent injury from repeated motion, halt the squat when your thighs are just above parallel with the floor. Do two sets of as many repetitions as you can. You may want to progress to using weights when this exercise becomes too easy.

Aerobic Fitness

Old guys with efficient hearts and lungs can literally run circles around younger guys on the basketball court. If you're aerobically fit, you don't just have get up and go, you have energy to keep going and going. The payoff: a better ticker and better oxygen delivery, which can also make your brain sharper.

The Test: Step-ups. This is a three-minute test for which you'll need to find or fashion an eight-inch step (a standard height for most household steps). Step up with one foot, then the other, then step down with one foot, followed by the other. Each up-up, down-down cycle is four counts. Using a watch to time yourself, move at a steady cadence of about 20 four-count cycles per minute. (To help yourself keep track, try counting cycles like this: 1-2-3-1, 1-2-3-2, 1-2-3-3, and so on until you hit 1-2-3-20.) When three minutes have elapsed, take your pulse: Put your index and middle fingers on the arteries of your wrist. Count beats for 15 seconds, then multiply this number by four to get the beats per minute. Now match your fitness level with your heart rate per minute, using the "average" numbers below. These are based on the assumption that you're moderately active, exercising between 10 and 60 minutes per week and regularly involved in recreation or work requiring some heavy effort.

Twenties: 120 beats per minute or less, average; 150 or more, poor; below 90, excellent

Thirties: 130 beats per minute or less, average; 160 or more, poor; below 90, excellent

Forties: 140 beats per minute or less, average; 170 or more, poor; below 95, excellent

Fifties and beyond: 145 beats per minute or less, average; 170 or more, poor; below 95, excellent

What to Do: To build aerobic capacity, do aerobic exercise at moderate intensity for at least 20 minutes three or more times a week. Good activities include: walking, running, cycling, cross-country skiing and, of course, stair-climbing. For a more detailed exercise prescription based on this test, contact the Step Company at 1-800-729-7837.

Flexibility

Does the word "creaky" mean anything to you? Feeling stiff and constrained is almost entirely a matter of flexibility—which is easily improved by making sure you put muscles through the motions they're designed for. One basic measure of flexibility is how far your back and legs allow you to reach.

The Test: Toe touches. Sit on the floor with your left leg straight in front of you. Tuck the heel of your right foot against your left thigh so that your legs make a figure 4. Reach your left arm as far as you can toward your toes. Flexibility doesn't necessarily change much from decade to decade, says Dr. Westcott—unless you're a couch potato. Between ages 20 and 40, here's how you rate, depending on your reach.

Wrist to toes: Good
Fingertips to toes: Average
Fingers to ankle: Fair
Fingers to sock line: Poor

Between ages 40 and 60, this scale shifts down a notch, so, for example, reaching fingertips to toes earns a "good" rating, with anything better being exceptional.

What to Do: The antidote to poor flexibility is stretching. Performing the fingers-to-toes stretch is ideal for stretching the lower back and hamstrings, which are essential for fluid movement in both the upper and lower body. When performing this move as an exercise, reach as far as is comfortable without bouncing, holding the position for 30 seconds. Repeat on the other side.

Body Fat

When doctors measure fat, they use high-tech flab-squeezing instruments called calipers. No access to current sports-medicine technology? Then close the fingers of one hand and make a C with the forefinger and thumb. What do you have? Right, a caliper.

The Test: Tricep pinch. Enlist a partner to hold a ruler. Extend your arm straight in front of you, palm up. Grab the skin on the back of your upper arm (the side facing down) between your thumb and fingers, and gently pull it away from the arm, trying not to pinch the skin too tightly. Have your partner measure the thickness of the skin held between your fingers and thumb (not the distance it's being pulled out).

Ages 20 to 39: ¾ inch of skin, average; ½ inch, good

Ages 40 to 60: ⅞ inch of skin, average; ⅝ inch, good

What to Do: The best way to cut down your body-fat percentage is to eat a low-fat diet (aim for 30 percent of calories or less) and take up aerobic exercise. The best fat-burning workouts are those that target as many of the body's muscles as possible, Dr. Westcott says. Good bets are rowing, cross-country skiing and hiking.

Skin

Wrinkles happen. Why? Loss of skin tone. As skin becomes less taut, sun damage, facial patterns and gravity conspire to make it sag and bunch together. It happens everywhere in the body, but the parts exposed to the elements take the worst beating. Changes in elasticity start during youth, but really kick in after about age 45.

The Test: Top-of-the-hand tug. The two areas that get the most sun are your face and your hands. To get an idea how supple the skin of your face is, pinch the skin on the back of your hand for four or five seconds, then let it go. Count the number of seconds it takes to snap back to its original smoothness. What you can expect:

25 to 34: 1 second

35 to 44: 2 seconds

45 to 64: 11 seconds

65 to 69: 20 seconds

70 and beyond: 50 seconds

What to Do: Forget the miracle cures like herbal baths and mud packs. Honest-to-goodness, scientifically proven wrinkle-erasers exist, in the form of Retin-A and its cousin, glycolic acid. Both make the outer skin shed dead cells faster, uncovering younger, less wrinkled skin. Ask your dermatologist for a prescription.

And while you're at it, stay out of the sun. It accounts for 90 percent of skin deterioration.

Nails

Granted, nails aren't exactly a top concern for most guys, but they do say a lot about how you're aging, if you look closely.

The Test: Hold any finger under a bright light so the light hits the nail. Now slowly turn your finger 45 degrees to the left, then to the right. What you'll see are the signs of aging, such as brittleness and ridges running from the tip of the nail to the cuticle, says Richard K. Scher, M.D., professor of dermatology and head of the Nail Section at Columbia-Presbyterian Medical Center in New York City. The changes come slowly, but here's what to expect.

Twenties to thirties: Few changes; maybe minimal ridging

Forties: Noticeable ridging; nails feel less flexible and are more prone to snags and breaks; may notice some peeling of the nail surface

Fifties: Changes from the forties become more discernible; may also start seeing slight discoloration and mild fungal infections

Sixties and beyond: Ridges become prominent; nails become significantly thicker, especially on the toes

What to Do: Nails may not be top priority, but they're dead giveaways for a man who keeps every other aspect of his age hidden. To keep nails healthy and youthful:

- Be protective. "Don't use nails for screwdrivers or tools," Dr. Scher advises. "The single most important thing you can do is protect them from trauma."
- Take nails to a professional. Guys are increasingly getting their nails "done," especially if they have careers like sales, where a polished appearance is a basic requirement for success. A manicurist can remove ridges and retard peeling by buffing and polishing the nail surface.
- Coddle your cuticles. Tell the manicurist to take it easy on

your cuticles, and not to push them back. They protect the growth center of the nail, and manipulation can interfere with growth.

Hearing

Noticeable hearing loss shouldn't even start until around age 60. "Still, we know that one in three men suffers some degree of hearing loss by that time," says John House, M.D., president of the House Ear Institute in Los Angeles. The implication is that some of us are losing hearing faster than we should, perhaps due to damage from earlier infections, common genetic defects or one too many reunion tours with The Who.

The Test: 25-decibel finger rub. In a quiet room, extend your arm straight out to the side and lightly rub your thumb and forefinger together. Slowly move the rubbing fingers toward one ear, taking note of how far away it is when the sound becomes audible. Repeat on the other side.

Under age 60, a person with normal hearing should be able to make out the sound at six to eight inches. If you're not able to hear at that range, you may not be catching everything people say to you—and that could put you out of the loop. If you can't hear beyond four inches, you have the hearing of a 70-year-old.

What to Do: Hearing loss is one of those things guys tend to ignore. Unfortunately, that leaves a lot of us saying "Huh?" all the time. Better you should see an ear specialist and get any existing problems corrected. The most common glitch is called otosclerosis, in which a bone that transmits sound to the inner ear hardens. The solution is to surgically replace part of the bone with wire. Micro-drills and lasers have improved the operation's success, minimized side effects, like dizziness, and shortened recovery time.

Smell

Smell (and taste) typically declines with age, especially in men. "One reason men have more high blood pressure may be that we're always reaching for the salt to add flavor," says Alan Hirsch, M.D., neurological director of the Smell and Taste Treatment and Research Foundation in Chicago. Again, declines usually aren't apparent until after age 60, but some men sense that their enjoyment of these tastes and smells isn't what it should be. And, says Dr. Hirsch, there's evidence that the midlife malaise many men experience may be linked to an inability to distinguish odors. Fortunately, there is a simple test you can use to make sure your senses are up to par.

The Test: Odor identification. Close your eyes and have a partner put two different-smelling foods under your nose, one at a time—pizza and chocolate, for example, or apple and Cheddar cheese. Under age 60, you should be able to tell them apart.

What to Do: If you can't distinguish odors well, try a food supplement called phoschol—short for phosphatidylcholine, a substance that raises levels of a neurotransmitter that sends olfactory signals to the brain. In one experiment by Dr. Hirsch, 40 percent of smell-impaired people reported improvement after taking phoschol.

Teeth

Healthy teeth can last a lifetime, but you may see some changes in tooth shape and color starting in the forties, says William Kuttler, D.D.S., a spokesman for the Academy of General Dentistry.

The Test: Texture test. Rub a fingernail downward from the gum line to the biting edge of the tooth. If you feel a ridge running across the width of the tooth, your gums have receded, leaving the bump as a sort of high-water mark. "Gum recession may be a sign of gum disease, which may lead to tooth loss," says Dr. Kuttler.

For an at-a-glance checkup, look for yellowness toward the gum, which indicates root structure peeking out. Check any crowns you've had ten years or more to see if the teeth next to them have become darker. Look at the pointed tip of the canines for flattening. What's typically found:

Forties: Pointed edge of the canine teeth may begin looking flatter; may see yellowness at the base of the teeth

Fifties: Canines and other front teeth become squarish; recession ridges may appear; teeth become noticeably darker

Sixties and beyond: Gums recede, and, if left untreated this gum recession can cause tooth loss

What to Do: The most important thing is to keep gums from receding. At home, this means flossing and regular, gentle brushing with a soft-bristle brush. It also means going in for regular dental checkups.

We know you've heard this before, but it's especially important because the tooth-robbing processes described above can occur at any time. Only a dentist will know whether changes are from aging or serious disease.

To keep front teeth looking sharp, which some dentists claim will give you an image that's tougher as well as younger, you can ask your dentist to reshape them. Since this process involves removing a certain amount of enamel, it's best done early on, while there's still plenty of tooth to spare.

Brightening teeth can be done either at your dentist's office or at home using bleaches applied and held in place with a molded mouthpiece. Dr. Kuttler recommends a combination treatment, with a start-up power bleach in the office and at-home follow-up. "My experience is that the home baths produce more lasting results," he says.

Posture

You're no slouch, so you certainly don't want to look like one. But that's what happens when muscles supporting the back become weak from disuse, causing the spine to shift out of alignment—an especially likely scenario if you have a few extra pounds in your gut to tug things off kilter. It's not strictly an appearance matter: If your posture is poor, you'll have less power in sports and more problems with your back, says Jeffrey Young, M.D., attending physician at the Center for Spine, Sports and Occupational Rehabilitation in Chicago.

The Test: Side bends. Posture is equal parts muscle flexibility and spinal mechanics, Dr. Young says. To measure them, stand with your feet about 12 inches apart. Slowly bend to one side, running your hand down your leg as far as you can comfortably go. For extra accuracy, have a partner watch you from behind, to observe exactly where your spine is bending.

Maintenance Schedule

Ages 20 to 29

Every year: Blood pressure test.

Every three years: Physical exam—should include checking eyes and ears, listening to neck and chest, thyroid exam, probe of abdomen, massages of chest and lymph nodes, hernia exam, checking testicles and penis, reflex and strength tests; blood tests, including those for cholesterol, glucose, kidney and liver function; urine tests for infection, diabetes, cancer, kidney and liver function.

Every five years: Tuberculosis test.

Ages 30 to 39

Every year: Blood pressure test, chest x-ray (if you're a smoker).

Every three years: Physical exam, blood tests, urine tests, electrocardiogram (if you have high cholesterol or a family history of heart disease).

Every five years: Tuberculosis test.

Ages 40 to 49

Every year: Blood pressure test, digital-rectal exam (DRE) for prostate cancer, hemoccult (blood-in-stool test) for colorectal cancer, chest x-ray (if you're a smoker), PSA (prostate-specific antigen) test for prostate cancer (if you have a family history of the disease or are African-American).

Every two years: Physical exam, blood tests, urine tests.

Every three years: Electrocardiogram (if you have high cholesterol or a family history of heart disease).

Age 50 and Beyond

Every year: Physical exam, blood pressure test, blood tests, urine tests, DRE for prostate cancer, hemoccult for colorectal cancer, PSA test for prostate cancer.

Every three to four years: Electrocardiogram, sigmoid-oscopy for colorectal cancer.

Twenties: You should be able to slide your hand past your knee; the spine should be pivoting from a point below the belt line

Thirties: Your hand should reach the knee; the spine should bend at or below the belt line

Forties: Your hand should reach the top of your kneecap; the spine should bend at the belt line

Fifties and beyond: Ideally, no different from the forties, but it's typical for your hand to reach only to your thigh and your spine to bend at navel level

What to Do: To ensure lifelong good posture, you need strong back, abdominal and gluteal, or butt, muscles. You can work them all in one move: Start by lying facedown, hands at shoulder level, as you would for a push-up. Keeping your hips against the floor, straighten your arms to lift your upper body. Return slowly to the starting position. If you can do this ten times easily, try doing the exercise with no hands, arms held against your sides. Once you've mastered ten repetitions of this, you're ready to try it with your hands beneath your chin and your elbows out. Finally, work up to ten reps in the "Superman" position: hips against the floor, chest up, arms extended directly in front of you.

Hair

Baldness patterns vary widely: Some guys are bald by 30; others have a full head right up to the end. There's really no measure of meaningful averages. Still, there are two things you should know. First, if you're going to go bald, your hair will start thinning early in the game, during your twenties and thirties. Second, men typically don't notice they're balding until they've already lost 50 percent of their hair, according to Clay J. Cockerell, M.D., clinical associate professor of dermatology at the University of Texas Southwestern Medical Center at Dallas.

The Test: In the interest of early detection, part your hair in an area of apparent thinness near the front of the scalp or at the crown of the head, where thinning generally occurs first. (You'll need a mirror.) Look for tiny, porelike indentations in the scalp. These are bare follicles—places where hairs should be rooted, but aren't. If you see them, you may be thinning.

What to Do: Detecting hair loss early will help if you want to use Rogaine, still the only drug for hair loss. It works best in men who still have 50 to 60 percent of their hair.

—Richard Allen

Gassing Up Your Gusto

A Primer on Fast Energy

Ultimately, everything comes down to energy. Without it, suns do not shine, life does not form from dust and fish don't grow legs to evolve into guys with careers, relationships and mortgages.

Energy is the ultimate commodity. When it becomes scarce, bad things start to happen. On a large scale, an energy shortage looks like an oil embargo or a potato famine. On a personal level, it looks like missed opportunities, annoyed spouses and a sag in your couch where your body inevitably settles for the weekend.

Sound depressingly familiar? Here's the good news: From a strictly physical standpoint, you have energy to spare. We all do. Our bodies store tremendous reserves of all the enzymes, acids, chemicals and other stuff that make us go. "Every couch potato has enough energy in him to get up and run 150 miles," says Edward Eichner, M.D., professor of medicine at the University of Oklahoma College of Medicine in Oklahoma City.

Where Do We Go Wrong?

Of course it sounds good to hear that we all have enough energy to run 150 miles. But this raises some serious questions. If we're all just brimming with untapped energy, why do we all wish we had more? Here's why. In many ways we unwittingly rob ourselves of energy. Let's use the time-tested metaphor of an automobile. Say the salesman claims you should get 50 miles to the gallon, highway. You pour in ten gallons of gas and head out of Knoxville to see your salty Aunt Minnie in Baltimore, 500 miles away. But lo and behold, you run out of gas 40 miles short of Minnie's house, right in that edgy area of Washington, D.C., that no congressman has ever seen. How come? Five reasons:

1. You need a tune-up—you're wasting energy.
2. You used the wrong gas. You should have chosen premium fuel.
3. External problems—traffic, fallen-rock zones—are slowing you down.
4. You have a leak in your tank.
5. The sales guy lied.

We can't do anything about the guy in the polyester suit, but we can help you steer clear of the other four problems. Here's a by-the-book energy maintenance program that will keep you running in high gear all day long.

Do-It-Yourself Tune-Ups

What do you have in common with Bill Clinton's '67 Mustang convertible? Both of you run on the same two things: oxygen and fuel. They're equally important, but fuel fill-ups you get maybe three times a day (we'll get to that in a moment), while oxygen uptake is constant.

Each breath of air enriches your energy mix, feeding your 75 trillion cells with more of what they need to regulate everything the body does moment by moment. You want to get as much as possible of the best air you can, says Sheldon Saul Hendler, M.D., Ph.D., of the University of California, San Diego, and author of *The Doctor's Vitamin and Mineral Encyclopedia.*

Make sure you're properly inflated. Breathe in. Breathe out. Good. Breathing seems pretty simple, but the fact is, we could do it better.

Most of us take a manly suck-in-your-gut approach to respiration, expanding the chest with each breath. This is the least efficient way to get oxygen surging through the body because it doesn't put enough air into the lower lungs, where blood flow is richest. The more blood that comes in contact with the oxygen, the more oxygen is delivered throughout the body. To breathe better:

- First, exhale fully. You'll take deeper breaths with empty lungs.
- Breathe through the nose, focusing on making your stomach move instead of your chest. This automatically expands the lower lungs, letting you take in more air than with shallower chest breaths. Aim for four to six breaths per minute.
- Optional extra: When you exhale, suck your stomach in. Because this is not a natural movement, it will make you concentrate more on your breathing, says Janet Burda, a registered respiratory therapist who is manager of respiratory care at University Hospital at the University of Colorado School of Medicine in Denver. It'll also give your gut muscles a mild workout.

Adjust your alignment. Try this: Slouch in your chair and lean to one side, then take a deep breath. Now sit up straight and take a deep breath. Which breath was easier? Right. You'll breathe better and have more energy all day long if your desk posture doesn't impede air flow. The best position is with your weight centered over your hips, head up and feet flat on the floor.

Rev the engine. One expert suggests you'll get more energy in the morning if you sing in the shower. Even if you do it badly, singing makes you breathe more deeply, especially if it's loud and involves a lot of words.

Take it out of the garage. Fatigue is a major symptom brought on by oxygen-poor, chemical-laden indoor air common in office buildings where windows don't open and there's little ventilation. According to David S. Bell, M.D., author of *Curing Fatigue*, 10 to 30 percent of people working in new or remodeled office buildings could be suffering the draining effects of bad air.

If your office windows are sealed or you don't have any windows, get outdoors for a shot of fresh air as often as you can. Think of it as a cigarette break without the smoke. Inhale some fresh air for a few minutes at least every two hours.

Keep the air filter clean. Speaking of smoke, you already know cigarettes gunk up the lungs, but they also steal energy by clogging airways with mucus, constricting blood vessels and making it harder for cells to tank up on oxygen.

Open 'er up once in a while. Vigorous exercise is the most effective energizer known. Not only does it immediately send more oxygen to the brain and body, it also prevents blood vessels from clogging, strengthens the heart, relieves the tiring effects of stress and improves your mood to help you kick back the dogs of depression.

When you do make time to get to the gym, save your harder workouts for after work. Your body will perform most efficiently between 4:00 and 7:00 P.M., when stress hormones wane and resting heart rate slows, giving the body more energy reserves. One Japanese study found that men who worked out in the afternoon also achieved greater increases in conditioning, boosting energy efficiency even more.

Even if you're chained to your desk, it's still time for a quick stretch. Stretching gets muscles working, blood moving and breathing going, all of which perk you up. Here are three quick moves that also loosen muscles likely to tense up deskside.

- Put your arms behind your back and intertwine your fingers. Straighten and raise your arms until you feel a stretch in the chest, shoulders and arms. Try not to bend forward. Hold for 30 seconds.
- While seated, intertwine your fingers and raise your arms straight overhead. Press your hands upward, lean to one side for ten seconds, then lean to the other side for ten seconds.

• Clasp your hands behind your head and push the palms together. You'll feel it in your chest and upper back. Hold for
30 seconds.

Putting a Tiger in Your Tank

What you give your body to run on has a direct bearing on your
energy. Here's how to make the most of your fuel to fight fatigue.

Use the right octane. Carbohydrates burn fast, clean and pure,
like liquid nitrogen. Fats and proteins don't. Fat is the lowest-octane
fuel around—it delivers virtually no energy to the body even though
it's packed with calories. The reason is that the body would rather
store fat than burn it, and in men it tends to get stored in the under-
carriage. That's why you want carbohydrates to make up the greatest
share, 60 percent, of what you eat.

Know your additives. There are plenty of things you can put in
your body to make it process energy more efficiently, says Dr.
Hendler. Here are some of the best.

• Multivitamins. Even mild vitamin shortages have a draining
effect, especially if you're exerting yourself. Studies in the Nether-
lands found that men who are just slightly deficient in thiamin, riboflavin and vitamins B_6 and C suffered a 20 percent decline in
athletic endurance. A daily multivitamin not only ensures that you
get enough of what you need, it also lets you absorb more. The
body takes up all the B vitamins together more readily than it does
one at a time. Look for multis that provide zinc, magnesium and
copper.

• Zinc. It helps with insulin storage in the pancreas, and insulin
is vital for the body's energy uptake. Furthermore, low levels of zinc
have been linked to decreased sex drive. Philip Reeves, Ph.D., su-
pervisory research chemist at the U.S. Department of Agriculture
(USDA) Human Nutrition Research Center in Beltsville, Maryland, recommends getting supplemental amounts of 10 to 15 milligrams per day—especially during the steamy months of summer,
since zinc is lost through sweating. Sources include beef, oysters
and wheat germ.

• Magnesium. One of magnesium's hundreds of jobs in metabolism is to package food into an energy form that the body can burn.

In one study of patients with chronic fatigue, magnesium injections boosted energy in half the cases. A man's diet should include 350 milligrams each day. Good sources: seafood, spinach, brown rice, oatmeal, beans and avocados.

• Copper. USDA studies find copper makes you sleep better at night, which improves daytime alertness. Look to get at least 2 milligrams daily. Good sources: avocados, bananas and mushrooms.

Keep the water pump working. Water not only contains energizing oxygen, it also helps transport it through the body in blood. Drink a couple of glasses morning, noon and night.

Jump-start with java. As a rule, you should keep caffeine consumption moderate. Too much causes a surge of adrenaline, but when the spurt is over, your power levels plummet. A single cup of coffee, though, can work wonders when you need it. British researchers gave caffeine to test subjects at night and found it gave them daytime-quality energy. Recommended dosage: one to two cups daily.

Read the fine print. It's fair to say most men don't read the instructions when they open a bottle of medicine, but labels often list fatigue as a side effect. Some common offenders are:

• Antihistamines. They impair the function of brain chemicals that keep thinking sharp.

• Pain relievers. Ibuprofen causes drowsiness or dizziness in 3 to 15 percent of people taking it.

• Cough suppressants. Use caution with products bearing the word "elixir"; all contain alcohol— some as much as 25 percent. Also note that those labeled "DM" include the drug dextromethorphan. It's a chemical cousin of codeine, with similar sedating effects.

• High blood pressure medications. Many have sedating effects. If yours is making you tired, ask your doctor to change your prescription.

Steering Clear of Energy Drains

Often it's not your internal combustion that's robbing you of energy, it's the route you have to travel. Here's how to avoid some common roadblocks along the energy expressway.

Prescribe some eye rest. Any weekend athlete knows that prolonged muscle exertion can leave your whole body feeling exhausted. And that goes not only for the arms and legs but for the tiny muscles in your eyes as well. According to Steven Montgomery, M.D., a resident at the University of Oklahoma's McGee Eye Institute in Oklahoma City, eyestrain can be a sign that you need corrective lenses. If you already have glasses or contacts, you may not be wearing them as often as you should, or your prescription may be weak or incorrect. How recently have you had your eyes checked?

Don't stare into cyberspace. Staring at a video screen makes you blink less and open your eyes wider, both of which cause the eye to dry out and fatigue, according to a report in the *New England Journal of Medicine.* Solutions:

• Take your eyes off the screen every few minutes and let them readjust.

• Lower your monitor so that you're looking down at it as much as possible; your eyes don't open as wide that way and don't dry out as easily.

Don't take a dim view. Bright light has caffeinelike alerting power, says Scott Campbell, Ph.D., professor of psychiatry at New York Hospital–Cornell Medical Center in White Plains. He's done experiments in which people exposed to intensely bright light performed 24 percent better in alertness tests than people who worked in customary office light. Since such bright lighting isn't exactly practical in the office, he recommends getting outdoors as much as possible.

Know which lights are heavies. Even if your lights are bright, they could be giving you trouble. Some fluorescent bulbs can cause fatigue and headaches, even depression. It's the rapid on-off pulsing of the fluorescent tubes that is to blame. British studies find that when fluorescents flicker faster than the eye can register, headache rates drop 50 percent.

What to do? If you're the boss, call maintenance and have them rewire the fluorescent bulbs in opposition to each other, so that when one bulb is on, another is off, delivering even light (and maybe getting more work out of your staff). Otherwise, head for your nearest garden store and pick up one of those Gro-Lite bulbs, which provide a better imitation of natural sunlight. Then simply screw it into a decent lamp, maybe one of those cool end-table jobs with a hula dancer on it.

Avoid heavy weather. It's the skin that registers air temperature, but it's the brain that responds to it. Mental sharpness is remarkably sensitive to temperature, with peak alertness concentrated in a narrow band between 65° and 72°F, says Alan Hedge, Ph.D., professor in the Department of Design and Environmental Analysis at Cornell University in Ithaca, New York. When the mercury goes below or above this range, studies find that lethargy increases and performance nosedives. Sleep studies find that people also rest best in this zone.

Break up boredom. If you're doing something dull or repetitive, take a break at least every 20 minutes. Even turning away from the task at hand for a few moments will improve your performance. Read a favorite magazine, call a client you like, play a computer game. Schedule small tasks you enjoy throughout the day: It'll give you something to look forward to.

ID-ing Mechanical Difficulties

Sometimes you need to pull 'er into the shop and have a professional look under the hood. Here are some problem areas you can get under control—if you know what to look for.

Keep tabs on your thyroid. What exactly is this thing? Essentially, the thyroid gland is the body's throttle, pumping out hormones that regulate metabolism. Too few hormones (hypothyroidism) and you're not revving at full power. It's a problem facing two million other bushed American men, and fatigue is often the only symptom.

"It's underdiagnosed in men," says Sara Schoman, executive director of the Thyroid Foundation of America. A thyroid gland can fail gradually over months or years, making changes in energy less noticeable. It also can pump too much (hyperthyroidism), often using more energy than you need and sapping your strength.

If you suspect a thyroid problem, see a doctor for a TSH (thyroid-stimulating hormone) blood test. In either case, proper treatment can return your hormone levels and restore your energy to normal.

Understand your immune system. Any bout with illness makes you tired because energy that could go elsewhere is instead channeled into mobilizing an army of immune cells. All in all, that's a good thing. The problem comes only when the army goes on unauthorized maneuvers. Of particular concern:

• Allergies. With allergies, immune forces mobilize but there's no real enemy. Ragweed, pollen, dust—all are innocent noncombatants that can nevertheless trigger retaliation from the body. You sneeze, you sniff and you get very tired. Antihistamines usually take care of most hay fever symptoms, but they'll make you drowsy. See a doctor for prescription medications like Hismanal that do the job without making your lids droop.

• Chronic fatigue syndrome. Studies find that the immune systems of people who have the disorder are constantly in overdrive, producing great quantities of certain defense-triggering chemicals. While it's a more common complaint among women, it's estimated that 30 percent of its victims are men. If you're just tired, you don't have it. If you did, you'd also experience symptoms including mild fever, sore throat, muscle pain, headache and sleep disturbances. You'd see at least a 50 percent reduction in your normal activity for at least six months. What you need is a complete medical exam, since fatigue isn't a complaint that can adequately be covered in a typical ten-minute office visit—and let them know ahead of time that your underlying complaint is tiredness.

Don't dawdle with diabetes. You need a little sugar in your blood. In the form of high-octane glucose, it's the body's gasoline. In people with diabetes, a shortage of the hormone insulin prevents cells from filling up on glucose. Instead, the glucose stays in the body's fluids and your energy literally goes down the toilet. Diabetes often goes undiagnosed for years. The best treatment for the most common form of diabetes is prevention.

• Take vitamin E. Studies suggest that daily supplements boost insulin performance.

• Drop pounds. Overweight people are more at risk for the disease.

• Do aerobics. Working out five times a week cuts the risk of diabetes by up to 42 percent.

Accept that sometimes you're not going to make it all the way to your destination without pulling over once in a while for a rest and a refueling. The key is not allowing low-energy periods to cut into your productivity.

—Richard Laliberte

Good As New

The Ultimate Guide to Keeping Healthy for Life

When it comes to recapturing your youth, time is a one-way ride. Even though you can't go home again, you can keep yourself from suffering from the more common age-related ailments. All it takes is a little common sense and self-care.

And it's worth it. After all, life as a guy can be scary. Consider this.

• Prior to age 65, men suffer heart attacks at almost four times the rate of women.

• By age 65, one in three of us will suffer from high blood pressure.

• One out of every eight of us will be diagnosed with prostate cancer, and from 1980 to 1990, the incidence of prostate cancer increased a remarkable 50 percent. Between one-quarter and one-third of those who contract it will die from the disease—an estimated 38,000 this year.

Care for Yourself

We face two challenges when it comes to caring for our own health. First, there's the macho ethic that tells us to suffer in silence, tune out pain and consider our bodies as nothing more than vehicles to get us from one place to another. That's one reason women visit doctors about 150 percent as often as men.

Then there's the second challenge. That's the opinion, on the part of the government, the medical community and society in general, that men's health somehow isn't as important an issue as women's is. For example, how many times have you seen television ads urging women to do breast self-exams and recommending regular mammograms? Ever see one telling young men about the importance of testicular self-exams? This despite the fact that testicular cancer is 95 percent curable if caught early.

We can start taking charge of our own lives by watching what we eat, cutting down on stress and getting more exercise. To help, we've compiled a brief man's guide to healthy living, providing you with the basics for staying young, active and productive for the long haul.

Eat Better, Live Longer

When we were kids, we selected our food on two criteria: what we could trade it for at school and what cool prizes were shown on the back of the box.

Today, eating has become a lot more complicated. It seems as though every day a new danger is discovered. To cut through the confusion, we've come up with simple, hard-and-fast rules for eating right. This basic overview should clue you in to whether your diet is the kind that will keep your engine revved up—or lead you to the great mechanic in the sky.

Cut the fat. High-fat diets have been linked to a wide variety of male diseases: heart disease, stroke, cancer and diabetes, to name a few. But many men are confused about dietary fat because it comes in three different forms. Here's a quick breakdown on each type and its relative merits.

- Saturated fat: This fat is bad for you.
- Polyunsaturated fat: This fat is bad, too.
- Monounsaturated fat: Ditto.

Most dietitians recommend a diet that's no more than 30 percent fat. (Most American men eat about 40 percent of their total calories in fat.) Here are some quick tips on cutting your fat intake.

- Watch the add-on fat. Pastas, breads and vegetables are naturally low in fat, but not when they're drenched in butter or sour cream. Look for better toppings, such as salsa, lemon juice or fat-free sour cream.
- Cut down on meats, especially red meats. Skinless chicken and fish are lower-fat alternatives.
- Try switching from whole-milk dairy products to low-fat or fat-free versions. If you drink whole milk now, switch to 2 percent, then gradually work your way down to skim.
- Adopt healthier cooking methods. Steaming, baking, grilling and microwaving are all better than frying, during which food absorbs oil (liquid fat).

Take your vitamins. A basic daily supplement should give you 100 percent of the recommended allowances for the following nutrients: beta-carotene (or vitamin A); the B vitamins (thiamin, riboflavin, niacin, biotin, pantothenic acid, folic acid, B_6 and B_{12}); and vitamins C, D, E and K. In addition, it should also contain 100 percent of what you need in the way of potassium, magnesium, selenium and zinc and at least 100 micrograms of chromium (but no more than the recommended limit of 200 micrograms), all of which are needed for a man's good health.

An even better supplement is one that's labeled "antioxidant-rich"—in other words, loaded with vitamins C and E and beta-carotene. That's because these three nutrients have been found to attack free radicals—loose oxygen molecules that hang around in the body and cause all kinds of damage, from wrinkling your skin to weakening your immune system.

Fill 'er up with fiber. In our grandparents' day, fiber was called roughage. Since it's hard to sell, say, breakfast cereal with big banners that say "High in Roughage," today we use the more marketable, less graphic term *fiber*.

A high-fiber diet fills you up without filling you out, keeps your plumbing in working order, helps lower your cholesterol level and may help reduce the risk of colon cancer. Nutritionists recommend you get at least 20 grams per day. How? Try starting out with a breakfast of oatmeal, whole-wheat toast and two pieces of fruit—that'll get you halfway there. Other good sources include most vegetables, beans and whole-grain breads and pastas.

Don't diet. Here's what happens when you go on a diet: Your body senses danger. Little primitive survival mechanisms, left over from the days when we scrounged for grubs on the high plains, start sending out messages that say "Conserve fat. Burn fewer calories." Now, is this your dieting goal? Of course not. How, then, do you lose weight? Eat more foods that keep your metabolism revving—the same carbohydrate-rich vegetables, fruits, grains and legumes that will also deliver vitamins and fiber.

Slash Stress from Your Life

Been a little tense lately? Join the club. Of all the health problems facing American men today, experts say that stress is priority one. Up to 90 percent of all visits to doctors are for stress-related illnesses, according to the American Institute of Stress.

What can we do to eliminate stress? Nothing. It's part of life, 1990s-style. But while we can't just make it disappear, we can take some major steps toward reducing the amount of stress in our daily lives. Here are some of the most successful anti-stress strategies around.

Get sweaty. Research at California State University shows that 30 minutes of aerobic activity immediately reduces body tension—and the more intense it is, the more effective. Weight training also helps: A study at Hofstra University in Hempstead, New York, found that weight lifting counters anxiety and depression and boosts self-esteem. And that's not to mention the numerous physical benefits of exercise.

Stay in balance. Most of us know the importance of having a hobby or favorite activity to distract us from the demands of work. But sometimes we make the mistake of choosing hobbies that are really extensions of our office life: for example, the computer programmer who designs video games in his free time. We certainly wouldn't tell you not to advance your career with outside activities, but if the words "tax deduction" enter your mind, you need a different hobby.

Look for something completely removed from your business activities. If you're a numbers cruncher, try something creative: painting, tinkering with an old car, tying flies, making pottery. If your job is high-tech, get back to the soil: Try gardening, bird-watching or hiking.

Ease your time crunch with a 20 percent solution. Expect everything you do to take 20 percent longer than you think it will, experts say. Time constraints have a hold on all of us, so don't beat yourself up over them. Take a hard look at what you've scheduled for the day and realize that unless you add another two hours to your workday, you're not going to be able to get it all done. Then reschedule accordingly.

Practice deficit reduction. Living beyond your means can actually make you sick. A researcher at the University of Alabama in Tuscaloosa studied British census data on 8,000 households and found that families that tried to maintain lifestyles they couldn't afford were more likely to have health problems. Before you spring for that Maserati, consider how much harder you'll have to work to afford it.

Find the meaning of life. Or at least the meaning of your life. One review of more than 60 studies of stress-busting tactics found that having a sense of purpose in life was the single most powerful way for men to gain peace of mind. It may come from religious involvement in a church or synagogue, from volunteer work or from political involvement. Or it may even come from just sitting alone for a few minutes a day trying to work out the ways of the world. The bottom line is to step back a bit from your day-to-day life, look at the big picture and realize that controlling your problems won't necessarily solve them.

Get in Shape

Maybe your college football chums are no longer counting on you to stick to your workout. But everybody else in your life is. That's because if there's one thing that every health expert in the world can agree on, it's this: Exercise is good for you. Any kind of exercise. And doing so might help keep you around longer for your loved ones.

There are two basic forms of exercise. Aerobic activities, like running, cycling, walking, stair-climbing and swimming, train the heart to pump blood more efficiently. Weight training keeps the muscles, joints and bones strong. To keep in shape, you need both—20 to 45 minutes of aerobics, and enough resistance training to target all the major muscle groups: legs, back, chest, arms, shoulders and abdominals. Do these three to five times a week and you'll get results. Your waistline will trim down, your muscles will bulk up, and most important, you'll be on the road to a longer, healthier life.

Having trouble sticking to it? Try this.

Put your money where your muscle is. A study at Michigan State University in East Lansing found that people who bet $40 they could stick with their programs for six months had a 97 percent success rate. Those who didn't bet succeeded less than 20 percent of the time.

Take it easy. It's far more important to be consistent in your program than to try to drain every bit of fitness benefit from each workout.

Vary the program. Nobody said your routine had to be routine. Run today, bike tomorrow—have fun.

Check your ego at the door. In a study, researchers at the University of Texas at Austin found that those who took up exercise mainly to improve appearance experienced a drop in feelings of self-worth. If you want to remember the real reason to stay fit, try hanging a picture of your family on your exercise-room wall.

Listen to Your Body

Here's a little secret—if you feel sick, you probably are. Nevertheless, most of us ignore our symptoms until, lo and behold, we wind up being poked and prodded by doctors. What we should do is manage our health the way we manage our business: Take on the responsibilities that we're qualified to handle and hire some part-time help when things get a little hairy.

Here's a list of body parts and their potential problems as well as what you should do about them.

Head. *Symptoms:* Headache that persists for more than 72 hours, prevents you from doing normal activities or is accompanied by vision or coordination problems; difficulty talking or thinking clearly; arm and leg weakness; fever or vomiting.

Possible problems: High blood pressure, brain hemorrhage, stroke, tumor, meningitis or Lyme disease.

Chest. *Symptoms:* Sudden, severe pain that lasts more than a few minutes; pain that gets worse with exertion or is accompanied by squeezing or uncomfortable pressure in the chest and dizziness, fainting, sweating, nausea or shortness of breath; or pain that radiates to the jaw, neck or arms.

Possible problems: Heart attack, angina or inflammation of the tissue sac surrounding the heart.

Neck. *Symptoms:* A severe sore throat that gets progressively worse and makes breathing or swallowing difficult, especially if accompanied by swollen glands in the neck or a fever of 101°F or higher.

Possible problems: Infection from mononucleosis or strep throat.

Abdomen. *Symptoms:* Pain that is sudden and severe, lasts more than four days, is only temporarily relieved by eating or recurs with constipation or diarrhea and bloating.

Possible problems: Appendicitis, gallbladder problems, ulcers, food poisoning or irritable bowel syndrome.

Back. *Symptoms:* Pain that lasts more than 72 hours or is severe enough to interfere with work or that radiates down the leg. Also any unexplained numbness or tingling accompanied by muscle weakness.

Possible problem: Herniated disk.

Genitals. *Symptoms:* Frequent urination or difficulty starting or stopping the flow of urine. A testicle that is tender to the touch or feels harder than usual or uneven.

Possible problems: Benign prostate enlargement or prostate cancer for urinary symptoms; infection or testicular cancer, a disease that is 95 percent curable if discovered early, for testicular symptoms.

Skin. *Symptoms:* Any sore that doesn't heal within a week, or a mole or birthmark that bleeds, develops irregular borders or changes color, size or texture.

Possible problem: Skin cancer.

—*Richard Laliberte*

How to Be Stronger Longer

55 Ways to Do Anything with Energy to Spare

"So I'm at this all-day business meeting with a bunch of the muckety-mucks, and the president of my division decides to go out for a lunchtime run," my friend told me. "I decide to invite myself along. I figure, I'm 30, and he's closing in on 50, so if I stick to a real leisurely pace, he'll have no trouble keeping up.

"But figure this," my friend continues. "We cruise along for about a mile or so, when suddenly he hangs a left and starts sprinting up the side of a mountain. I make it halfway and let him go on without me. So I'm sitting there panting, my heart is pounding in my ears, and my first thought is, 'Geez, I'd like to have that kind of energy when I'm 50.' And my next thought is, 'Geez, I'd like to have that kind of energy now.'"

My friend made the mistake of buying into a myth that energy and vitality are the province of the young. "In the eyes of society, when you're 20, you're hot; when you're 40, you're not; and when you're 60, you're shot," says Stanley Teitlebaum, Ph.D., a clinical psychologist at the Postgraduate Center for Mental Health in New York City.

Fortunately, you can disprove that wisdom. Whether you're in your thirties, forties, fifties or beyond, you can still amaze people with your energy, drive and raw strength. You can push a little harder on the playing field, come through a 12-hour workday with loads of energy to spare and still make love like you did back in your college days. In most cases this energy and vigor is already inside you. You just need to learn how to unleash it. Here's how.

Lead the Pack in Any Game

Whether it's that fifth set of tennis, a full-court game of hoops or even a group hike up a mountain, you don't want to just keep up—you want to lead. Even when you're working out on your own, squeezing out one more bench press or one more lap in the pool can make the difference between meeting a personal goal and falling short. To help you push it to the next level, we polled the experts for their best energy-boosting secrets. Here's what they said.

Beef up on breakfast. Energy begins with fuel. Even if you are getting the recommended 60 percent of your calories from high-powered carbohydrates, that may not be enough to sustain you through intense workouts. The best place to add energy is breakfast: Eating a big meal in the morning restores energizing blood sugars depleted during sleep. For a quick 400 calories of carbohydrate, have a banana (which also adds potassium, a high-energy nutrient lost in sweat), an orange, a bowl of cereal in skim milk and toast with jam.

Stock up on power snacks. Common wisdom has it that you shouldn't take in extra calories an hour before exercising, because digestion will draw energy away from working muscles. For a moderate workout, that's true. But if you're planning to train hard and long, you'll need extra energy. Load up on carbohydrates in the days before your workout, and tank up on a high-carbohydrate sports drink right before. In a study of runners who ran for 35 kilometers, then were asked to finish their workout by going all out for 5 kilometers, those who'd had a high-carbohydrate sports drink just before their run could maintain their pace longer and with greater power than runners who'd had nothing beforehand.

Be a daydream achiever. Letting your mind wander during prolonged exercise staves off fatigue and can make you feel much more energetic, suggests a study at the University of Alabama at Birmingham. Good subjects to let your mind roam to include the scenery around you, projects at work and even hassles from your daily life. On the flip side, researchers found that dwelling on the specifics of your workout—worrying about form, for example—can increase fatigue.

Construct muscle with carbohydrates. Can what you eat make the difference in how much muscle you have? Yes, according to researchers at the University of Illinois at Chicago. When they put 18 people on a low-fat, high-carbohydrate diet for 20 weeks, they found the subjects lost an average of 11.3 percent fat. Makes sense, but here's the kicker: Those individuals gained an average of 2.2 percent lean muscle. More muscle, without lifting weights. Researchers speculate that because our bodies don't turn carbohydrate into fat very efficiently, a high-carbohydrate diet may make us more prone to gain muscle.

Make a rite choice. One study of Olympic athletes found that competitors who used a consistent, systematic training ritual before exercising tended to be more successful than those who didn't. And the ritual itself didn't matter—what mattered was that the Olympians were religious about using it. For your own personal ritual, try finding a spot by yourself to gather your thoughts, doing a specific warm-up routine of stretches performed in order, or saying mantralike phrases like "loose and easy" or "Olivia Newton-John" to yourself.

Beat the heat. Outlast younger competitors by being smart about how your body reacts to the heat—whether it's outside on a balmy spring day or inside an overheated gym. First, drink even if you're not thirsty; by the time you are, you could be well on your way to dehydration. Sunburn will cause your body temperature to rise, making you lose more fluids. To help ward it off, wear light clothing instead of going without a shirt. In hot weather, soak those clothes with water before you put them on and you'll be wearing portable air-conditioning.

Start big and work your way down. Want to lift more weight in the gym? You can keep your body from tiring too quickly with the right sequence of lifts. Experts recommend starting out with the exercises that hit the larger muscles or with exercises that target more than one muscle group—such as bench presses, military presses and most back exercises. Finish up with exercises that work the smaller muscles, such as biceps and triceps curls. Here's why: Smaller muscles tire faster than bigger ones. If you exhaust your triceps with, say, a few sets of dips, they won't be able to assist the chest and shoulders as well in the bench press.

Reward yourself. Sometimes all it takes to find energy midway through a tough workout is the knowledge that there's an ice-cold beer at the finish line, or even just a hot shower. The point is that we're not that far removed from Pavlov's favorite pet, and small rewards can go a long way to motivate us.

Outwork Your Co-workers

Like most companies, yours probably has its share of energetic upstarts gunning for a place higher up on the ladder—and you can be dead sure some of them are aiming for the rung you happen to occupy.

You hold the cards of experience, but in a business climate that puts a premium on change and new ideas, the higher-ups are entranced by youth for its own sake. To keep up with the upstarts, you need more vigor day-to-day. Forty-four percent of American men admit to frequently feeling "used up" by the time they leave the office. For more energy on the job:

Stroll around your neighborhood before starting your day. Twenty minutes of bright outdoor light provides a caffeinelike boost in alertness that indoor lighting can't match.

Take a breathing break. Most men breathe too shallowly, and that limits the amount of energizing oxygen the body gets. Try this five-minute energizing break offered by Robert Fried, Ph.D., author of *The Psychology and Physiology of Breathing*. Sit quietly at your desk. Close your mouth and breath in slowly and steadily through your nose. As you breathe, make sure your belly rises before your chest does, which will ensure that you're drawing oxygen deep into your lungs. Slowly release each breath in the same way.

Energize with lunch. Put protein on your plate in the form of foods such as sliced turkey breast and skim milk: They prime the brain with chemical messengers that carry alertness signals. Balance with carbohydrate from such sources as whole-wheat bread and fruit to keep muscles supplied with fuel.

Rest your eyes. Staring at a computer screen dries and tires eyes, partly because you don't blink enough to lubricate them. Let your vision roam to more distant objects every few minutes. Also, make sure your monitor is at eye level or lower—higher elevations cause eyes to open wider, making dryness worse.

Outsmart Your Co-workers

Okay, those tips will help you get more energy. But just having energy isn't enough—you need to exude energy. Make people excited about working with you. Revitalize your image so that you come across as a younger, on-the-rise player. This is a political problem and it has some political solutions.

Join the gang. Unless you're a pro solitaire player, when you're at work, you're part of a team. "Practice collegiality like a religion," ad-

vises Marilyn Moats Kennedy, managing partner at Career Strategies in Wilmette, Illinois. Invite new guys to lunch, and always join after-hours gatherings when invited, even if you stay only a short time. This makes you part of the "young" crowd, not an old guy.

Project vitality. Don't just sit at your desk all day long, which makes you seem static and dronelike. Get up every now and then, move briskly through the office, greet people heartily but briefly, advertising the base of support and rapport you have. As much as possible, stand when doing business that doesn't necessitate sitting, such as talking on the phone or reading reports.

Never underestimate yourself. Research at Pennsylvania State University in University Park found that it's not so much our mental powers that suffer as we get older—it's our confidence in them. When the scientists asked 837 people, ages 29 to 95, to predict how they'd do on a series of tests, it was the older participants who consistently underestimated how well they'd perform.

Exercise your arteries. Regular aerobic exercise does more than burn fat and keep your heart healthy. It also helps keep you mentally sharp. Research shows that exercise can prevent arteriosclerosis—that old "hardening of the arteries" that we blame Grandpa's forgetfulness on. One study found that endurance-trained older men had significantly reduced arterial stiffness, compared with their less active peers.

Judge not. Let's just say you hate rap music—you wouldn't know Snoop Doggy Dogg from Snoopy the dog. Or suppose you fail to see the humor in the moronic adventures of Beavis and Butt-Head. Well, shut up about it. You don't have to love this stuff. But you can keep your opinions about music, clothing and personal adornment to yourself.

Make Love Like You Used To

The message we men sometimes get from our partners is that being a good lover equals having staying power during sex. And staying power means two things: physical endurance and sexual endurance. Here's how to gain both.

Change position. During sex, try a variety of positions. Let your partner be on top or lie with you side by side, for example.

This accomplishes two things—it provides opportunities for your mate to do a little more of the work, and it allows you a greater degree of ejaculatory control. Many men find their, uh, composure disappears fastest in the traditional missionary position.

Change your mind. Don't try to distract yourself. Old tricks like trying to take your mind off what's happening by thinking about baseball won't work. "You need to pay more attention to sexual feelings and sensations, not less," says Al Cooper, Ph.D., clinical director of the San Jose Marital and Sexuality Center in California. Being mentally focused makes control easier to achieve. Focusing on your own physical sensations also makes foreplay more enjoyable, and increased foreplay can help enhance your image as a "slow hand."

Change the game. Start the seduction long before bedtime. "Look for opportunities to share activities that are different and exciting," advises Martin Goldberg, M.D., director of the Penn Council for Relationships at the University of Pennsylvania School of Medicine in Philadelphia. "Think of yourself as literally still 'going out' together." A romantic day followed by a torrid night is really a marathon lovemaking session, no?

Change the frequency. Make love often. Practice makes perfect, and the practice isn't bad, either.

Call the doctor. If you have real concerns about premature ejaculation, you may want to investigate drug therapy. Ask your doctor about the antidepressant clomipramine (Anafranil). In a study at Case Western Reserve University in Cleveland, the drug increased men's ability to delay from an average of 81 seconds—about a minute and a half—to an average of 409 seconds—or nearly seven minutes.

Keep Healthy for the Long Haul

History is written, they say, by the men who outlive their rivals. So when it comes to that ultimate goal—immortality—the closer you get to it in the physical sense, the better chance you have of achieving it in the metaphysical sense. That means taking care of your body and your mind. To finish first by finishing last:

Exercise regularly. One hour a week. Is that too much to ask?

Especially considering that one study found people who don't exercise regularly are 100 times more likely to have heart attacks under stressful conditions than those who get regular exercise. A three-times-weekly program of 20 minutes in the gym or on the track is all it takes to be a "regular."

Take your pulse. Your resting heart rate might be the most important indicator of how long you have to live. Not only does a lower heart rate indicate a healthy heart, but research shows it may also protect you from cancer and other diseases. In a study of more than 7,000 British men ages 40 to 59, those with resting heart rates above 90 beats per minute were more than twice as likely to die of cancer or other disease as those with heart rates below 60 beats per minute, even adjusting for smoking behavior. To change your forecast, you need aerobic exercise, which will strengthen your heart and lower the number of times it needs to beat per minute.

Eat a few fruits and vegetables. If you had all day, we'd cite chapter and verse the reams of studies showing that fruits, vegetables and the stuff in them ward off a multitude of cancers and other problems both big and small. The point is, this is easy. You don't have to force down artichokes every night. Just pick a few fruits and vegetables that you like and eat five of them every day. Throw some fruit on your breakfast cereal, snack on an apple, order a salad with your lunch, eat a baked potato and some spinach for dinner. There. You have one of the most important building blocks of a good diet.

Keep moving and shaking. So you were a go-getter right out of college, but you're kicking back and enjoying your current job? Better keep trying to get ahead. In a review of several studies, researchers found that middle-class men who progressed early in their careers but then remained stable later had a higher risk of death than those who progressed in midlife as well.

Keep optimism alive. Studies find that men who are pessimistic in their twenties are 30 percent more likely to be in poor health two to three decades later. The key to positive thinking is learning to control your response to tough times, says Martin Seligman, Ph.D., author of *Learned Optimism*.

- Always tell yourself you can do better. Even if the boss loves your newest report, tell yourself you can do better. That way, if he hates the next one—well, no big deal. You're getting better all the time, right?
- Keep looking at the big picture. You've made it this far, all the while supporting a family and keeping your sanity. Keep patting yourself on the back for everything you've accomplished.
- Remember, there are very few fatal flaws in life. A screw-up is not some preternatural manifestation of your own lack of worth. It's a screw-up. You've done it before; you'll do it again. So will everybody else.
- Finally, never attribute success to luck. Yours or anybody else's.

Laugh at fate. Just believing you are in control of your destiny can lengthen your life. Researchers looked at Chinese-Americans who were born in years that were traditionally believed to be ill-fated for certain diseases. Those individuals died as many as four years earlier than Chinese-Americans whose birth years didn't harbinger health problems. Are the ancient myths true? Not likely. The unlucky Asians also died younger than Anglos born in the same years—apparently because the Anglos simply didn't believe they were doomed to die young.

Keep your friends close. In a study of 1,368 heart disease patients at Duke University in Durham, North Carolina, those with even one good friend were three times less likely to die after a heart attack than those with no close relationships. Why? Perhaps because friendships protect us from stress. In another study, men with a social network had lower levels of stress hormones in their blood. Building your social bases is largely a matter of removing the obstacles, according to Robert Pasick, Ph.D., author of *What Every Man Needs to Know*. Here are some suggestions.

- Don't wait for old friends to come to you. Make the call. Write the letter. "Don't assume a one-up, everything's-fine posture," Dr. Pasick says. "If there might be unresolved hurts between

JUST THE FACTS

Number of men in every thousand who are hearing impaired: 369 you, mention them and express a desire to get past them."

- Follow up. You do it for your business associates, so why not for friends? Keep track of birthdays and drop a line. Call them up every so often just to touch base. Try to do them favors when they're down because of work troubles, illness or marital strife. Keep important dates in your friends' lives written in your day planner.

Celebrate your birthday. Your attitude about aging can affect your life expectancy, too. In one study, older adults who believed their health status was a function of age had a 78 percent greater risk of dying than those who believed their health was a function of controllable factors, such as how they took care of themselves.

Take vitamin E supplements. More and more research seems to indicate that E is the king of vitamins. In two studies, people who took at least 100 international units of vitamin E a day for two years had about a 40 percent lower risk of heart disease than those who relied on diet alone for their vitamin intake. This is important, because E is hard to get through diet alone—it's mainly found in foods like canola oil and nuts. The vitamin has been shown to keep fat in the bloodstream from turning into artery-clogging cholesterol.

Don't diet. As bad as being overweight is, losing weight and gaining it back may be worse. In a study of more than 11,000 men, those whose weight fluctuated more than 11 pounds over the course of 15 years showed a significantly increased risk of mortality. If you are overweight, the key is to lose the weight slowly through lifestyle changes like exercise, which will help you keep the weight off.

—Richard Allan

PART 3

Muscle
Mastery

A Year of
World Records in Sports

Here are some of the latest feats of the world's greatest sportsmen.

1. U.S. track-and-field star Leroy Burrell set a new world mark of 9.85 seconds in the men's 100-meter race.

2. Swiss cyclist Tony Rominger pedaled 55.291 kilometers in just 60 minutes for a new world record.

3. Olympic speed skater Dan Jansen carved his name in the record books by skating 1,000 meters in 1 minute, 12 seconds.

4. The largest stadium in the world is Maracaña Municipal Stadium in Rio de Janeiro, which can hold 205,000 people, roughly twice the size of the largest U.S. stadium.

5. Wayne Gretzky became the National Hockey League's all-time scoring leader when he netted his 802nd career goal.

6. Jerry Rice, the National Football League 49ers wide receiver, scored his 127th career touchdown to surpass the great Jim Brown on the all-time list.

7. A nine-man team from the Forum Health Club in Chelmsleywood, Great Britain, set a world 24-hour bench-press record of 8,873,860 pounds.

8. Pole vaulter Sergei Bubka soared to a new world-record height of 20 feet, 1¾ inches in Sestriere, Italy.

9. Russian Alexander Popov posted a new world mark of 48.21 seconds in men's 100-meter freestyle swimming.

10. Cross downhill skiing with mountain biking and what do you get? Most likely you get a nice memorial service—unless your name is Christian Taillefer. Then you get a new downhill speed record of 111 miles per hour, beating the old world record by almost 20 miles per hour.

Firming Up the Fat Farm

Chisel Out a Stronger Self with this Three-Part Plan

The mystery at first seems as perplexing as the allure of polka music. The bathroom scale says you've gained a modest five pounds since college, but the way your trousers are squeezing your midsection says something entirely different. It's a common conundrum, and the simplest explanation is this: Over the years, your body, totally unbeknownst to you, may have been shedding muscle and replacing it with fat.

There are a number of reasons for this cruel trick of nature, explains James Graves, Ph.D., associate professor and chair of the health and physical education program at Syracuse University in New York. "For one thing, as we get older, we tend to become less active, so the fat we used to burn off begins to collect," he says. "For another, the male body begins to put out less human growth hormone, thus it's harder to build or keep muscle mass as we age."

Luckily, what once was can be once again. In a study at Washington University School of Medicine in St. Louis, researchers showed that the male tendency to swap lean muscle for fat is anything but inevitable, if you throw exercise into the equation. The researchers divided older men into two groups, exercisers and nonexercisers. Then they compared them with two similar groups of younger men. They found the older couch potatoes were carrying an average of 22.2 pounds more pure fat than the younger couch potatoes—but the older exercisers were less than 9½ pounds fatter than the younger active men.

63

And when it comes to losing muscle mass as the years tick by, that process can be reversed. According to studies by William J. Evans, Ph.D., director of the Noll Physiological Research Center at Pennsylvania State University in University Park, men on a weight-lifting program can increase muscle strength more than 200 percent, even at the age of 96. A bonus is that weight training may help slow the age-related decline of human growth hormone, making it easier to maintain muscle once you have it.

Now for the big questions: How many pounds of fat need to be converted to muscle to make your body look brand new? And more important, how long will it take? The answers: not as many as you might think—and not as long as you might expect.

According to Dr. Graves, the average middle-age man in the United States is carrying around 20 percent body fat, whereas the reasonably active college-age male has about 15 percent body fat. That's not a huge difference, particularly when you figure that for a 160-pound man to drop from 20 percent body fat to 15, he has to lose only eight pounds of fat. "If that eight pounds could be replaced with eight pounds of muscle, that guy would be looking really good," says Dr. Graves.

Following is a three-part program designed to beef up your muscle mass and make fat a thing of the past.

Part 1: Food

Because we're all men here, we can safely say that none of us fears hard work. What makes us uncomfortable, however, is anything that threatens to restrict our pleasure. That's why you'll be glad to know that the menu changes we're suggesting are modest—painless, even. Consider: The typical male diet is about 35 percent fat, 45 percent carbohydrate and 20 percent protein. If you can just reduce fat to 20 percent, raise carbohydrate to 60 percent and leave protein at 20, the payoff is huge.

Research shows that subjects placed on a simple diet of lean meat, fruits and vegetables can lower their body-fat ratios even without exercise. What's lean meat? "Chicken and fish are lean enough to do the job," says Loren Cordain, Ph.D., director of the Colorado State University Human Performance Research Center in Fort Collins. "And you can even find some lean cuts of beef and pork that won't upset your program."

A word of caution: The one thing you don't need to worry about is protein. "Men trying to gain a little muscle mass often get fixated on the concept of needing more protein," notes Dr. Graves. "But most of us are already getting the appropriate amounts of protein."

Part 2: Aerobic Training

The word here is "moderation," in both amount and intensity. Your body adapts to the demands you put on it, and if you overdo the aerobics, your body will mold itself into a marathoner, not a weight lifter, says Don Chu, Ph.D., author and training consultant for the Ather Sports Injury Clinic in Castro Valley, California. In other words, you'll shed fat well enough, but you won't build muscle.

"For this kind of program, where muscle growth is as important as fat loss, I recommend people start with 20 minutes of aerobic activity three times a week," Dr. Chu says. "Over the next three or four weeks, you should move up to about 30 to 40 minutes per session."

As for exercise, anything that gets you puffing will do. Bicycling, fast walking, jogging, climbing stairs are all fine choices.

Part 3: Weight Training

Welcome to the bottom line. Aerobic exercise will help you shed fat. The right diet will help you keep fat off and provide the right fuel for muscle growth. But if you want to pick up muscle, you have to pick up some weights.

The following exercise plan is designed to build weight slowly at first, then faster toward the end. You'll work half your body one day, and the other half the next. Then take a day off. Plenty of rest

(continued on page 70)

The Exercises

Okay. You know how to exercise, you know how to eat. But what exactly should you be doing once you pick up a barbell or dumbbell? Here's a workout routine to turn that fat into muscle. But remember, for any free-weight exercise you do that requires you to hold the weight above your head, use a spotter. This is not a namby-pamby program here, and serious weight lifting means serious safety.

MONDAY AND THURSDAY
Chest, Shoulders and Triceps

Dumbbell fly. Lie on your back on a flat exercise bench with a dumbbell in each hand. Raise your arms straight above your chest, palms facing each other and elbows slightly bent. Slowly lower the dumbbells in an arc away from your body, so your hands end up out to your sides. Now gradually raise the weights, again following the same curving trajectory, until the weights are once again nearly together above your chest.

Incline dumbbell bench press. Sit on an incline bench with a dumbbell in each hand. Raise them to your chest, keeping your hands shoulder-width apart, palms facing away from you, elbows at your sides. This is the starting position. Now slowly raise the weights, pressing them up above your chest and touching the weights together. Be sure not to lock your elbows at the top of the movement. Slowly lower the weights back to the starting position.

Decline dumbbell bench press. Lie back on a decline bench with your head at the low end and your feet secured at the high end. Have a spotter hand you a pair of dumbbells and position them above your head as you grip them with arms extended straight up, shoulder-width apart, palms facing each other. Now slowly lower the dumbbells to your chest, keeping your elbows back and wide. Push them back into the starting position, making sure to avoid locking your elbows.

Twisting military press. Stand straight, feet shoulder-width apart, with a dumbbell in each hand. Bring the weights to shoulder height and in close to the chest, palms facing your chest. Now slowly push the weights upward while rotating your wrists outward. (At the top of the movement, your palms should be facing away from you.) Slowly lower the weights back down, rotating the palms back inward.

Side lateral. Stand straight with a dumbbell in each hand, arms at your sides. Begin by raising your arms out from your sides until they are parallel to the floor, palms up, with elbows slightly bent. At the top of the movement, rotate your wrists forward as if you were pouring two pitchers of water. Hold briefly and slowly lower the weights to the starting position.

Bent-over lateral. Sit on the edge of a bench with a dumbbell in each hand, so the weights hang at your sides. Slowly bend at the waist until your chest touches your thighs. Your arms should be hanging straight down with the weights by your feet. Slowly raise the dumbbells out to each side until your arms are parallel to the floor. Hold for a second, then return to the starting position.

Two-hand triceps extension. Standing naturally, feet shoulder-width apart, grasp a dumbbell with both hands and raise it above your head so the weight is vertical and the top plate rests comfortably on the palms of your hands, thumbs around the handle, palms facing up. This is the starting position. Now, keeping your feet in place, your back straight and elbows close to your head, slowly lower the weight behind your head as far as is comfortable. Finish by raising the weight back to the starting position. (But don't lock your elbows.)

Rope pull-down. Thread a thick rope or a small towel through the hook of a lat pull-down machine. Stand facing the machine, about a foot away, and hold both sides of the rope about eight inches below the hook, hands six inches apart. Keeping your back straight and elbows at your sides, slowly pull down until your arms are beside your thighs, elbows locked. Slowly bring your hands back to the starting position.

(continued)

The Exercises—*Continued*

TUESDAY AND FRIDAY
Back, Biceps and Legs

Dead lift. Stand facing a barbell on the floor with the bar over your toes. Keeping your head and back straight, bend your knees and grasp the bar with a shoulder-wide alternating grip (one palm facing you, the other facing away). Your arms should be extended but not locked. With your back straight, slowly stand up, keeping the bar close to your body throughout the lift. Slowly return to the starting position.

Stiff-arm seated pulley row. Sit at a pulley machine with your feet against the foot rest, knees slightly bent. (Keep your knees in this position throughout the movement.) Bend forward and grab the handles with both hands, palms facing each other. Keeping your elbows slightly bent and back flat, lean your torso back until you are sitting up straight. Arms should remain extended throughout the exercise. Slowly lower to the starting position.

Reverse-grip pull-down. Stand facing a pull-down machine and grab the bar with an underhand grip, hands shoulder-width apart. Kneel in front of the machine, letting the resistance extend your arms overhead. Keeping your back straight, slowly pull the bar down to the front of your chest. Hold, then return to the starting position.

Seated biceps curl. Sit on the edge of a bench with a dumbbell in each hand. Drop your arms toward the floor, keeping your palms facing inward. With your back straight, slowly curl both dumbbells up toward your shoulders. Hold, then lower to the starting position.

Reverse-grip E-Z curl. Standing with your feet shoulder-width apart, hold an E-Z curl bar (shorter, angled bars) with a palms-down grip. Keep your elbows close to your sides. Slowly curl the bar to shoulder level, then lower it slowly back into starting position.

Leg press. Sit in a leg press machine with your back flat against the pad and your feet firmly on the platform 12 inches apart. Release the weight and slowly lower it until your legs are bent slightly less than 90 degrees. Slowly raise the weight until your legs are straight, but don't lock your knees. Return to the starting position.

Leg extension. Sit on a leg extension machine with your feet beneath the pads so your knees are snug against the seat. With your head and back straight, raise both legs until they're fully extended. Hold, then gently lower to the starting position.

Leg curl. Lie facedown on the leg curl machine, placing your feet under the pads with your knees just over the edge of the bench. Curl your lower legs up until your feet almost touch your buttocks. Hold, then lower to the starting position.

Seated calf raise. Sit at a seated calf machine with your back straight and your knees under the pads. Place the balls of your feet on the foot bar, toes facing forward. Release the safety bar and drop your heels as low as possible. Loosely grip the knee pads for stability and push up as high as possible on the balls of your feet. Lower to the starting position.

MONDAY THROUGH FRIDAY
Abdominals

Abdominal muscles are one of the few you can work every day. They respond better to high-repetition sets, so stay at between 12 and 16 repetitions for the following two exercises during all 12 weeks of the program.

Seated leg tuck. Sit on the edge of a flat bench. Straighten your legs and lean your torso back until your body forms a 45-degree angle. Bend your knees as you raise them to your chest. Hold for a second, then extend your legs back out in front of you. Keep continuous tension on your lower abdominals throughout the movement.

High-pulley crunch. Thread a rope or towel through the hook of a pulley machine. Get on your knees facing the machine about three feet away. Both your knees and thighs should be touching. Hold the ends of the rope against the top of your head and slowly curl your torso forward. You'll be using your abdominal muscles to lift the weight stack. Return to the starting position.

is included, and that's deliberate, because what people don't realize is that muscle isn't being built during the workout. It's being built during the repair process, which occurs during rest. "All that extra rest time is going to add up to the increased muscle growth you're looking for," says Dr. Chu.

By the way, there's a little anatomy lesson that goes with this program. You don't need to know it, of course, and if you'd rather just follow us blindly, you can skip the next few paragraphs and get to work. If you'd like to know why this workout will build muscle, however, here are the facts.

Within your muscles are two kinds of fibers: slow-twitch and fast-twitch. Slow-twitch fibers are the ones that provide endurance. They'll take you through Hell's triathlon. But, unfortunately, they don't distinguish themselves in the area of building bulk. They are developed by lifting lower amounts of weight many times. Fast-twitch muscles are the big, bulky kind that make you look impressive in a T-shirt and provide short bursts of explosive power. These dynamos are best worked when you lift a lot of weight a few times.

Anatomy lesson over, but keep these different muscle fibers in mind as you progress through the following three phases. Each phase is designed to attack these fibers in a steadily more challenging way. Happy lifting.

The Program
Weeks 1 to 4: Getting Toned

The beginning part of your regimen is designed to get your slow-twitch muscles up to speed. Without building proper endurance, you won't have the stamina to build well-balanced muscle. So the order of the day is many repetitions, many sets, but not many pounds on the bar. As for what exercises to do, do the ones we've included with this chapter.

Week 1: You'll want to do each of the exercises in this program 12 times. Then do them another 12 times—and finally do them another 12 times. In gym lingo, that's "three sets of 12 repetitions." You'll want to use weight light enough that you can lift it for three sets of 12 without too much trouble, but heavy enough that you'll be exhausted after your third set.

The Fat Index: How Much Is Lean, How Much Is Lard?

A scale will tell you what you weigh, but not how much of that weight is pure fat. If you were an Olympic athlete, you might have your trainer use a set of fat-measuring calipers on you, or submerge you in water to check the displacement. However, since you probably aren't heading for the Olympic Games this year, odds are no one's clamoring to gauge your body composition for you.

No matter. Here's a simple way to get an approximate figure, courtesy of Jack Wilmore, Ph.D., an exercise physiologist at the University of Texas at Austin and author of *Sensible Fitness*. All you need is your waist measurement and your weight. Measure your midsection at the exact level of your belly button (or just take the waist measurement you use when you buy pants) and draw a line from that number to your weight, using the chart at right. Your body-fat percentage is where the straight line crosses the percent-fat line.

Weeks 2 to 4: Now that you have a feel for the exercises, see if you can't boost yourself to five sets of 15 repetitions. "If you find yourself progressing quickly, you can go as high as 20 reps per set, but no more than that," says Dr. Chu. The reason is simple: If you can do more than 20 reps at a time, you're not using enough weight to give your muscle fiber the challenge it needs. Only when you find yourself breaking the 20-rep limit should you add some extra weight. Rest 30 seconds to one minute between sets.

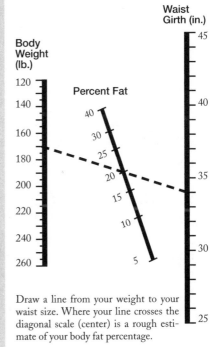

Draw a line from your weight to your waist size. Where your line crosses the diagonal scale (center) is a rough estimate of your body fat percentage.

Weeks 5 to 8: Building Up

Once you've gotten up to four or five sets of 15 repetitions, it's time to start lifting more weight, but lifting it fewer times. This is the phase that will trigger serious muscle growth.

Week 5: Start with three sets of 8 repetitions. Since you're doing fewer exercises, you'll be able to use more weight. In phase one, for example, you might have been bench-pressing 100 pounds 15 times. But if you're lifting a weight only 8 times, you might be able to press 150 pounds.

Weeks 6 to 8: Once you're comfortable with three sets of eight repetitions, step up the number of repetitions to ten for each set. Now you're really working. By Week 8, progress to four sets of ten repetitions. It'll be during this phase that you'll start to notice some growth as opposed to the subtle toning and mild definition brought out earlier. That's because you've begun to awaken those fast-twitch fibers. Rest one to two minutes between sets.

Weeks 9 to 12: Bulking Up

Now it's time to really coax some growth out of your muscles. This part of the program intensifies the muscle-building strategy in order to give you the body buildup you want.

Week 9: Start this phase the way you ended the last one, with four sets, but this time lift the weight only five times per set. That means—you guessed it—adding more weight. Add enough iron so your muscles reach fatigue in a mere five repetitions.

Weeks 10 to 12: Keeping the weight the same, work up to five sets of six repetitions. Rest two to three minutes between sets.

Continuing Education

True progress in weight lifting doesn't come by reaching your goal, then quitting. It's an evolution. So after 12 weeks, look at your progress. If you've accomplished what you wanted to accomplish, then go back and concentrate on whichever routine you felt most comfortable doing. If your goal is to continue building mass, stick with that program, but increase the poundage as you progress.

—*P. Myatt Murphy*

Brilliant Exercise

Maximize Workouts by Flexing Mental Muscles

"Pretend your arms are meat hooks."

"What?"

"Pretend your arms are meat hooks," my workout partner repeats. I have 110 pounds of iron suspended in front of me, my muscles are screaming for mercy, and this guy wants me to make believe I'm the bad guy in *Peter Pan*? "You're cheating—you're using your forearm muscles to pull the lat bar down," he says.

"Oh."

"If you think of your arms as hooks, that'll keep your wrists straight and you'll use your back muscles instead."

He's right. With this little mind game, I'm able to relax my arms and let the muscles of my back pull the bar down to my chest. The effort goes where I want it to, and the muscles I want to develop get a full workout.

Unbeknownst to me, I've just engaged in a tactic called imagery, using the creative powers of my mind to enhance my exercise routine.

More and more, researchers are beginning to take notice of the role that the mind plays in exercise—as well as the role that exercise plays in enhancing the mind. Getting the most from your workout, it seems, means bringing more than just your muscles into play.

In fact, there are plenty of ways to engage your brain at the same time you engage your body. Simple mind games, motivation tactics and relaxation techniques can help a guy stick to, and get more from, his workout.

And no, we're not going to get all weird and New Agey on you—no stuffing crystals down your pants, no pyramid hats. The techniques that follow are simple and effective, designed for the guy who simply wants to get the most he can from exercise.

The Mind-Body Link

Researchers have known for a long time that exercise can boost brainpower and creativity. "For some people, the creative thinking that occurs during and after exercise is quite pronounced," says Kenneth Callen, M.D., an associate professor of psychiatry at the Oregon Health Sciences University School of Medicine in Portland.

In one study, Joan Gondola, Ph.D., of Baruch College of the City University of New York, found that students who participated in aerobic fitness and dance classes were able to think of more uses for an ordinary object, such as a pencil, than those who didn't participate in aerobics.

Why the increase in original ideas during exercise? Some experts believe that exercise increases oxygen flow to the brain. "As you become aerobically trained, the body becomes more efficient at transporting and utilizing oxygen," says Robert Dustman, Ph.D., a researcher at the Veterans Affairs Medical Center in Salt Lake City. Other researchers speculate that exercise triggers the release of hormones that enhance creativity. Some even theorize that aerobic exercise may suppress activity in the left hemisphere of the brain, the half that is responsible for logical thought, and stimulate the right hemisphere, which regulates intuition and creativity.

All this is great news but what does that

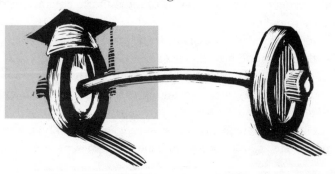

mean to our biceps and our waistlines? Plenty. In fact, creativity and imagination can work wonders on your workout—if you know how to use them right. Here's how.

Drive yourself with distraction. One of the most effective mental techniques available to athletes—and the rest of us—is a strategy called dissociation. It's essentially a form of controlled daydreaming, consciously directing your mind away from the task at hand and on to more pleasant thoughts. The result is a more enjoyable workout, a less boring workout. In short, a workout that you'll look forward to instead of dreading.

Researchers at Smith College in Northampton, Massachusetts, studied the effects of dissociation on exercise in women. Student subjects cycled for 15 minutes while their heart rates were monitored. Some were asked to concentrate strictly on their exertion levels during the exercise; others were asked to try to remember the names of every teacher they'd had since kindergarten. While the actual exertion was similar for both groups, those who were busy conjuring up schoolmarms of yore rated their level of exertion as significantly less than their self-focusing peers did. And while these test subjects were women, researchers say that dissociation tactics work as well in men.

Exercise your mind first. The technique is called visualization. When you imagine yourself exercising before you actually begin working out, you get tangible, muscle-building benefits as well as better performance. In one study, subjects were asked to use three different mental strategies to prepare for a grip-strength test. One strategy consisted of psyching themselves up by getting mad or pumped up. Another was visualizing themselves squeezing the grip-strength meter as hard as they could. The third was counting backward out loud from 20. Those who visualized themselves squeezing the meter did far better on the test than those who prepared by using the other methods.

There's evidence that this type of mental preparation may have some direct impact on the nerves, effectively "priming" the muscles needed for a specific task. Some studies have measured a 30 percent contraction in the biceps of test subjects who simply envisioned flexing the muscles, says Diana McNab, assistant professor of sports psychology at Seton Hall University in South Orange, New Jersey. Some exercise therapists use this imagery tactic on patients recovering from surgery. Even though they can't, say, perform a sit-up, if they imagine themselves performing one, they'll get a slight muscular contraction that will encourage recovery.

Give yourself an imaginary helping hand. Any psychological ploy to make your task seem easier than it is can improve performance. In his *Winning Guide to Sports Endurance,* triathlete Scott Tinley notes that seven-time world professional marathon swimming champion Paul Asmuth sometimes imagined he had something attached to his head that was pulling him through the water. This kind of positive thinking can help anyone perform better. For example, McNab recommends that a way to squeeze out a few more crunches in a routine exercise plan is to envision a string connecting your navel to your spine. As you curl up, imagine that string pulling down on your navel, tugging it toward your backbone. "That image will help you get a fuller contraction," she says.

Help comes in different forms for different people, of course. If you need some inspiration to complete that three-mile run, turn your last laps around the high-school track into the final stretch of the Boston Marathon, the crowd cheering as you close in fast on the leader.

It may also help to ease up once in a while. "You don't have to be in a competitive mood all the time," says sports psychologist Michael Sachs, Ph.D., associate professor of physical education at Temple University in Philadelphia. "Remember to relax and enjoy your workout."

Focus on form. Sometimes it's hard to let your mind go, especially when it starts to wander toward things like your mortgage payments, for example, or that weasel in promotions who keeps claiming credit for your ideas. In times like these, you still want to distract your mind away from your exertion level, so think positively and focus it instead on your form. Some examples from Tinley: Keep your stride long, turn your pedals in a circle, pull all the way through with your swimming stroke, make your bench press slow and even. "You'll find those niggling doubts and fears melting away as you concentrate on the mechanics of your efforts," he says.

Live in a dream world. If you still doubt that subconscious thought and performance are linked, we have news for you. In a study of masters track-and-field athletes, researchers in Arkansas and Oregon found that those who dreamed about competition, particularly those who dreamed of success, tended to report faster personal times for some events. Even if you're not a competitive athlete, go to bed with exercise on your mind, and you may just sleep your way to a better workout.

The Body-Mind Link

Just getting to the gym is more than half the battle. The problem is that when there are a thousand other things screaming for your attention, skipping a workout is often the easiest thing to do. What you need is a dose of motivation. But here's a secret: Motivation is inextricably bound with self-esteem.

To keep on coming back to the gym, you have to put value on what you're accomplishing—that is, taking care of yourself. A study at Texas Tech University in Lubbock rated the self-esteem levels of 31 people with sports- or job-related injuries whose rehabilitation included physical therapy. Researchers found that those who ranked low in self-esteem were the same people who skipped or canceled the most therapy appointments.

On the other hand, regular exercise has been shown to build self-esteem and fight depression, possibly by speeding more oxygen to the brain. "You get more circulation to the brain, so you're more likely to have normal recall instead of getting bogged down in unpleasant memories," explains Robert S. Brown, Sr., M.D., Ph.D., clinical professor of psychiatric medicine at the University of Virginia School of Medicine in Charlottesville. In short, regular workouts build self-esteem, but self-esteem is crucial in getting you to

JUST THE FACTS

Here's how to maximize your running: Don't think about it. Researchers at the University of Alabama say that runners whose minds wander during a run feel more invigorated than runners who monitor things like heart rate or breathing.

work out. Well, don't fear. Here are some simple mental tricks that can improve your outlook—and your exercise habits.

Get S.M.A.R.T. The key to maintaining any fitness regimen is to set reasonable goals for yourself. If you start out with the objective to get in the best shape of your life in six weeks, guess what, fella—you're not going to make it. Focus your goals on performance rather than winning and frame them in positive terms. Dr. Sachs recommends that you use the acronym S.M.A.R.T. and set goals that are:

*S*pecific: You want to set a certain pace, run for a certain period of time, lift a set amount of weight—something you can determine that you've accomplished.

*M*easurable: You should be able to show proof of your progress, be it with a watch or set of weight plates.

*A*ttainable: A goal that a sensible workout program should put within your reach—not so difficult that you're frustrated, not so easy that you're bored.

*R*ealistic: Before you decide where you want to go, make sure you've made a reasonable assessment of where you are. If you know you can get to the gym only three times a week, be sure your goal is attainable with that level of exercise.

*T*ime-bound: Set a specific time frame for reaching your goal.

Get creative in monitoring your progress. Most any book on exercise you pick up will tell you to keep a log as a motivation tool. If you're the diary-writing sort, fine. If not, try some more creative tactics. Let's say you're planning on running three miles a day, three times a week. Get a map of your state, draw a line across it, and trace nine miles along the line for each week you meet your goal. You should make it across the widest part of New Jersey in less than eight weeks. Before long, you'll be on your way to navigating the whole country.

Bank on your progress. If you run, walk or cycle, each day after you finish, toss a penny or a nickel (or more if you're so inclined) into a jar or bowl. As weeks go by, you'll see ever-increasing evidence of the progress you've already made.

Take some affirmative action. Affirmations have nothing to do with joining a religious cult or contacting your inner child. They're simple phrases or words you can repeat to yourself whenever you feel a funk coming on. Thinking about skipping today's workout? The minute the thought crosses your mind, simply say to yourself, "Stop." Take a deep breath. Now refocus your thoughts in a positive light: "I'm on the road to fitness. I want to stay there."

Remember, you'll feel better if you exercise. In one study, researchers asked subjects suffering from depression to memorize a list of words such as "pretty" and "ugly." Then, 90 minutes later, they asked the subjects to recall all the words. A majority of them recalled mainly negative ones. After the same depressed folks participated in an aerobics class, the memorization drill was repeated. This time, there was a significant upsurge in the number of positive terms recalled.

Take up a demanding sport. In a study conducted by Dr. Brown, student athletes at the University of Virginia were given mood-evaluation tests at the beginning and end of their sport seasons. Result: Those who participated in high-energy sports such as basketball and wrestling showed a greater improvement in mood than those who participated in low-intensity sports such as golf.

But even challenging sports can get old if that's all you do. If you want the psychological lift that exercise can deliver, don't get stuck in a rut. On one level, this means if you don't enjoy biking, don't bike. Take up racquetball, swimming, weight training, whatever. Look for a sport that fulfills your emotional needs as well as your physical ones. On another level, it also means breaking up even the sports you do like with a variety of different activities. Cross-training is all about this kind of change—different workouts not only challenge different muscles, but they may stimulate different parts of the brain.

The Body-Stress Link

High-tension living has been linked to everything from cardiovascular diseases to immune dysfunction. Yet exercise seems to keep some of these problems at bay. A study done with the Honolulu Heart Program found, for example, that among older men who lead active lifestyles, the incidence of stroke is about one-third of that for inactive men.

Why exactly do men find stress relief from exercise? One theory suggests that exercise triggers the release of brain chemicals, such as endorphins, that have a positive effect on mood. In a study at Ohio State University in Columbus, students who participated in aerobics three times a week not only improved their fitness levels but also significantly lowered their test anxiety levels in less than two months. In another study, researchers in Kansas found that men who jogged at least 20 minutes a day three times a week were less anxious and expressed less anger, hostility and aggression than nonexercisers.

That's good, not only for your mind but for your body as well. Ask any member of the losing team in the Super Bowl how too much stress can affect athletic performance. After he's finished wiping the floor with you, he'll probably tell you that when your mind is stressed out, your body is prone to making mistakes. This is not something you want, especially if you're going to be bench-pressing your weight this afternoon.

Take your meditation. Meditating for as little as 20 minutes twice a day can be remarkably effective in improving general well-being, according to some experts. It can also help you get more from your workout, since a relaxed body performs better than a tense one. If you're not one for meditation, three-time Ironman World Series champion Tinley recommends a practical alternative. Before, say, a session of weight training, find a spot where you can be alone, close your eyes briefly and see yourself moving through the exercise.

"The idea is to calm yourself," says Tinley. Envision yourself moving easily through the motions, maintaining your form and exhaling with each repetition.

Hop on the table. Athletes in every sport, from three-time Tour de France champion Greg LeMond to horseshoe pitcher George Bush, rely on massage, notes Tinley. Anyone who trains regularly subjects muscle and mind to substantial strain. Physically, massage reduces muscle tightness, aids circulation and relieves soreness. Mentally, the soothing salve of massage eases tension—and where a soothed mind leads, rigid muscles often follow.

"On the massage table, you learn how it feels to be relaxed," says Bob McAtee, a Colorado Springs massage therapist who works extensively with athletes. "If you carry that feeling of relaxation over into training—remember what it's like for your shoulders to be relaxed, your legs to be relaxed—you're much more likely to perform better."

No time to book the services of a massage therapist? Self-massage can be a valuable addition to your training routine, and you can reap the benefits in as little as 10 to 15 minutes a day, says McAtee. Here are some pointers for the neophyte.

- First, use large, vigorous strokes along the length of the entire muscle. Large strokes might include rolling, kneading or long, gliding strokes. To help circulation, direct these strokes toward the heart.
- Follow with smaller strokes, working across the grain of the muscle to help separate and relax the muscle fibers.
- If you encounter pain, leave it be. "There's good pain and there's bad pain. Massage can relieve good pain, such as muscle soreness. But bad pain means you're working too deeply or working on something that shouldn't be massaged. If it's painful, stop," advises McAtee.

Stretch your mind as well as your body. "Every athlete performs better when relaxed," says Bob Anderson, a runner and cyclist and author of the book *Stretching.* And, he says, incorporating regular stretching sessions into your training routine is one of the most effective ways to teach your mind and your muscles how to relax. The key is to try to relax physically and mentally during your stretches.

Unfortunately, most of us who do bother with stretching rush through it briefly before breaking into a jog or jumping on the bike. If you can't fit a relaxed stretching session into your daily routine, pick a relaxed time during your day to stretch—say, right before *Home Improvement.* As long as you stretch slowly and gently and remember to focus on the feel of the stretch, you can do this any time without warming up first, says Anderson. Here are a few quick tips to remember.

- Slow and steady. Never bounce, and never stretch to the point where you feel pain.

- Avoid stretches that use your body weight to stretch a muscle—the old standard toe touch, for example. Throwing your body weight behind a stretch may force you to go beyond your natural limit, and presto, you're injured.
- Hold each stretch for 15 to 30 seconds to allow time for the body to relax.

Don't buy the couch-potato excuse. So you're not a regular exerciser? You can still blow off stress with a brisk 20-minute walk, says David Roth, Ph.D., associate professor of psychology at the University of Alabama in Birmingham. "The one-shot exercise session does appear to have anti-anxiety effects," he says. That's not to say that an occasional walk is a substitute for a regular exercise program. Expect the relaxing effects of that walk to last about an hour.

—Stephen Perrine

The Sinful Seven

Avoid the Most Common Exercise Mistakes

Back when you played sports in high school or college, you didn't have the option of slacking off in practice. You had a coach with eagle eyes and drill-sergeant vocal cords, threatening you with extra wind sprints the first time he saw you dog it around the track.

But now that you're training on your own, it's easy to pick up bad habits, fall prey to poor advice and—there's no kind way to say this, fellas—just get lazy. One look down at an expanding middle is enough to make a guy nostalgic for the bark of Coach Crackwhip.

Since there's no one around now to blow the whistle on you whenever you cheat on your workout, it's up to you to make sure you're not taking the easy way out and robbing yourself of the health-and-fitness benefits you're there to achieve in the first place. All you need are some reminders—a few gentle boots in the pants, if you will—to knock you back on track. "A simple correction in your training or technique could make all the difference in the world," says Randy Huntington, a Fresno, California, coach and fitness consultant whose client list has included Wayne Gretzky and world-record long jumper Mike Powell.

With the help of Huntington and other coaches, trainers and exercise physiologists, we've identified the most common training mistakes men make. Our quick fixes will help you get more from your workouts, spare you needless injury and boost your performance in your chosen sport.

Mistake: Swimming with a kickboard. Using a kickboard would seem to be a good way to train your legs, since the foam board holds your body above water while your legs do all the work. In fact, a kickboard causes the hips and legs to drop lower, so they drag underwater, says Michael Collins, coach of the Davis, California, Aquatic Masters and the 1990 United States Masters coach of the year. "Good swimmers keep their bodies horizontal on the surface, making them more streamlined."

Quick Fix: For a better workout, leave the kickboard on the pool deck, Collins suggests, and flutter-kick on your side. For proper freestyle form, extend your underwater arm in front of you and rest your surface arm against your side; every 10 to 12 kicks, take a stroke to switch sides. This drill keeps your legs in alignment with your torso, the perfect position for slicing through the water.

Mistake: Lifting with cold muscles. "Ninety percent of men who work out with weights do not warm up before lifting," says Edward Jackowski, owner of Exude, a nationwide fitness training company based in New York City, and author of *Hold It! You're Exercising Wrong.* "If they warm up at all, it's with a light set of bench presses, which does nothing but shock your muscles." Lifting with cold, tight muscles is the number one reason lifters suffer injuries and muscle soreness after a bout with the iron.

Quick Fix: "Break a sweat before you lift," suggests Jackowski. Don't worry about warming up particular muscles. What you need are some aerobic exercises that increase blood circulation to the entire body. The best aerobic warm-ups are: five to ten minutes of pedaling a stationary bicycle at between 60 and 90 revolutions per minute with the bike set at low to moderate tension, ten minutes of walking at a pace of three to four miles per hour, five minutes of running at five to seven miles per hour or five minutes of jumping rope.

Mistake: Lifting with bad technique. The top enemy of building stronger, bigger muscles is poor form. Without proper technique, you tend to cheat, which not only cuts into your strength gains but also increases your risk for injury. One of the most common of these mistakes, says Jackowski, is arching your back off the bench as you're pressing up a heavy weight. "Arching is using leverage; it's artificial strength," he says. "Besides, it's a surefire way to strain your back muscles."

Another common mistake—and dangerous bad habit—is using momentum to do a biceps curl. During a standing biceps curl with a barbell, men tend to bounce their hands off their thighs to help them curl the weight upward. That's cheating, and it isn't doing anything to make your muscles stronger.

Quick Fix: Flatten your lower back against the bench as you press upward. There are two tricks to ensure that you do this: First, lower the poundage about 20 percent—that's the typical extra amount of weight most guys try to lift that they can't handle. Second, bring your feet off the floor and place them flat on the bench, just in front of your buttocks. Doing so will help keep your lower back against the bench as you lift.

For the biceps curl, lower the weight very slowly on the negative phase of the curl, using a count of 1-2-3-4, and hesitate a split second after you reach your thighs. This will keep you from bouncing or rocking.

Mistake: "Yo-yoing" at cable stations. By their very design, the cable stations on weight-stack machines encourage a common mistake that Jackowski calls yo-yoing. It's when you allow the descending weight to yank dangerously on your arms at the end of the move.

Quick Fix: Stay in control of the weight by working slowly and limiting your range of motion. On triceps push-downs, for example, press downward until your arms are straight, using a two-count. Then, ease the bar back up, very slowly, using a four- or even a five-count. And stop as soon as your hands reach chest level.

Mistake: Rocking on a rowing machine. The most common error men make on a rowing machine is putting too much back and not enough legs into the stroke, risking injury to overused muscles and cheating idle ones out of a strength-building workout. "The correct rowing motion requires a precise sequence that you rarely see being used at your local health club," says Larry Gluckman, former Olympic rower, coach of the national rowing team and a training consultant with Concept II, maker of rowing ergometers. "Guys tend to drive backward with their backs first, which wastes the power of the legs and can strain muscles."

Quick Fix: Follow this sequence as you begin rowing: legs, then back, then arms. Keeping your upper body at a slight forward angle, first drive back with your legs and hips. Then lean slightly backward and pull the handle in toward your abdomen. On the return, follow the sequence in reverse, extending your arms and leaning forward before you bend your legs.

Mistake: Overstriding while running. It would seem logical that lengthening your stride would help you run faster. But taking

JUST THE FACTS

If you're exercising to keep blood pressure down, don't run yourself ragged. Canadian research finds that light aerobic training (about half your maximum intensity) lowered blood pressure as effectively as moderate training (about 70 percent of maximum intensity).

longer steps actually slows you down by creating a braking action every time your foot meets the ground.

Another problem with overstriding is that it overextends muscles and tendons, which can lead to injury. It's estimated that about 20 percent of distance runners make this mistake.

Quick Fix: "Taking more steps, not longer ones, is the key to going faster," says Jeff Galloway, former Olympian and author of the perennial best-seller *Galloway's Book on Running*. Taking more rapid steps will naturally shorten your stride. To monitor your progress, run around a track at a race pace and count the number of times your right foot strikes the ground over a minute. Research by State University of New York College at Cortland running coach and exercise physiologist Jack Daniels, Ph.D., suggests that the best rate for most runners, weekend and elite alike, is about 90 strides per minute. If yours is less than that, shorten up your gait and regularly monitor your pace. Taking shorter strides will feel awkward at first, but you'll adjust within a few weeks.

Mistake: Always standing up to cycle uphill. You've been doing it since you were a kid: Come to a hill on your bike, and, automatically, you're out of the saddle, legs driving down, arms jerking the bike side-to-side in a sinuous weave. It seems like the logical way to attack a hill, but it's really a huge waste of energy that's not helping you get up the hill any quicker.

Quick Fix: You need to approach hills with momentum and technique in mind, says John Howard, three-time Olympic cyclist and one of the most respected technicians in the sport. Attack the hill with as much speed as possible, keeping the wheels straight and remaining seated for as long as you can. As you near the hill, shift into an easier gear and slide back in your seat slightly. Concentrate on punching the pedals forward with the balls of your feet instead of hammering them straight down, which drives your energy into the ground. "Exiting the saddle should be your last resort," says Howard.

—Jeffrey Csatari

Getting
Ripped

Coax Out Mucho Muscle in 60 Days or Less

You know how it is: You start working out and in no time, you can feel the results—a little more room under your belt, a little more bounce in your step, a little more fire in your sex life. It's good, yeah, very good, but something's missing. What about seeing the results? Where are those big, strong, defined muscles the guy at the gym promised you when you signed up?

They're in there somewhere, trust us. All you need to do is make a few adjustments in how you exercise and how you eat, and those muscles will grow like mushrooms after a rainstorm. Regardless of whether you're a skinny guy, an average Joe or a beefy hulk, your muscle fibers—the building blocks of bulk—have the ability to increase in size by 25 to 40 percent, according to William Kraemer, Ph.D., director of research at the Center for Sports Medicine at Pennsylvania State University in University Park. And you don't have to commit the rest of your life to building muscles. Commit for the next two months and you'll see results. Below we offer you a complete nutritional program as well as a blueprint designed by Dr. Kraemer, one of America's top weight-training experts, for putting the finishing touches of muscularity on your body.

Eat More—And Smarter

It takes up to 2,500 extra calories to build a pound of muscle, so you're going to enjoy the next two months. But when it comes to putting on muscle, what you eat is every bit as important as how much you eat.

Listen to your body. "When you lift weights, your muscles grow and take away nutrients that normally would have been burned for energy, so your appetite grows," says Jay Kenney, Ph.D., nutritionist at the Pritikin Longevity Center in Santa Monica, California. So the advice is simple: Eat when you're hungry. Your body will let you know when it needs more calories for the muscular construction work you're about to undergo. One small note: Don't take this to mean you can eat anything and everything. If you pile on the junk food, your body will turn a lot of those extra calories into fat. You want to look like a Greek god, not Jimmy the Greek.

Go easy on the meat. Part of muscle is protein, and many body-builders swear by protein powders and shakes—not to mention steak dinners. But most experts don't believe extra protein is necessary. "Gorillas are strict vegetarians, and nobody would argue that they can't grow big muscles," says Dr. Kenney.

The average fit guy already gets more than enough protein in his diet to build all the muscle he needs. In fact, your body needs about 35 grams of protein daily to function properly. To build a pound of muscle a week (quite a task), you'd need to add just 16 grams of protein each day, for a total of about 51. Yet the typical American man already eats twice this amount—more than 100 grams daily. Instead of eating more meat, focus on making sure the meat you do eat is lean. "Fat in your diet is more likely to be stored as fat in the body and won't help muscle growth," says Dr. Kenney. The best bets are fish, skinless chicken or turkey or lean beef (top round is leanest). If you do eat pork, avoid the chops and opt for tenderloin.

Have plenty of potatoes. A quick lesson for those of us who are not professional athletes and/or seeing a biology major on the side: Your body, particularly your muscles, runs primarily on a substance called glycogen. Your body makes glycogen out of carbohydrate, found in potatoes, pasta, rice, bread and oatmeal. Now, if you skip ahead to the exercise portion of this chapter, you'll see that to build muscle, you're going to be working your muscles very hard in the gym. That means you'll be exhausting your stores of glycogen. Solution: more carbohydrate. "Try to get at least 20 to 25 servings of high-carbohydrate foods a day," says Dr. Kenney.

Whoa, doc—25 servings a day? It's not as hard as it sounds, says

Dr. Kenney. Every slice of bread, every small piece of fruit counts as a serving. The average restaurant portion of pasta counts as 6 to 8. For breakfast, three shredded-wheat biscuits with a banana delivers 5-plus servings. For lunch, a couple of sandwiches (four slices of bread) gives you 4 more. For dinner, a hearty pasta salad and a baked potato would add at least another 9. That means to round out the plan, you'll only need to fit in a bagel or muffin for a mid-morning or midafternoon snack.

Trade vegetables for fruits. "While vegetables are a good source of nutrients, they tend to be low in calories," says Dr. Kenney. "If you fill up on them, you'll have a tough time gaining any weight." He's talking, of course, about the good kind of weight, namely muscle, not fat. For the extra calories you need, get the bulk of your vitamins and fiber from fruit. One serving at about 60 calories more than doubles the calories you'd get from a typical serving of vegetables. "You still need to get two servings of vegetables a day," cautions Cheryl Hartsough, registered dietitian and nutritionist with the Professional Golfer's Association National Resort and Spa in Palm Beach Gardens, Florida. "But if you want more calories, stop at the second serving and go for the less bulky foods that have more calories." Take your pick of these single fruit servings: one medium apple, one peach, three apricots, one medium orange, 15 grapes or 1½ cups of strawberries.

Lift More—And Smarter

The food is the fuel, but there's only one way to make your muscle cells grow like a bunch of beachfront condos: progressive resistance training. (That's weight lifting to you and me.) Here are a few key elements to keep in mind.

Build muscle by twos. "One set each of ten different resistance exercises is fine for people interested primarily in health-and-fitness benefits," says James Graves, Ph.D., associate professor and chair of the health and physical education program at Syracuse University in New York. "But if the goal is to develop mass, you need to do more sets." This means lifting a weight as many times as you can (that's one set), resting for a minute or so, then lifting again. For more muscle, plan on doing two or three sets of each exercise.

Balance your assets. Don't make the mistake of concentrating on, say, your chest muscles and ignoring your back. What's that? You don't see your back? Doesn't matter. "You need to arrange the exercises so that you hit all of your joints from both sides equally," adds Dr. Kraemer. "If you do a squat, leg press or leg extension, for example, you've only worked the muscles in the front of your legs. You need to do leg curls (which exercise the hamstrings, or back of the legs) as well, or you risk creating an imbalance in the leg muscles." And that could lead to injury. The same goes for exercising your chest and upper back, abdominals and lower back, and your biceps and triceps muscles.

Start big. For maximum growth, exercise your muscles from large to small. For example, exercise your chest and back before you exercise your arms. "We've done studies that show that people who do large-muscle-group exercises (also called compound exercises) at the end of their workout typically choose lighter weights than they would have had they done them at the beginning," says Dr. Kraemer. And to build muscle, you want to be lifting heavier weights.

Here's a sample beginner's workout that starts with large muscle groups and ends with small.

- Legs: Squat
- Chest: Bench press
- Shoulders: Military press
- Hamstrings muscles: Leg curl
- Back: Seated row and lat pull-down
- Quadriceps muscles: Leg extension
- Abdominal muscles: Crunch
- Triceps muscles: Triceps extension
- Lower back: Back hyperextension
- Biceps muscles: Arm curl

JUST THE FACTS

If you're having trouble building muscle, take a break. A study from the University of South Carolina says you can gain muscle faster by getting two days' rest between weight-lifting sessions, instead of one.

Vary the load. To encourage maximum growth, you'll need to vary the number of repetitions and the amount of weight lifted. That's because your muscles need to be trained for both endurance and power. Doing more repetitions with less weight builds endurance, and doing fewer repetitions with more weight builds power. By combining light, moderate and heavy workouts, you'll give your muscles the variety of work they need. Here's the plan.

- *Monday:* Light workout. "Nobody likes to start the week off by doing a heavy workout," says Dr. Kraemer. So give yourself a break. Do two or three sets with a weight you can lift 12 to 15 times.
- *Wednesday:* Moderate workout. Today you're using a slightly heavier weight, one you can lift for eight to ten repetitions. "Moderate days will provide just the right number of repetitions and weight to achieve muscle growth," Dr. Kraemer says. Here you're easing off the endurance-building work and starting to build strength.
- *Friday:* Heavy workout. For this session work with weights you can lift a maximum of four to six times. "Heavy days will ensure that you lift with maximal force," Dr. Kraemer says. At this point, you're exclusively working for short-burst power and muscle mass.

Rest. Believe it or not, rest may be the most influential variable of your workout—if you use it productively.

"We've found that if you can cut down the amount of rest between each set, you'll stimulate your body to produce more natural steroids," says Dr. Kraemer. With lighter sets, you can get away with about 30 to 60 seconds of rest. Heavier sets will still demand a good two minutes of rest.

—Mark Golin

PART 4

Disease
Free

Hot Health Facts

We've distilled the essence of the latest medical research to give you exactly what you need to know.

1. AIDS. HIV is now the number one killer of young men ages 25 to 44.

2. Exercise. A study examining the fitness of almost 10,000 men over five years found that unfit men had the highest death rate, while fit men had the lowest death rate. The men who improved their fitness during the study had a 44 percent reduction in the risk of death.

3. Diet. In a study of 832 men, men who ate the most fruits and vegetables had the least risk of stroke.

4. Cholesterol. Men with a total rating of more than 240 are 80 percent more likely to have erection problems.

5. Alcohol. Men who drink the equivalent of four drinks a week have higher blood pressure than nondrinking men. On average, their systolic pressure, the top number, was 4.6 points higher, while diastolic pressure was 3 points higher.

6. Aspirin. Taking low dosages to prevent heart disease may reduce your risk of colon cancer up to 50 percent.

7. Iron. This mineral remains an enigma. Diet analyses of more than 4,000 U.S. men and women found that higher iron levels in the blood were not positively linked to the risk of heart attack.

8. Sex. One study found that almost 17 percent of men experiencing fertility problems had experienced "blunt testicular trauma," even if the injury occurred 15 years earlier.

9. Prostate. The prostate-specific antigen (PSA) test for prostate cancer really works. One study found that PSA tests correctly predicted 91 percent of the cancers.

10. Drug side effect. Proscar, a prostate-shrinking drug, may promote hair growth in men with male-pattern baldness.

The Hole Truth

Research Uncovers the Mystery of Ulcers

Living with an ulcer is kind of like hosting the house guest from hell: It rarely kills you, but you want to send it packing nonetheless.

Chances are one in ten that you'll develop an ulcer. And if one is or has been a part of your life, you probably know that they're notorious for return engagements: You get one, you take your medicine and it goes away. But then it comes back. It can become a vicious cycle, something you think you just have to live with.

Think again.

Over the last ten years, medical research has turned the notion of ulcer redux on its ear. The blame for ulcers used to rest squarely on your excesses—your high-pressure job, your taste for five-alarm food or your penchant for smoking or drinking or taking too much aspirin. Now, overwhelming evidence points to a bacterial infection as the major cause. The culprit? A spiral-shaped bug called *Helicobacter pylori*. Wipe out that bacterium and you wipe out that ulcer.

An ulcer, a peptic ulcer actually, is an inflamed and worn-down patch of tissue in the lining of the stomach or small intestine. It's the digestive equivalent of a rug burn that won't heal. Every time food drops in, the lining is awash in acid-rich digestive juices. The acid switches on the protein-chopping enzyme pepsin, and together they team up to corrode stomach and intestinal walls.

Normally, stomach lining rebounds fairly well from this wear and tear, but infection with *H. pylori* literally adds insult to the acid injury. Acid kills most bacteria; *H. pylori* survives because it churns out an enzyme that neutralizes surrounding acid. Shielded from the acid, the bug corkscrews its way through a protective layer of mucus, latches onto the lining and inflames acid-worn sites. If this happens in your stomach, you get a gastric ulcer. More commonly, the damage is done to the upper part of your small intestine, and you get a duodenal ulcer. Either way, you also get agony.

How *H. pylori* triggers this inflammation still isn't clear. "The bacteria may interfere with normal repair processes," says Andrew H. Soll, M.D., associate director of the Center for Ulcer Research and Education at the University of California, Los Angeles.

The promise of a cure came to light in the early 1980s when two Australian doctors found a link between *H. pylori* and gastritis, or stomach inflammation. One of them even went so far as to infect himself with the bacteria to prove the point—and he did; his stomach lining swelled up shortly after he drank a bacteria-laced solution.

Earlier this decade, leading ulcer experts meeting at the National Institutes of Health (NIH) in Bethesda, Maryland, to assess the results of ten years' worth of studies were convinced enough to officially lay the blame for 80 percent of all gastric ulcers and 90 percent of all duodenal ones on *H. pylori* infection. This is major news.

"Eradicating the infection prevents the recurrence of ulcers," says Tadataka Yamada, M.D., head of internal medicine at the University of Michigan Medical Center in Ann Arbor and chairman of the NIH conference on *H. pylori*'s role in peptic ulcer disease. The proof is in the numbers.

"If you had an ulcer today and we healed it and didn't do anything else, you would have a 75 percent chance of that ulcer coming back in a year," says David Peura, M.D., a gastroenterologist at the University of Virginia Medical Center in Charlottesville. "But if you have *H. pylori* and we eradicate it, it's less than 5 percent."

The cure is simple. All it takes is a short course of drugs normally used to heal it and about two weeks of intensive double- or triple-antibiotic therapy to kill the bacterial invaders. Talk to your doctor about which treatment is right for you.

One question: If you've never had ulcers, do you need to worry about the bug? Your actual risk of ulcers from *H. pylori* depends on a number of factors. First, you have to be exposed to the bacterium; unlike a cold virus, you can't catch it out of thin air. The primary means of transmission are person-to-person or through infected human waste. Contaminated water can be another culprit, which helps explain why rates of *H. pylori* infection are higher in countries with poor sanitary conditions.

Age is another factor. There's a higher incidence of ulcers among older men. Dr. Soll theorizes that many were infected as children and then harbored the bacteria without symptoms for years.

A genetic link is also possible: A study from Baylor University in Waco, Texas, found nearly identical infection rates among sets of twins raised together and those who grew up apart. Studies also suggest that risk rises as income and education levels fall; race seems to be a factor as well—research controlling for age and income found infection rates among African-Americans and Hispanics to be twice those of Whites.

Though the infection is quite common, it does not automatically sentence you to an ulcer. While just about everyone with ulcers is infected, not everyone infected develops ulcers. "Only about 1 percent a year of people who have the bacteria develop ulcers," says Dr. Soll.

If you have an ulcer or a history of one, the infection itself is fairly easy to confirm. There's a simple, five-minute blood test that detects antibodies to the bacteria and that your doctor can do in the office. Major research centers are also using breath tests to detect increased levels of the enzyme released by the bacteria. Compared to blood work, these tests are simpler to perform and just as accurate, but they're also more expensive—up to $150—and, because they haven't yet received government approval, they're probably not covered by most insurers.

Specialists agree that the word on *H. pylori* has been slow in getting out to general practitioners. If your doctor isn't up to speed on antibacterial treatments for ulcers, write the Digestive Health Initiative at 1201 Connecticut Avenue NW, Suite 300, Washington, DC 20036, for more information. Meanwhile, here's a list of common misbeliefs about ulcers and what does and does not cause them.

Aspirin. Regular use of aspirin and ibuprofen can cause ulcers in some people even when *H. pylori* isn't present. If the source of the ulcer is bacteria, these common anti-inflammatory drugs can worsen symptoms. In fact, daily use of aspirin for preventing arthritis and heart disease is estimated to quadruple your risk for gastric ulcers and cause more than half of all bleeding ulcers, according to Dr. Soll. He advocates a cautious approach. "If I were going on aspirin long-term, I would check my *H. pylori* status and get rid of it," he says.

Stress. Stress can't give you an ulcer. But if the stage is set—*H. pylori* infection or too many aspirin—it can bring one on and make the symptoms a whole lot worse. A study of 8,000 men from Case Western Reserve University in Cleveland suggests that men with stressed marriages who didn't feel that they had their wives' love and support were twice as likely to develop ulcers as those with happy marriages.

Blood type. People with type-O blood appear to be most susceptible to ulcers. It seems they have more of a specific type of receptor on their stomach cells that attracts *H. pylori*.

Smoking. While not a direct cause, smoking increases your ulcer risk. Leave *H. pylori* to its devices, and smoking can slow healing, encourage recurrences and increase the risk of bleeding or the need for surgery to remove ulcerated tissue.

Alcohol. High concentrations of alcohol can stimulate acid flow and damage your stomach, but alcohol use alone won't cause ulcers.

—*Carol Ann Shaheen*

Cholesterol by the Numbers

Figuring Out and Improving Your Ratings

You walk out of the doctor's office with a little piece of paper in your hand, and it has a number on it, something like 240, 250, even 270. It's your cholesterol count, and it's high. Too high.

Before you panic, before you start mulling over cholesterol drugs, before you race out to buy more life insurance, here's what to do: Stop. Breathe in. Breathe out. Now relax, because you have a little work to do.

About half of us have cholesterol that's high (240 or above) or borderline high (200 to 239), which may put us at risk for heart disease and possibly a handful of other health problems, including stroke and impotence. But numbers alone don't tell the whole story, says James Cleeman, M.D., coordinator of the National Cholesterol Education Program (NCEP) at the National Institutes of Health in Bethesda, Maryland. The important thing to remember is that cholesterol can be lowered with the right plan. So when the doc starts throwing big numbers at you, here's what to do.

Look at the Numbers

The blood test that measures total cholesterol is also designed to measure something called high-density lipoprotein, or HDL. This is the "good" form of cholesterol that scours roadblock-forming plaque out of your system. If your HDL reading is 35 or above, that's good news. Relax, and jump ahead to step two.

If your HDL level is below 35, you could be in potential danger, even if your total cholesterol is less than 200. "If HDL is low, you could have a coronary risk tremendously higher than a guy whose total is elevated," says Carl Lavie, M.D., medical co-director of Cardiac Rehabilitation and Prevention at the Ochsner Heart and Vascular Institute in New Orleans. But wait—it's still not time to worry. There's more figuring to do.

Count Risk Factors

What you're about to do next also depends on circumstances outside of your cholesterol status. So give yourself a pop quiz:
- Do you smoke?
- Do you have high blood pressure?
- Do you have diabetes?
- Do you have a family history of heart attacks or sudden death, striking a father or brother before age 55 or a mother or sister before age 65?
- Finally, are you over age 45?

Saying yes to any of these questions suggests a risk of coronary disease.

Also keep in mind that being overweight or not getting enough exercise can increase the risk from any of these factors.

Take a New Test

What you want is more precise information about a substance called low-density lipoprotein, or LDL. That's the "bad" choles-

terol, which leaves waxy deposits all along your circulatory system. You particularly need to be tested for LDL if your total cholesterol is in the borderline range (200 to 239), or higher, and you answered yes to at least two of the risk-factor questions in step two. Schedule an appointment with your doctor for an LDL test. It'll require drawing more blood, and you'll need to fast beforehand.

The number to hope for is something under 130. If your LDL count is below this range, there's a lot less to be concerned about.

You still need to cut down on dietary fat, particularly the saturated kind, and cholesterol—and a little more exercise wouldn't hurt, either. You're at no immediate risk for cholesterol-related disease, but plan on being rechecked in five years.

If your measurement is over 130, however, it's time to look seriously at your individual risk factors again.

Plot Your Course

If your LDL is 160 or above, it's too high, plain and simple. You'll be put on a strict diet and exercise program to start, and you'll need to be under a doctor's care. Your first goal is to bring LDL down to below 160.

If your LDL is between 130 and 159, your course of action depends on your risk factors. If you answered yes to one or none of the risk-factor questions in step two, you probably won't need to be under a doctor's care. You can take charge of the situation by reducing your intake of saturated fat and cholesterol, controlling your weight and exercising regularly. Your goal is to bring LDL below 130.

If your LDL is between 130 and 159 and you have two or more risk factors, you're in the same boat as the 160-and-over group and are looking at an increased risk of heart disease. The difference is that your goal will be to bring your LDL under the 130 line.

If you've ever had a heart attack, angina or heart surgery, no matter how high your LDL is now, you'll need to work to bring it down to 100 or below.

Change Your Diet

A good diet is the most important line of defense against the effects of cholesterol, says Scott Grundy, M.D., Ph.D., director of the Center for Human Nutrition at the University of Texas Southwestern Medical Center at Dallas. "Sixty-four percent of your risk for heart disease is from diet alone."

And simple changes can give you dramatic results fast. One review of different cholesterol-lowering studies found that dropping total cholesterol by 10 percent and sustaining that level can cut the risk of heart disease by an average of 25 percent at age 40. According to Dr. Grundy, that kind of reduction is possible in a mere two to four weeks through diet changes alone, especially when cholesterol levels are very high. Your priorities, in order, are:

• Cut back on foods high in saturated fat, like whole-fat dairy products and fatty cuts of red meat, and cholesterol, like eggs. This is the big one, the single move you can make that will change your cholesterol level and lower your risk. You should know, too, that there's an added benefit to cutting back on saturated fat: It may help you lose weight. And that's important not just for cosmetic reasons. Dropping five to ten pounds and keeping them off can double the LDL reductions you get from reducing saturated fat and cholesterol alone, according to an NCEP report.

• Boost your fiber intake. An international study found that eating a diet high in soluble fiber reduced LDL an additional 4.8 percent in people who were already eating a low-fat diet. And that's key. Soluble fiber didn't do the job by itself; it enhanced the drop in LDL that came from eating less fat. Foods high in soluble fiber include beans, whole-wheat pastas and oat and wheat-bran cereals, fruits such as apples (with the skin on) and oranges (eat the white stuff, too) and most vegetables, such as broccoli and carrots.

• Take your vitamins. Especially antioxidants. People who get plenty of vitamin C also have high levels of HDL, according to research from the U.S. Department of Agriculture and the National Institutes of Health. The effect appeared strongest in older men. The best dietary sources of C are oranges, grapefruit and other citrus fruits and juices as well as green and red peppers and broccoli. Research in Finland has also determined that artery clogging progressed more slowly in men with high LDL who had the highest blood levels of beta-carotene (found in carrots and sweet potatoes) and vitamin E (found in wheat germ and mangoes). Make sure your diet includes plenty of antioxidant-rich foods, such as broccoli and carrots, and consider taking a daily multivitamin supplement.

• Eat seafood. Plenty of studies suggest that fish-eaters are less prone to heart disease. A low-fat diet that included a daily serving of fish increased subjects' HDL and decreased their LDL, according to a study in Australia. Subjects ate salmon, tuna and sardines; these and other cold-water fish are your best bets. Opt for broiled or baked, not fried.

Add Exercise

Physical activity directly affects cholesterol by lowering LDL and raising HDL. According to Dr. Lavie, 30 to 45 minutes of exercise three to six times a week can raise HDL by 5 to 10 percent over a period of three to six months. One study conducted at NASA found that employees who spent eight weeks on a combined diet and exercise program reduced heart disease risk by 30 percent from cholesterol changes alone. Beyond that, the men in the study lost an average of five pounds.

Consider Medication a Last Resort

As a rule, doctors are slow to prescribe cholesterol-lowering drugs, for a number of reasons. First, diet and exercise need about six months to kick in. Beyond that, drugs add cost to treatment, can have side effects and usually need to be taken long-term—perhaps for the rest of your life—to be effective.

So drugs are the last step, but if you've already tried diet therapy and exercise to no avail, they can save your life. You're a candidate for medication if your LDL score is 190 or higher, if it's 160 or higher and you have two or more of the risk factors mentioned in step two or if it's 130 or higher with heart disease. What drug you take, however, depends on what your doctor thinks is best for you. Choices include:

• Bile acid sequestrants (like cholestyramine and colestipol), which help the liver dump cholesterol out of the body and promote the removal of LDL from the blood. They have relatively few side effects and are considered ideal for younger men.

• Nicotinic acid, or niacin, which both lowers LDL and raises HDL by roughly equal amounts, in the 15 to 20 percent range. Niacin delivers good results, but side effects like flushing, nausea and activation of ulcers can make it unbearable. In one study of the drug, 78 percent of participants dropped out before the research was complete.

• Statins (fluvastatin, lovastatin, pravastatin and simvastatin), which block certain enzymes in the body that help synthesize cholesterol, producing LDL reductions as high as 40 percent, but with only modest increases in HDL. Patients tolerate the drugs well—those on them as long as five years have not experienced any serious side effects. But because they're relatively new, there's not enough known about long-term use. For that reason, they're recommended only for men under 45 whose extremely high LDL levels warrant it.

With a little effort, you can take steps to lower your cholesterol without drugs. As you see, much of this starts as soon as you open your mouth to eat or as soon as you strap on those running shoes for a walk or jog. "Our genes predispose us to certain cholesterol levels, but what we eat and what we do can have a tremendous impact," says Dr. Cleeman of the NCEP.

—*Richard Laliberte*

Race, Health and You

A Hard Look at the Pros and Cons of Genetics

There are no six-foot-eight Yamashitas in the National Basketball Association. An awful lot of O'Briens have freckles. And not very many Rodriguezes have blue eyes. This much about our heritage is clear: For better or worse, how you appear to the outside world is largely shaped by your origins.

But what about matters beneath the skin, such as susceptibility (or immunity) to certain diseases? Does ethnicity matter? The answer is yes, but perhaps a qualified yes. As James Reed, M.D., professor of medicine at Morehouse School of Medicine in Atlanta and author of *The Black Man's Guide to Good Health*, puts it: "The leading cause of death in the Western world is cardiovascular disease—and that's what you should be most concerned about, whether you are white, black, yellow, purple or chartreuse."

But even though almost any disease can strike across the board, there are clear variations among men of differing ethnic backgrounds. For example, Blacks are up to twice as likely to have high blood pressure as Whites. And Mexican-Americans are more than twice as likely as non-Hispanic Whites to have diabetes.

There is big controversy over the extent to which these risk factors are genetic or lifestyle-related, in the sense that a meat-and-fried-potatoes kind of guy is more likely to have gummed-up arteries than a raw-fish-and-rice kind of guy.

In truth, all diseases have a component of both. "Everything is genetic; the question is how much the environment will color it, mollify it or modify it," says Aubrey Milunsky, M.D., director of the Center for Human Genetics at Boston University School of Medicine and author of *Heredity and Your Family's Health*. In other words, we have varying degrees of susceptibility to ailments such as heart disease and cancer, and how we live our lives will largely determine how well we can dodge these bullets.

This chapter will help you determine your susceptibility so that you can live smartly. Knowing your heritage is an important key to figuring that out. Just two caveats: First, you're about to see a few stats that may startle you, possibly worry you. Remember that statistics point out norms. That's all. Don't assume that if a certain disease is common among your ethnic group, you are doomed. Similarly, don't be lulled into thinking you are immune from a disease simply because it's rare among people of your type. Second, remember that your immediate family gives you the best picture of what evils may be lurking in your gene pool. Knowing your ethnic background is helpful; knowing your personal family history is crucial.

Europeans

Special Concerns: White men are, medically speaking, the baseline. When you hear of, say, the "increased risks" of high blood pressure among Blacks, what experts are usually referring to is the difference in risk between Blacks and Whites. Reams of data compare the health status of various minority groups with that of White people, who make up about three-quarters of the American population. (Unfortunately, very little data exist comparing Whites to Whites—say, Italians to Swedes or Irish people to Poles.)

The most obvious and dramatic increased health risk for all Whites is melanoma, the deadly kind of skin cancer. The disease has become epidemic in the last few decades, with the incidence rate climbing by about 4 percent a year. Simply by virtue of your fair skin and its vulnerability to the sun's ultraviolet rays, you are ten times more likely to get melanoma than a Black man. The lighter your skin, the more susceptible you are.

You are also more likely to lose your hair as you age than are men of other ethnic backgrounds. The reason is assumed to be overwhelmingly genetic. Plus, you may be more prone to arthritis, particularly osteoarthritis of the hip. According to a few studies comparing Whites with Chinese, Asian Indians, Native Americans and Pacific Islanders, Whites appear three to six times more likely to have hip problems. "It probably has something to do with the structure of the skeleton itself," says Roy Altman, M.D., professor of medicine and chief of arthritis at the University of Miami School of Medicine and Miami Veterans Affairs Medical Center.

Good News: As a White man, it's easy for you to get health advice. Pick up just about any newspaper or magazine—they're written for you. Most medical studies look primarily at Whites, and most drugs are formulated with Whites in mind. In only a few categories, such as those we just mentioned, are White men clearly at higher risk of disease than men of color.

Smart Strategies

• Trim your diet. When a White man dies, the chances are more than 40 percent that the cause was heart disease or stroke. Largely responsible for these appalling stats is the typical American diet.

You've heard the litany before, but it bears repeating: Cut fat in your diet to less than 30 percent of total calories. (Most of us eat about 40 percent of our total calories in fat.) The way to do it is to cut down on fatty meats, switch from low-fat dairy products and go for steamed, baked and grilled foods over fried. You should also make a concerted effort to get more fiber in your diet by loading up on vegetables, beans and whole-grain breads. These diet adjustments will not only lower your risks of cardiovascular disease but also help prevent cancer, the second most fatal disease among men.

• Work out regularly. We all spend far too much time in our easy chairs and not enough time exercising. Regular exercise is crucial to warding off sickness, including heart disease, cancer and high blood pressure. Research shows, for example, that people who don't exercise are 35 to 50 percent more likely to develop high blood pressure.

• Take a load off. Losing weight by exercising and eating lean can also reduce your risk of osteoarthritis. Dropping just ten pounds and keeping it off, no matter what your current weight, can cut your risk of osteoarthritis in the knees by 50 percent. But take it easy. This disease is sometimes called the wear-and-tear kind of arthritis, so your best exercise bets are low-impact workouts, such as swimming, biking or walking.

• Cover up. For that special Caucasian curse, melanoma, get in the habit of wearing a full-spectrum sunscreen that blocks both kinds of ultraviolet radiation (UVA and UVB). Twice a year, go over your body very thoroughly, looking for any dark spot that has changed color, texture or size or has started to bleed. Better yet, schedule a yearly appointment with a dermatologist and let him give you the once-over.

• See your doctor. Even in seemingly perfect health, you should get to the doctor regularly, just to make sure. If you're over 20, get your blood pressure checked yearly and have a full physical exam every three years. Guys over 40 should have a physical every two years, and men over 50, every year.

African-Americans

Special Concerns: As a Black man, your number one health concern is high blood pressure. It's closely related to heart disease and even more closely to stroke, and it's up to two times more common in Blacks than in Whites. Even worse, it's likely to do more harm to you than to a man of another ethnic group. Research at the University of California, San Francisco, has identified a gene form—one linked with an increased risk of stroke, heart attack and kidney failure—that occurs much more frequently in African-Americans with high blood pressure. This may explain why young and middle-age Black men reportedly have the highest rate of stroke of all groups in the United States, and a heart disease rate that's one-third higher than that of Whites.

Prostate cancer occurs at much higher rates in Blacks than in Whites. Black smokers are at greater risk than White smokers of developing lung cancer—although, interestingly, Black men who smoke have a significantly lower rate of emphysema. Death rates from asthma are six times higher among Blacks than Whites. And glaucoma, a group of diseases related to increased pressure in the eye, is four to five times more common in Blacks, who are assumed to have a genetic susceptibility. Glaucoma is the leading cause of blindness in the United States.

Good News: Your heritage actually helps protect you from some common diseases. Osteoporosis—an age-related loss of bone mass—affects about 10 percent of American men, but according to a study at Dartmouth Medical School in Hanover, New Hampshire, the risk among African-Americans is half that of Whites. The most likely explanation, the researchers say, is that Blacks are protected by denser, stronger bones. As a dark-skinned man, your chances of developing a deadly melanoma are a fraction of those of a White man, and on a vanity front, you are somewhat protected from hair loss as you age. Balding is four times more common in Whites.

But let's take another look at that first major concern—blood pressure. Some well-publicized studies in past years have tried to explain the high blood pressure rates in African-Americans by pointing out possible genetic deficiencies in the way Blacks process salt and in the elasticity of their blood vessels. But doctors are adamant that lifestyle is more important than genetics, for a very telling reason: Blacks in rural Africa are practically free of high blood pressure. The evidence suggests that by making some smart lifestyle choices, you can dramatically cut your risks.

When it comes to the eyes, you may be more susceptible to glaucoma, but you are dramatically less susceptible to macular degeneration, the third leading cause of blindness in the United States. Doctors aren't sure why, but your chances of suffering from this disease are slim, simply by virtue of your heritage.

Smart Strategies

• Monitor your blood pressure. If you don't already know what your reading is, that's mistake number one. Have a blood pressure test every year.

• Skip the salt. "African-Americans get too much salt and too little potassium," says Dr. Reed, who is also president of the International Society on Hypertension in Blacks.

There is evidence that even if you consume no more salt than a White man, it could have a greater effect on your blood pressure. For this reason, it's critical that you avoid high-salt foods, like peanuts, pretzels, potato chips and just about anything you get in a fast-food joint. To increase your potassium levels, have lots of fresh fruit and fruit juice.

• Start a stress-reduction program. Stress is a major factor in high blood pressure, and "simply having grown up a Black man in this society adds a great deal of stress," Dr. Reed says. "It's incredibly important for Black men to learn stress reduction." Make an effort to seek out leisure activities that bring you pleasure. Experiment with various stress-reduction techniques, such as brisk walks, to find one that works for you.

• Get to the gym. According to the American College of Sports Medicine in Boston, regular aerobic training can reduce blood pressure by as much as ten points.

• Find the right medication. If you've been diagnosed with high blood pressure, be aware that certain blood pressure medications seem to work better for Blacks. A number of studies show that Blacks don't respond to ACE inhibitors or beta-blockers as well as Whites and may need stronger doses. Similar studies show that Blacks seem to respond better to diuretics. You should make certain that your physician is familiar with these studies.

• Avoid secondhand smoke. To guard yourself against lung diseases of all sorts, including cancer and asthma, the most important thing you can do is steer clear of tobacco. "And that includes sidestream smoke. Don't smoke, and remove yourself from those who do," urges Floyd Malveaux, M.D., Ph.D., of Howard University College of Medicine in Washington, D.C.

• Go for a checkup. Because of your increased risk of prostate cancer, you should receive a prostate-specific antigen test and digital-rectal exam every year after age 40. Because of your susceptibility to glaucoma, you should get a comprehensive eye exam every two to four years.

Asians

Special Concerns: We're talking about Asians and Pacific Islanders, men whose families originated somewhere between Istanbul and Honolulu. So it's not surprising that there are huge differences in the health problems within this group. On the whole, however, differences in health risks between Asians and Whites are less striking than those between Blacks and Whites.

But there are exceptions. In Hawaii, for example, men of native descent are particularly prone to diabetes and cardiovascular disease—with a death rate double that of the state's overall population. Asian-Indians have the highest heart disease rates of any ethnic group in the United States. This is most likely because of the genetic makeup of their blood, which tends to have low levels of artery-protecting HDL cholesterol. And among Filipinos, the rate of high blood pressure may be as high as the rate for Blacks.

Cancer rates overall tend to be lower among Asians than among Whites. One notable exception is stomach cancer, with rates for Japanese-Americans and native Hawaiians about three times the rate for Whites. And cancer of the liver, which is extremely rare in Whites, is the second leading cause of cancer deaths among Vietnamese and other recent Asian immigrant groups.

Good News: On the cancer front, you may have a degree of inherited protection. If you're a Chinese-American man, for example, your risk of prostate cancer is less than half that of Whites. And if you're of Filipino or Hawaiian heritage, your risks from colon and rectal cancer—major killers of American men—are considerably lower than for Whites. There's probably a strong genetic link.

Even better news is that most of the increased health risks you face are probably because of factors under your control. Stomach cancer, for example, is known to be closely related to diet. And liver cancer, linked to a virus, is preventable through immunization. Another reason to toast your Asian heritage is that there is some evidence Asians may be less prone to alcoholism than men of other backgrounds. Scientists can't say for sure yet, but it seems that Asian men are genetically programmed to get sick on alcohol before they can imbibe the unfathomed quantities sometimes consumed by others.

In Asian and Pacific Islander groups prone to cardiovascular problems, such as native Hawaiians, known risk factors include obesity, smoking and stress—all within your control.

Smart Strategies

• Cut fat from your diet. For most men of Asian ancestry, such as Japanese-Americans living in California, the heart disease rate is similar to that of Whites, which is to say it's far too high. For most groups, the blame can be placed squarely on Western diets, says Dan Sharp, M.D., Ph.D., director of the Honolulu Heart Program at Kuakini Medical Center. "The best thing that, say, a native Hawaiian can do for his health is to return to the native diet," he says. That doesn't necessarily mean taro root for lunch every day, but it does mean lots of vegetables and little fat, and treating meat more as a condiment than as a main course, which is good advice no matter what your heritage.

• Emphasize aerobics. Pacific Islanders, such as native Hawaiians, come from ancestors who spent much of their lives traveling long distances by slow boat. Those who were able to conserve body fat enjoyed a distinct survival advantage. This genetic legacy could go a long way toward explaining why so many modern-day Hawaiians need to let out their belts as they age. The best way to battle the bulge is with a regular exercise program and a low-fat diet. These same two steps can also raise the "good" HDL cholesterol— particularly good news for those of Indian descent.

• Get immunized against hepatitis. Liver cancer in Asian men, particularly among first-generation immigrants, is so high because of the prevalence of the hepatitis B virus, a disease that weakens the liver, making it susceptible to cancer, says Chris Jenkins, project director of the Vietnamese Health Promotion Project in San Francisco. Hepatitis B, which can be sexually transmitted, also makes you vulnerable to cirrhosis.

• Avoid pickled and char-broiled foods. Certain traditional Asian foods, such as barbecued meats (which contain potentially cancer-causing nitrites) and pickled vegetables, such as cabbage and radishes, are believed to be a major reason stomach cancer is so high among some Asian groups, says Don Ng, M.D., assistant clinical professor of medicine at the University of California, San Francisco. He recommends cutting down on these foods and letting your doctor know that you are at increased risk for stomach cancer.

Native Americans

Special Concerns: Diabetes. Native Americans are ten times more likely than other Americans to develop the disease. One tribe, the Pimas of Arizona, has the highest rate of diabetes in the world—about 50 percent of Pimas over 35 are afflicted. Severe kidney disease resulting from diabetes is ten times more common in Navajos than in Whites. Your susceptibility to diabetes is very likely linked to your genetic makeup.

A discussion of Native American health risks would be lacking if it didn't mention alcohol. According to the Indian Health Service, four of the ten leading causes of death among Native Americans are alcohol-related. Why are Indian people so susceptible? There are many theories, including high cross-cultural stress and peer pressure. But while the causes aren't fully understood, the effects are. Drinking contributes to a host of diseases—including diabetes.

Good News: As a Native American, your risks of most forms of cancer are remarkably low. Overall incidence of cancer among American Indians is less than half that of Whites. As far as diabetes is concerned, whatever genetic risks exist can be minimized with the right lifestyle. Early reports by doctors working with Native Americans indicated that diabetes was once quite rare.

Smart Strategies

• Lose weight. Obesity and inactivity are your worst enemies. Most guys with non-insulin-dependent diabetes are 30 to 60 pounds overweight. Several studies show that you don't necessarily need to trim down to fighting weight to make a difference. Losing even ten pounds can result in a big drop in blood sugar.

• Give your lungs a workout. One study found that performing an aerobic activity just once a week reduced the risk of non-insulin-dependent diabetes by 23 percent. Exercising two to four times a week cuts your risk by 38 percent.

• Give your muscles a workout. In another study, a single weight-lifting session improved the efficiency of insulin in men with or without diabetes.

• Take your vitamins. Studies show that vitamins E and C, in

What the Statistics Say

If You Are ...	Your Child May Have ...	Chances Are ...	How Bad Is It?
Black	Sickle-cell disease	1 in 650	Ultimately fatal blood disorder
	Thalassemia	8 in 1,000	Similar to sickle-cell disease
White	Cystic fibrosis	1 in 2,500	Causes chronic lung infection
	Phenylketonuria	1 in 25,000	May cause mental retardation
Jewish (non-Sephardic)	Tay-Sachs disease	1 in 3,600	Brain disorder
	Familial dysautonomia	1 in 10,000	Affects involuntary nervous system controlling blushing and blood pressure
Italian or Greek	Thalassemia major	1 in 400	Fatal blood disorder
Armenian/ Jewish (Sephardic)	Familial Mediterranean fever	1 in 8,000	Causes short, recurrent attacks of fever with pain

particular, tend to be lacking in the diets of men with diabetes. You'll find C in citrus fruits, potatoes and broccoli. Vitamin E is harder to come by—it's found in wheat germ, corn oil and nuts.

• Avoid alcohol. If you think you have a drinking problem and need some help, contact your doctor or tribal health department. The vast majority of tribes have some kind of program for treating drinking problems.

Hispanic-Americans

Special Concerns: Hispanic men are a blend of many races, so it is difficult to make generalizations about Hispanic health. Nevertheless, one generalization that can be made is that diabetes is a major concern.

"It's the most important health problem for Hispanic adults," says Eliseo J. Perez Stable, M.D., associate professor and general internist at the University of California, San Francisco, School of Medicine. You are twice as likely to develop diabetes if you are of Mexican or Puerto Rican descent; if you're Cuban-American, you are 1½ times as likely. There's probably a genetic factor, but one you can ameliorate by adjusting your lifestyle, says Dr. Perez Stable.

Respiratory problems, such as asthma, also tend to be higher among some groups of Hispanics—Cubans and Puerto Ricans in particular. Mexican-Americans, on the other hand, are at no increased risk.

Good News: Your overall risk of cancer seems to be lower than that of most ethnic groups. Colon cancer as well as lung cancer is

about half as common in Mexican-Americans as in Whites. And although diabetes, a risk factor for heart disease, is prevalent in Hispanic populations, the death rate from heart disease is lower than for other Americans. This is particularly true for Mexican-Americans, whose increased risks from high rates of diabetes seem to be offset by a genetic predisposition toward lower cholesterol levels.

Smart Strategies

• Target diabetes. The same diabetes-busting advice recommended for Native Americans holds true for Hispanic people as well—exercise, decrease your fat intake and tank up on vitamins.

• Know the warning signs. Studies show that Mexican-Americans with diabetes are more likely than either Whites or Blacks to suffer the disease without seeking treatment. You should consult a doctor if you experience unusual thirst or hunger, frequent urination, fatigue, weight loss, frequent infections or slow healing of cuts and bruises. Urge your family members to do the same.

• Avoid asthma triggers. Some experts say that asthma rates are so high in some Hispanic groups because they tend to live in urban areas. City apartments can be filled with such asthma-boosters as cigarette smoke, dust mites (live in curtains and rugs) and cats. If you have a tendency toward asthma, do yourself a favor and snuff out the cigarettes, lead all smokers to the balcony, go for tile over carpeting and give the kitty to your girlfriend.

• Visit the produce department. Eating more fresh fruits and vegetables should also be a top priority for Hispanic men, says Amelie Ramirez, Dr.P.H., director of the South Texas Health Research Center at the University of Texas Health Science Center at San Antonio.

"A 1994 survey by the National Hispanic Leadership Initiative on Cancer showed that less than 15 percent of Hispanic men are eating three servings a day of fruits and vegetables," Dr. Ramirez says. Most nutrition experts recommend at least five. By boosting your intake of fresh produce, you will tend to lose weight, lessen your risk of diabetes and reduce your risk of all cancers.

—*Russell Wild*

The Bottom Line on Impotence

Straight Talk on Man's Worst Problem

Consider a disorder of epidemic proportions that can profoundly alter the quality of a man's existence—destroy his sex life, his marriage, his self-esteem. Consider that this condition is so ruinous, in some states it's grounds for divorce. And finally, consider the fact that until only ten years ago, even doctors didn't fully understand what caused it or how to cure it. Now, don't you think you should have seen something on the evening news?

What we're talking about is impotence. Despite decades of misunderstanding about its cause, this is a medical condition like any other, both preventable and treatable. And unless you educate yourself about it, your odds of falling victim are higher than you might think.

Epidemic might seem like a strong word to use for a problem that no one's talking about. But in the Massachusetts Male Aging Study, researchers who interviewed 1,290 randomly selected men between the ages of 40 and 70 found that 52 percent reported some impairment in their ability to have an erection. In other words, approximately half of American men in their middle years can't perform the way they'd like sexually.

"This study shows that erectile problems are much more than a rare inconvenience," says Irwin Goldstein, M.D., professor of urology at Boston University School of Medicine. "We're talking about an estimated 18 million American men with some form of the disorder."

So why the silence? Two reasons:

1. Men are ashamed. The same guys who readily complain to their buddies about a wrenched back or tennis elbow would never acknowledge that they're having trouble getting or keeping erections. We can't even talk about erectile dysfunction with our doctors: "Most of my patients have had the problem for a year or two before finally coming in," says William Richards III, M.D., a urologist in St. Joseph, Missouri, and a regional adviser for the Impotence Institute of America. And he's only talking about men who seek help. It's estimated that less than 10 percent of all impotent men do.

2. Women are ashamed. We men aren't renowned for our willingness to seek medical care. A lot of us wind up at the doctor's office only after prodding from our wives or girlfriends. But what separates impotence from other male maladies is that women, those gatekeepers of medical attention, often are not willing to address the problem either.

"Women are very protective about their partners, so they seldom talk about their husband's sexual problems," says Dr. Goldstein. "And there's also the fear that it's all because she's not attractive enough or that in some other way it's her fault."

A woman can be as deeply in denial about impotence as her partner. The trouble is that it's this very denial, this silence, that allows impotence to destroy men's sex lives. To understand why addressing the problem is critical—why we should all be talking about prevention and treatment—it helps to understand the mechanics involved.

The Mechanics of Manhood

As men, we've been blessed with a miracle of hydraulics right inside our trousers. Like a balloon that enlarges when filled with water, the penis gets bigger and harder when filled with blood. But the success of an erection hinges on three things happening in the appropriate order: (1) The arteries must carry blood into the penis, (2) the muscle tissue in the penis must relax to allow the blood to flow in and (3) the penis must temporarily store the blood. If any step goes awry, the result is likely to resemble a candle left out in the sun.

All these operations are heavily dependent on one element: oxygen. The penis is like any other muscle or organ in the body. To reach peak performance, it needs plenty of oxygen and other nutrients, and it needs a rich supply of blood to deliver them. Research by Dr. Goldstein and his colleagues suggests that it is only during erections (when blood volume is at the max) that there's enough oxygen present in penile muscle to produce prostaglandin E_1. This natural substance helps keep penile arteries clear by preventing the buildup of fibrous tissue in them.

In your teens and twenties, your body ensures that the penis gets enough oxygen by triggering nocturnal erections—an average of two or three hours' worth every night. Dr. Goldstein describes this as the body's way of recharging its sexual batteries. However, with each successive decade of life, these nighttime erections become less frequent, so it's even more important to have regular waking erections. Tough assignment, we know, but think of it as doctor's orders. In fact, Dr. Goldstein recommends at least three erections per week. How you meet this quota is entirely up to you. But let's just say, if your partner isn't around, you know what to do.

Now, if you're already experiencing technical difficulties, you're going to need a little more than just the attempt to have sex on a regular basis. You're going to need to get to your doctor for a complete physical. (Hey, he's a doctor. Get over it.) That's because erection troubles could well be symptomatic of a serious underlying medical condition, such as:

- High cholesterol. Just as cholesterol creates a buildup of plaque in the arteries of your heart, it can also clog the arteries of your penis, hindering blood flow.
- Diabetes. This disease not only damages the blood vessels supplying the penis but can also deaden the penile nerves that control erections. Diabetes currently afflicts six million men in the United States; sometimes impotence is a precursor to diabetes.
- High blood pressure. It can damage the lining of the arteries, making them more susceptible to plaque buildup and

hindering their ability to deliver blood to the penis.

Erection troubles can also develop from blood vessel damage that's the result of a blow to the groin area, such as from an accident or sports. Even an injury in young adulthood can manifest itself later in life. It's estimated that there are 600,000 men in the United States with such trauma-related impotence, a quarter-million from sports injuries alone.

All these problems can be addressed, treated, sometimes even reversed. "There's no reason that a man who's continuing to breathe should not continue to enjoy sex," says Neal Brown, the founder and director of the Society for Impotence Research and Support.

So make it a point to have your doctor give you a thorough going-over—cholesterol, blood sugar, blood pressure and all—as soon as possible. In the meantime . . .

Check your medicine cabinet. If you're already on blood pressure medication, or if you take antidepressants or drugs for ulcers, arthritis or anything else, ask your doctor if they might be the problem. There are dozens of medications that have been linked to erectile troubles.

Check your head. About one in every ten impotence problems is psychological, usually stemming from a souring relationship or poor self-esteem. Failing to get it up once or twice is not impotence; the true medical condition is a gradual problem, not a sometime occurrence. That's why you need to have a physical. If there's no apparent medical cause, you may want to ask your doctor to recommend a psychologist specializing in men's issues.

Check the equipment. Finding out whether or not you're having nocturnal erections may help your doctor find the cause of your problem. If you can get erections in your sleep, then obviously you are not fully impaired. Before you go to bed, take a strip of postage stamps and wrap them around the base of your penis. To keep them from uncoiling, dampen a back corner of the top stamp and stick it to the one underneath. If you're still having erections, the stamps will pop loose during the night as your penis enlarges.

Take it easy. During vigorous sex, you're demanding that your circulatory system supply blood not only to your penis but also to your hard-working hip and leg muscles. For some men, this deprives their members of enough blood to maintain an erection, what's known as the pelvic steal syndrome. The solution: Conserve your energy and let your partner take the more active role.

Polish off the chromium. The trace mineral chromium helps insulin stabilize your blood sugar and may help prevent non-insulin-dependent diabetes. You can find it in broccoli, wheat germ and bran cereals, but you might want to supplement your diet to meet the recommended dose of 50 to 200 micrograms a day for men.

Drop the chips; try the nuts. One important link that has emerged from research is the one between high levels of the "good" cholesterol, HDL, and better erections. This is because HDL helps remove plaque from the circulatory system and keep the arteries that supply the penis clear. In the Massachusetts Male Aging Study, for example, no man over age 55 who had an HDL level above 90 suffered from complete impotence. And while you need to limit the total amount of fat in your diet to less than 30 percent, one great way to keep your HDL up is to trade saturated fat—the kind in butter, meats and fried or processed foods—for monounsaturated fat—the kind you get from olive and canola oils, avocados and nuts.

Start circuit training. This is a workout technique that intersperses weight lifting with aerobic exercise, keeping your heart rate high. This constant movement helps burn fat while simultaneously building muscle, and that's just what your body needs. Combusting fat helps you lose weight; building muscle helps you burn more calories when you're at rest and keep the extra weight off. Both protect you from diabetes and high blood pressure and, therefore, impotence.

—David Sharp

PART 5

Women and Sex

Recent Sex Books for Men

Whether you want be kinky or just work the kinks out of your sex life, there's a book for you. They're new, they're hot and they just might answer that eternal question, Who wrote the book of love? Here is a list of male-oriented sex books that have recently hit the shelves.

1. *Seven Weeks to Better Sex* by Domeena C. Renshaw.

2. *Erotic Games: Bringing Intimacy and Passion Back into Sex and Relationships* by Gerald Schoenewolf.

3. *My First Time: Gay Men Describe Their First Same-Sex Experience*, edited by Hack Hart.

4. *One Hundred Fifty Most-Asked Questions about Midlife Sex, Love and Intimacy: What Women and Their Partners Really Want to Know* by Ruth S. Jacobowitz.

5. *One Thousand One Sex Secrets Every Man Should Know* by Chris Allen.

6. *Prostitutes Discuss Male Sexuality* by Samantha Miller.

7. *Sex Is a Serious Pleasure* by Norman Able.

8. *Sex: Real People Talk about What They Really Do* by Harry Maurer.

9. *Women, Sex and Rock 'n' Roll: In Their Own Words* by Liz Evans.

10. *Women Who Love Sex* by Gina Ogden.

The Books of Love

Take a Lesson from an Ancient Text or Two

I have attended countless management workshops and been tutored on Windows. I have taken cooking classes, karate classes, scuba classes and fly-fishing classes. I've been taught the proper posture for walking ("Get those shoulders down!") and even how to breathe ("Stick out that belly!").

But one thing I've never really been workshopped on is sex. And neither have you.

Now, does that make sense?

Most men regard themselves as Studley Doright when it comes to sex. But let's be honest. If we have room for improvement on our fly-casting strokes, isn't it likely that we have a little room for improvement on people strokes?

Since most real-life workshops are somehow designed to be embarrassing, if not downright humiliating, we've decided to give you a workshop in the privacy of print. Based on my reading of countless (that is, more than three) sex manuals, and some field testing as well (I'm a bachelor), what follows is hereby rated R, so if you don't want this kind of thing, read something else. Another word of warning: When the situation warrants, wear a condom when you try any of the ideas that follow.

For the Tongue-Tied

If you're still with me, we'll begin at the beginning with some basic but often overlooked stuff. For example, the most important body part for perfect sex is the tongue, but not necessarily used in the way you're thinking.

"Though a man loves a girl ever so much, he never succeeds in winning her over without a great deal of talking," says the *Kama Sutra,* the world's oldest and most famous sex manual, written about 2,000 years ago and based on writings that go back even further—no one really knows how far.

This observation hit me like a bolt of lightning. It was nothing less than a double-millennium male bonding experience. You guys had to talk, too? Oh, my Indian brothers, what did you talk about? Tigers? Elephants? Monsoons? No, you probably talked about what I must speak of—the feelings of your beloved, which I doubt have changed in all those centuries.

But wait, the tongue has a second role to play. Leaping ahead one hundred generations or more, here is the advice of sex therapist Irene Kassorla, Ph.D., author of *Nice Girls Do—And Now You Can Too,* on talking during sex.

"Let your partner in on all the sensations you're feeling; everything that's happening to your body and how excited you are. When you hear your partner saying 'I'm having such a good time!' it will be easier for you to relax. Silent lovemaking breeds alienation, increases anxiety and squelches performance. Talking promotes self-confidence, stimulates action and encourages intimacy."

So we have to talk not only before but during, too, lest we alienate and squelch. Fortunately, according to Michael Morgenstern, author of *How to Make Love to a Woman,* "it doesn't really matter what you say. She just wants to know that what has just happened has some importance." ("Honey, that was like . . . major.")

And Morgenstern must know what he's talking about, because he's a lawyer. On reading his counsel, I immediately imagined myself getting hauled into sex court.

"Is this gonna be another laryngitis plea?" the judge says snidely.

"No, Your Honor, I just couldn't think of anything intelligent to say," I whimper.

But that won't get me (or you) off the hook. Start talking and don't stop until you're unconscious or out the door.

Field test report: Hey, it works.

Food for Thought

Talking isn't the only form of "preliminalia." The connection between food and sex has been considered important for more than 2,500 years. But some of the advice of sexual dietitians tends to be extremely arbitrary. By arbitrary, I mean stupid. *The Perfumed Garden,* a book written six centuries ago in North Africa, reveals, for instance, that the secret of an especially lusty man was a regular diet of "yolks of eggs fried in fat and swimming in honey"—topped off with "well-aged muscatel."

This guy obviously did not have a personal nutritionist aboard his camel train. Or, for that matter, a proper wine steward. ("Master, this muscatel is very well aged. Forty-eight, even forty-nine, hours.")

No, it's not the exotic positives but rather the commonsense negatives that mean most in this age of hypernutrition. Avoid big-time fat and cholesterol (as in those egg yolks). Over time, our modern doctors tell us, a diet of scrambled eggs, cheeseburgers and pizza will literally clog up the plumbing of love just as it clogs the plumbing of life.

That's long-term. Short-term, alcohol is the greatest performance-squelcher of all. After two, maybe three glasses of wine, your skill curve begins to plummet like a mud hen hit by a sidewinder.

Big pre-thang meals can have the same effect. For one thing, they make you sleepy. But you could run into worse trouble. *The Perfumed Garden* warns that "coitus after a full meal may occasion rupture of the intestines." I don't know about you, but I hate it when that happens. Even though there appears to be no scientific basis for this warning, I now follow this advice religiously.

One final note on "preliminalia": "Candlelight," advise David and Ellen Ramsdale, authors of *Sexual Energy Ecstasy,* "flatters the human body by making it look more fluid and smooth."

Field test report: Quite true, I found. Removing my reading glasses has pretty much the same effect. Both at once is miraculous.

Fingers For-Play

In *Ananga-Ranga* (Theatre of Love), an Indian sex classic written in the fifteenth and sixteenth centuries, I learned that even royalty needs a little foreplay. This Muslim-era tome reminds readers what the court physician said to Maria Theresa, Empress of Austria: "Furthermore, I am of the opinion that the sexual organs of your Most Sacred Majesty should be titillated for some length of time before coitus."

That same book gives this practical tip for accomplishing same: Make an "artificial elephant trunk" by bringing together the first three fingers of either hand, and thus stimulate the woman.

Another unusual technique—this one for the nipples—is suggested by the Ramsdales. Here it is: Clasp your partner's nipples between two fingers, the nails held flat against her skin. Then, take your thumb and caress her gently and directly.

Field test report: The three-finger technique did, in fact, prove surprisingly effective, although as my partner signified pleasure, I had to repress the sudden impulse to trumpet like a big bull elephant.

The nipple technique varies in effectiveness, I found, and is somewhat complicated by an urge to say, or at least think, ding-dong, ding-dong.

Posturing and Positioning

From here on, the going gets somewhat, well, complicated. At least for me. You see, I have a form of dyslexia when it comes to spatial relations. I can't assemble *anything,* and I'm not exaggerating.

After doing weeks of book research on various postures, I felt a desperate wish for an overhead projector in the bedroom. So, if you ask me for detailed results of field testing, you'll have to wait another year or so. It'll take me that long to sort things out. On the other hand, my research taught me several quite unexpected facts.

1. The favorite positions of most men and women are the good old missionary position and the also familiar woman-astride position. It's by no means a sure bet that satisfaction will be greater if more exotic positions are employed.

2. According to the *Hite Report*, only about half of sexually ac-

tive women experience orgasm on a regular basis. And since modern moralists declare that it is each and every individual's responsibility to ensure his or her own climax, one can safely say—even if in a muted voice—that if she doesn't make it, it isn't necessarily your fault.

3. Now, put 1 and 2 together and you get . . . Hey! The pressure is off! You don't really have to master any new weird and wonderful techniques to please yourself or your partner. But what you can do is introduce new elements of novelty, variety and perhaps delight as you learn them together.

That said, try the following:

Cozy and intimate. This position is said to be ideal for those who want a relaxed posture, one that in fact is perfect for falling asleep in each other's arms (after, not during).

Begin in the missionary position, fully engaged. She then draws up her right leg (you can do this for her) and you both roll over to your left, until you're on your sides facing each other.

"In this position," says Whit Barry in *Making Love: A Man's Guide*, "you don't have to worry about supporting your weight on your elbows and knees.

"Many couples find that this position encourages a kind of cozy intimacy that suits them perfectly," he adds. Another big plus: You're not crushing her.

Hitting the spot. Here's a favorite from 500 years ago: It's another simple approach from that Arabic classic *The Perfumed Garden*, and it is said to have been developed in India, where it was counted as "the thirteenth manner" of making love.

The method is called *dok el arz*, which in simple English—perhaps too simple—means "pounding on the spot."

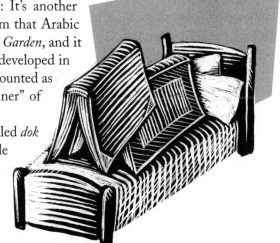

According to the author, one Sheikh Nefzawi, no position was so enthusiastically approved of by his fifteenth-century buddies—and their wives. In his own words (translated by Sir Richard Burton, the great-something-or-other of the actor): "The man sits down with his legs stretched out; the woman then places herself astride on his thighs, crossing her legs behind the back of the man." Lining things up, the woman guides her lover into her. "She then places her arms around his neck, and he embraces her sides and waist, and helps her to rise and descend upon him. She must assist in his work."

Nefzawi relates that a long-frustrated wife whispered to her husband, "This is the veritable manner of making love!"

X-cellent positioning. Alex Comfort, M.D., D.Sc., author of *The Joy of Sex*, is fond of this approach, which he calls "a winner for prolonged slow intercourse."

His instructions: "Start with her sitting facing him, penis fully inserted. She then lies right back (so do you, but slowly) until each partner's head and trunk are between the other's wide-open legs, and they clasp hands. Slow, coordinated wriggling movements will keep him erect and her close to orgasm for long periods."

The splayed-out legs of each partner explain the "X position" name. Take your time with this one, and when you lie back, do so gradually, until you both feel comfortable.

Get in bloom with the blooming lotus. Before describing these next two approaches, from the *Ananga-Ranga*, I feel I should mention that in the Indian tradition, love and sex can be central to spirituality. Rather than diverging from the spirit and plunging into the physical—as in the Puritan tradition—the ancient Indians who followed the path of the Kama regarded sex as a major portal of entry into the world of pure spirit. *Ananga*, from the title of the book, designates the Indian god of love. There are many ways to know him, including the following:

The woman lies on her back, with her head lower than the rest of her body, either from lifting her hips with her hands or with the help of some supporting pillows. In this position, she swings her feet outward and bends her knees so her heels wind up in contact with her hips.

There is a reverse version of this in which the woman lies on her stomach, with her knees against the bed. She grasps her feet and pulls them around and up to her hips. This tends to direct her center region downward. Her partner then moves behind her, raises her thighs further up and pushes his knees under them.

Just in case your partner should ask what exactly you have in mind as you begin to orchestrate this, you can say, without any trace of hesitation, "In ancient India, they called this *Vyaghravaskanda.*" While that may take some practice to pronounce (can you say vee-ah-krah-vah-skon-duh?), it is probably a better choice than the translation from the Sanskrit, which works out to "attack of the tiger."

—*Mark Bricklin*

Basic Training for the Mating Game

A Total-Body Workout for Super Sex

Remember when you first learned about sex? Remember how you decided there and then that your parents absolutely, positively did not do that because the thought of your dad and your mom doing that thing was just too horrible to imagine?

Well, guess who's that age now, guy? Except the problem isn't whether your kids can imagine you having sex—it's whether you can imagine you having sex. Your early twenties are over, and those marathon lovemaking sessions are gone—along with the days off spent in bed that ended after your first promotion. It's easy to start wondering if perhaps the party's over, libido-wise. Well, we have a message for you: The party's far from over. In fact, the dance has just begun.

"I hear this fear articulated all the time," says Eric Gronbech, Ph.D., professor of physical education at Chicago State University, who researches the link between fitness and libido. "It's true that the aging process changes all aspects of your physicality. But that doesn't mean you can't be as sexually athletic and daring as ever."

In fact, your level of desire—and performance—can be enhanced with a simple program of exercise, one that will keep you as primed and eager as a sophomore on spring break.

The Exercise-Sex Link

Sex is like any other physical activity that involves muscles and sweat: Proper training is paramount for primo performance.

"Training and exercise are at the foundation of peak performance," says Dr. Gronbech. "If you're in your thirties, forties or fifties, your physical performance can be maintained—even improved."

A moderate workout regimen designed specifically to add endurance, strength and flexibility to key muscles and joints involved in sex—including those that control orgasm—will help keep you lively between the sheets. Anyone who works out knows that exercise makes you feel good. But researchers are finding that it's also a turn-on.

"Men who work out moderately and regularly report increased libidos, more satisfying sex and fewer erectile failures," says James White, Ph.D., an expert on physical fitness and sex and professor emeritus of exercise physiology at the University of California, San Diego.

In a landmark study, Dr. White had 78 men follow a moderate aerobic regimen four times per week. After nine months, the men reported their rate of sexual intercourse had leaped an average of 30 percent, with 26 percent more orgasms. An increased frequency of masturbation was also recorded.

Research suggests that workouts themselves can be a turn-on. In a study of women, Chicago State University researchers learned that almost one in four had experienced sexual arousal or even orgasm while exercising. (Makes you want to look into those step aerobics classes after all, huh?)

What about men? Dr. Gronbech, who directed the Chicago State study, says that exercise increases the flow of endorphins and adrenaline, which play key roles in the chemistry of arousal for both sexes. Also, moderate exercise boosts levels of testosterone, the male sex hormone. Finally, by increasing the capillary network throughout the body, regular exercise can increase a man's blood flow. That means there's plenty of blood to spare when the brain signals for an erection.

Psychological factors may be just as important. The process of getting into shape can enhance a man's self-image and confidence. "Even the soreness you feel after working out can give you an intense feeling of self-satisfaction," explains Dr. Gronbech. "You feel good about yourself, and that feeling overflows into your relationship with potential partners."

Honing Your Skill with Exercise

Ready to get lucky? To bolster your desire, performance and pleasure, we've constructed a three-part better-sex workout, incorporating general fitness, sex-specific training and exercises that can give you more control over your lovemaking. Here's all you need to go for the gold.

A general fitness regimen should build a solid aerobic capacity and overall strength, tone and flexibility. "The goal here isn't to become muscle-bound, but simply to remove physical and psychological impediments to sex, like flab, fatigue and stress," says Dr. Gronbech.

Another point: Take it easy. In the sex-exercise connection, more isn't better. Too much muscle soreness and fatigue can put a damper on romance. Marathon runners, triathletes and Ironman competitors find that their sexual desire greatly decreases, says Dr. White. One theory holds that during heavy exercise, the body channels blood away from the genitals, where the testicles normally promote testosterone production, and into the muscles where it's most needed. The result: a very fit man who always has a headache.

Here's how to design a workout that won't wear you out.

Start with low-impact aerobics. To get through an evening-long lovemaking session, what you need first and foremost is stamina. Unlike in most full-contact sports, you can't call time-out during lovemaking while the team trainer administers oxygen.

To build endurance, your best bets are low-impact aerobic exercises, which will do the job without straining your body. Go for at least three sessions a week of 20 to 30 minutes each. Swimming, stair-climbing, rowing and running are all fine options.

Pump the iron first. Moderate your aerobic conditioning with weight training. Alternate your aerobic days with a lifting regimen that covers the full body—arms, legs, abdomen, chest and back. Use either free weights or a Universal- or Nautilus-type system.

"The goal is to increase strength and tone muscles. Don't try to lift massive amounts of weight—remember, you're not trying to bulk up," advises Dr. Gronbech.

Work with a moderate weight, maybe half of what you're capable of lifting. Do two or three sets of 10 to 12 repetitions for each muscle group.

Fine-Tuning the Hot Spots

All right, you've built stamina, trimmed off flab and toned your muscles. These are the first steps toward actually getting sex. (A nice car and a powerful deodorant help, too.) With a regular workout routine, your energy is up along with your libido. Now it's time for some target training.

Unless you know some sexual positions the rest of us haven't heard of, bulging neck muscles aren't going to make a whole world of difference between the sheets. What you need to do is add in some exercises and stretches that target the parts of the body called into play during lovemaking. The following moves will help boost your performance.

Turn your beer belly into a "six pack." Your abs are important in sex, and note we said abs, not flabs.

"These muscles are used for the thrusting motions of sex," says Dr. White. They also help hold your belly in, which is important when it comes to luring a partner to willingly do the aforementioned thrusting motions with you.

To work your stomach, simple crunches are the safest and most effective exercise to develop strength. Lie on your back, knees bent, feet flat on the floor. Fold your arms across your chest. Keeping your lower back flat against the floor and your neck relaxed, slowly curl your torso upward until your shoulder blades are four to six inches off the floor. Hold for a moment, then relax and repeat.

Begin with three sets of 10. As your endurance increases, work your way up by fives. "If you can get up to three sets of 20 repetitions," says Dr. Gronbech, "you'll have all the thrusting strength you need for sex."

Keep the calves from crimping. When it comes to your calf muscles, the issue is flexibility, not strength. During orgasm, men sometimes overflex their calf muscles. "Didn't you ever get a knot in one of your calves during sex?" asks Dr. Gronbech. Either of these two stretches will help.

- *Classic runner's stretch.* Stand about four steps from a wall. Shift one leg forward about eight inches, bending it at the knee, while keeping the back leg straight. Now reach out and grab the wall at about chest height, leaning into it as you keep your back leg straight, heel flat. As you lean forward, you should feel the stretch from your heel to the back of your knee. Hold it for a count of 20, then relax and shift feet.
- *Bedtime calf stretch.* Lie flat on your back on the bed with one leg bent, foot flat against the mattress. Keeping the opposite leg straight, raise it as far as you can until it's pointing

at the ceiling. Hold the leg steady and exhale as you slowly flex your foot, pointing your toes down toward your chest. Hold the stretch, relax, then lower your leg and repeat with the other one. Complete this exercise three times.

Hit below the belt. As the key pivot point in the thrusting motion, your hip joint and the muscles that support it must remain flexible. Here's what to do.

- *Butterfly stretch.* To loosen the groin, lie flat on your back in bed with both legs bent, feet flat on the mattress. Reach down and pull your heels toward your buttocks. Now, using your hands to guide them, turn your ankles so the soles and heels of your feet touch together. Your knees will angle out to the sides. Exhale. Let the natural weight of your legs push your knees toward the bed. When your knees are as far apart as possible, hold the stretch for ten seconds. Do this several times until your groin muscles are loose and limber.
- *Hip stretch.* Lie flat on your back with your legs dangling off the edge of the bed. Pull one knee toward your chest, locking your hands over your upper shin. Inhale and pull the knee closer. Hold the stretch for a count of ten, relax and repeat with your other leg. Complete this exercise three times.

Get shipshape shoulders. Most people associate shoulder injuries with activities such as hurling baseballs and breaking down doors. But sex takes its toll, too.

"Especially in the missionary position, when the man tries to support his weight on his elbows," says Dr. Gronbech. "All that stress ends up in the shoulders."

Here's a simple stretch. Sit up in bed, hold your arms above your head and cross your wrists. Inhale, straighten your arms and extend them back behind your head as far as you can, still keeping your wrists crossed. Your elbows should be behind your ears. Hold the stretch for a count of ten, then relax. Repeat three times.

JUST THE FACTS

A 170-pound man burns an average of 5.25 calories per minute during sex.

Motions for the Machinery

Any man who's limber, toned and in shape can make love like a rabbit. But sex, as an athletic event, is more akin to synchronized swimming than to water polo. Timing, in other words, is everything. Here's an exercise you can do that can give you more control over, and more intensity during, your orgasm.

The muscles involved are called the pubococcygeus. We're not even going to try to tell you how to pronounce them—let's just call them the PC muscles. In men, they anchor the base of the penis several inches within the pelvis; in women, they surround the vaginal wall. In both sexes, the muscles surround the urethra and control everything that passes through.

In the 1940s, gynecologist Arnold Kegel discovered that stronger PCs meant better bladder control for women. Dubbed Kegels, his simple exercises—tensing and relaxing the PCs—had a welcome side effect: heightened pleasure during intercourse. And during the last decade, sex researchers have realized that men can strengthen their PCs, too. The results are more intense orgasms, better staying power, a greater number of orgasms and firmer erections.

Here's how you can cash in on the Kegel. To find your PCs, use the men's room. The muscles you clench to stop the flow of urine, or to force out the last few drops, are your PCs. Now that you have the location, try this three-part Kegel regimen developed by psychiatrist and sex therapist Alan Brauer, M.D., of the Brauer Medical Center in Palo Alto, California. The three moves thoroughly exercise the PCs in the ways in which they're called upon during sex, he explains.

Begin training your PCs by doing 10 slow reps of each of the Kegel variations below five times a day. After a week, increase to 15 repetitions per set. Continue adding 5 repetitions each week until every set includes 30 of all three variations. Once you've reached this level, practice at least 150 Kegels a day.

1. Slow clenches. Squeeze down on your PC muscles as if trying to stop urine flow. Hold for a slow count of three.
2. Flutters. Clench and relax your PCs as rapidly as you can.
3. Push-outs. Bear down on your PCs as if to force out the last

drops of urine. You'll feel your abdominal muscles clench as well.

What's nice about Kegels is that you can practice them almost anywhere, notes Dr. Brauer. "When you're driving, walking, watching TV, doing dishes, sitting at a desk or lying in bed. No one will ever know."

What's even nicer is that this technique gives you control over your sexual performance like you've never experienced before. Dr. Brauer explains that after you've followed a routine of regular Kegels for a few weeks, you'll feel an increased awareness of the impending orgasm, so you'll have more time to decide whether to follow through or back off.

You'll also be better able to hold back your ejaculation by squeezing—or doing an extended Kegel—as the moment of inevitability approaches. And when you do finally climax, the newly toned musculature will result in a heightened orgasm.

Kegels may also give you a longer-lasting orgasm, according to Dr. Brauer. Typically, a man feels three to eight pleasurable contractions during orgasm, and the first is the most powerful. By tightening your PC muscles during orgasm, you can stretch the experience out. "Many men eventually double the number of contractions and may reverse their intensity," he says. "The latter ones become the most pleasurable."

About the only body part we haven't talked about is the penis itself. And let's face it, they haven't developed a Nautilus machine yet that can work this baby.

But there is an exercise that may help make for a harder and more sensitive erection—though you'll have to do it in the privacy of your own home. Sit on the edge of the bed with your legs spread apart. While you're fully erect, locate the muscles that move your member up and down and from side to side. Practice flexing these muscles—you'll most likely use some abdominal, thigh and buttock muscles as well. By exercising these muscles, you'll increase blood flow to your groin, says Dr. Brauer. And that means a firmer you.

—*Mark Roman*

Doctors' Orders

Sex Therapists Expose Their Cravings and Inhibitions

They've seen the latest research. They've read every book. They've experimented with all the tapes, toys and techniques. They have an antidote for every possible problem. And there's nothing they haven't heard from their clients or colleagues.

They're experts, pros . . . sex maestros.

And just as you would expect your mechanic to have a perfectly tuned car and your doctor to lead a very healthy life, wouldn't you also think that sex experts would be having some incredible fun?

That's what prompted us to ask some of the country's leading sex therapists and sex educators about their private pleasures. We wanted to get past the client case studies to learn what these experts have distilled for themselves—the tips that are so effective, so delightful, they've taken them into their own bedrooms.

But something strange happened. Some doctors didn't return our phone calls. Others listened and then politely declined. And a few clearly got nervous. Now, keep in mind that these are people who normally discuss such things as anal eroticism the way we talk about carburetor care.

After a long and, we might add, tireless search, we did find four experts who were willing to speak to us—all women, as it turns out. And here's the thing: Once they started talking, it was our turn to squirm. What they covered is all really good stuff, mind you, ranging from creating the most sensual evening possible to eroticizing safe sex. It's just that some of the details like, um, masturbation, aren't in our normal conversational repertoire.

So if you're embarrassed easily, you'd better turn the page. Otherwise, read on for some enlightening and frank advice on matters sexual.

The Ultimate Sensual Evening

Barbara Keesling, Ph.D., a sex therapist practicing in Santa Ana, California, who authored *How to Make Love All Night*, seemed most appropriate for this topic. Dr. Keesling was a surrogate partner for 12 years. In case you're wondering, yes, that does mean what you think it means. She had sex with male patients as part of their treatment. Although she no longer does this, she says the experience "taught me how to understand men, how to make them happy" and contributed to a personal sex life that she rates as "above average."

"But let me tell you something," she adds, "I have the same sexual problems everyone else does—not enough time, and I'm frequently too tired."

Thus, her fantasy of a "totally sensuous evening" has a lot to do with putting life on hold and simply relaxing. Dr. Keesling points out that when you're anxious, blood vessels constrict and less blood flows to the genitals, whereas when you're relaxed, vessels expand and more of it heads to the, er, important organs. If this is the type of thing that turns on a former sex surrogate, then chances are it'll work with your partner, too.

For Dr. Keesling, a sensuous evening begins with sensual food. She'll start with hors d'oeuvres, such as juicy fruit slices, meat that can be pulled from a bone, creamy foods that can be licked and some champagne. "After a few glasses of champagne, I get in a very sexual mood. My husband would prepare the food, but we'd eat it together, slowly, savoring it for about an hour," she says.

No props, erotic movies or sexual devices, she says. In fact, Dr. Keesling's idea of a turn-on surprisingly doesn't even include music or candles, or a lot of talking. "I just want a big bed, some baby oil, dim lights and naked bodies."

Next comes the touching part: "He would start sensuously stroking me—not a massage, just really into touching me all over, caressing. He would start on the periphery with my arms and legs, staying away from my genitals. Next, he'd turn me over and start on my back. As my arousal increased, he'd gradually begin some genital caressing. He would rub baby oil, warmed by his hand first, all over me. Then he'd perform oral sex on me lasting many, many minutes. Eventually, he'd get on top of me, play with me, tease me, rub his penis all over me before finally penetrating me. The intercourse itself would be real slow. He would ride each orgasmic wave with me."

Okay, wipe the steam off your glasses. According to Dr. Keesling, there are two especially instructive points here. The first is something you've probably heard before, but it bears repeating: Men need to take their time more and set the mood. The secret is, again, not to worry about playing the right music or lighting candles. It's simply to explore the other person. "Women love you to pay attention to them," she reminds us.

Second, it's important to learn the art of touching. Dr. Keesling offers the following suggestions for developing a sensuous touch. First step: Scrub the grease out from under your fingernails. Then:

- Keep your touch light and move your hands very, very slowly.
- Touch for your pleasure, not your partner's.
- Concentrate on where you are touching or being touched. Be comfortable, relax, soak up the sensations like a sponge.
- Use warm oils and lubricants to help your touch linger, or dust the skin with baby powder to smooth your stroke.
- Don't try to increase your arousal, fight it off or control it— just enjoy the pleasures of the moment.

The most important lesson in all of this, Dr. Keesling says, is to learn to appreciate the exquisite range of sensation of which the body is capable. As she puts it, "The feelings in your fingertips and skin are the central elements of satisfying sex."

Heating Up Safe Sex

Patti Britton, Ph.D., a sex counselor in New York City, terms herself a child of the 1960s who had always viewed sex as a "divine birthright." But then came AIDS and what she describes as a general shutting down of sexuality as we knew it.

"I saw it in myself and in my client base," she explains. "There was a move toward monogamy, an abnegating of our right to be sexual and an attempt to divert desire into something that felt safe, usually a long-term relationship. I shut down myself. I had to get beyond HIV and discover that safer sex could be hot and fun."

Dr. Britton, whose postgraduate work included certification as a "Safer Sex Educator," uses a bedside "treasure box" filled with condoms, lubes and toys to enhance her sex life. "One of the gifts from HIV is that we're learning to eroticize many things beyond the penis and vagina," she explains. "The penetrative part of sex is only one component of sexual expression." Variety, experimentation and, most important, play are what make safer sex fun, she says.

The logical place to start is with the condom. "Just putting on a condom can be a very pleasurable experience," she says. "One thing I love to do is put the condom on with my mouth. This allows for a steamy connection between two lovers. It fulfills one of the man's favorite things, which is oral sex, plus it's fun for the woman."

Dr. Britton recommends that you experiment with a variety of condoms—masturbate with them if necessary—to discover the kind that's most pleasurable. Yes, there are differences from one to the next. In particular, check out the Pleasure Plus, a condom with a large pouch toward its head that creates stimulating friction for both partners during intercourse.

Lubricants may also help enhance sensation when you're wearing a condom. Dr. Britton's tip: Put a tiny dab of lubricant inside the tip of the condom before you don it. Another is to take periodic breaks from intercourse to slowly and luxuriously lubricate the vagina, because condoms can dry it out. (If you're using a latex condom, though, be sure to use a water-based lube to protect its integrity.)

Oral sex can be a risky act for HIV-conscious men and women, but Dr. Britton says there are ways to do it enjoyably and safely. "I engage in licking, sucking, caressing or gently biting parts of the male anatomy, the shaft, the testicles, while being careful not to permit any transmission of body fluid," she says.

"I feel a lot more confident now, and I'm willing to use what I know," she says. "It still means I have to be choosy, but I'm not shutting down sexually out of fear. I'm wisely, and joyfully, moving forward."

Pumping Up Your Partner's Desire

Patricia Love, Ed.D., a marriage therapist practicing in Austin, Texas, and co-author of *Hot Monogamy*, has been telling people for years how to turn each other on. It's surprising, then, to hear her admit that "the needle on my sex meter points to zero most of the time."

Although she says her lack of desire never jeopardized her own marriage, Dr. Love admits, "If I were to list its big problems, that would be right up there . . . I dealt with it by feigning interest, making excuses, shaming my husband, picking a fight, faking orgasm or avoiding sex altogether."

Any of this sound familiar? If you always want to and your partner rarely does, then there should be some solace in Dr. Love's estimation that a third of all women may have similarly low sex drives. But a marked desire discrepancy can eat away at a relationship, raising doubts of fidelity, attractiveness and endearing love.

"I felt very inadequate," says Dr. Love. "I couldn't understand why I wasn't turned on, and neither could my husband. We both took it personally." Then, while doing research for her book, she came across a study in which older women were given injections of testosterone and estrogen. These are two of the body's main sex hormones, and levels of both decrease with age. Although testosterone is considered a male hormone, women have it, too, though in smaller quantities. Studies show that it's partly responsible for fueling the sex drives in both genders. Estrogen, meanwhile, plays a role in female mood elevation, among other things. Supplementing with the two can apparently have powerful effects.

Or at least they did in the study that Dr. Love found. Those women experienced dramatically higher levels of desire and arousal, to the point where—get this—some of their men complained. Intrigued, Dr. Love decided to experiment on herself. She began taking testosterone and estrogen and felt totally different almost immediately.

"I thought about sex constantly," she says. "It was like night and day. I had this simmering sexuality. It was easy to get aroused and easy to come to orgasm. I wanted to have sex."

Dr. Love took the magic potion for three months, under a doctor's care, before starting to temporarily acquire some unwelcome side effects. She actually started to grow a bit of facial hair, and she broke out with a bad case of acne. When she quit the treatment, the problems went away, but she'd learned a valuable lesson: A large part of our sex drive is purely biological.

"Once you get the facts, you realize that much of your partner's desire has little to do with you," explains Dr. Love. "My situation wasn't about being adequate or inadequate. It wasn't anything about my partner or our relationship. It was hormonal. Once I realized this, I felt normal for the first time in my life."

If a low drive is keeping your bedroom too neat, Love recommends first having a complete physical exam to rule out such other possible causes as depression, side effects from prescription medicine and chronic disease. If blood tests indicate a hormonal deficiency in either you or your partner, then testosterone supplementation, taken through injection or a transdermal patch, is an option.

If you and your partner don't want to be lab rats, there are other things you can do to ease the difference, says Dr. Love.

For the person with greater desire:

- Be more direct in asking for sex.
- Initiate sex out of love and desire, not out of habit. In other words, don't dim the lights just because it's Saturday night.
- Become an expert in creating desire in your partner. Talk. Ask what turns her on. Then try it.
- Don't deliberately heighten desire with fantasies or pornography. This simply widens the sexual gap.
- Masturbate more frequently to control your sex drive.

JUST THE FACTS

According to the American Optometric Association, women who take birth control pills blink an average of 19 times a minute, or one-third more often than women who aren't on the Pill.

For the person with low interest:

- Accept more responsibility for personal arousal. Try a little. Sometimes if you begin to act aroused, you start becoming aroused.
- Be clear and reasonable about sexual preconditions. For example, you may be a more willing partner if you've had a relaxing massage or a hot bath. Speak up and explain what you need.
- Make room in your life for sex. Schedule a "sex date" with your partner and let your libido cook slowly.
- Act on the slightest pulse of desire, rather than waiting for the earth to shake.

Loving Yourself

Betty Dodson, Ph.D., has been dubbed the Mother of Masturbation for having personally taught thousands of men and women how to guiltlessly get off in the self-love clinics that she leads. And we're not talking John Madden chalkboard lessons, either. Rather, Dr. Dodson actually reaches orgasm along with her class in these "masturbation workshops." That's about as public as you can get with your sex life.

As Dr. Dodson, a New York City sex educator and author of *Sex for One*, explains it, self-love is "the missing link in our understanding of human sexuality. It's a natural part of our sex lives. Everybody pretends it doesn't exist, but the first form of sex we experience is with ourselves."

As a case in point, she cites the *Sex in America* study, which declared that more than 10 percent of us aren't having sex at all. "Once again, that's assuming sex can only be partner sex. Our culture denies masturbation as a possibility. It blows my mind. We have to acknowledge our self-sexuality."

Beyond simple self-pleasure, Dr. Dodson says masturbation has many important benefits. For instance, it's an excellent way to:

- Explore your body and learn about your sexual response.
- Take the anticipatory edge off a hot date so sex isn't the only thing on your mind.

- Provide sexual satisfaction for those without partners.
- Learn to control ejaculation.
- Handle an irrepressible sex drive.
- Teach a partner what feels best.
- Practice safe sex.
- Relax.
- Learn to accept and like yourself.

This last point is perhaps the most important—it's central to Dr. Dodson's philosophy. While she was married, she admits to often masturbating after sex (while her husband slept) to reach a climax she couldn't achieve through intercourse. But she was "sick with frustration and guilt" for doing it. It was only after the marriage ended that a new partner helped her become comfortable with something as simple and human as touching her body.

"I got up enough nerve to watch myself masturbate in front of a mirror," Dr. Dodson recalls. "When I saw I didn't look funny or strange, but simply sexual and intense, I was amazed. Until that moment, I had no visual image of myself as a sexual being."

Now, most men probably don't have a tough time masturbating. But Dr. Dodson points out that many men feel tremendous guilt about it. She says you should try what she did—masturbate in front of a mirror in order to get truly comfortable with the idea. Another tip: Actually set aside some special time for a kind of date to make love to yourself. "I'm not talking about a two- or three-minute number here," she says. "Bring yourself up slowly with self-massage, oils, vibrators, whatever. Get close to orgasm, then back off. Take 30 minutes or more."

According to Dr. Dodson, masturbation will enhance partner sex, not eliminate the desire for it. This is especially true if the self-loving is shared. "Watch each other masturbate," she says. "Learn each other's techniques. What's most important is the dialogue it will open between you and your partner.

"When men finally learn to be comfortable with masturbation," she continues, "they'll stop being so needy and dependent on women. Better love comes from abundance. We'd all be better lovers by loving ourselves more."

—Joe Kita

Sex Education from a Lady

A Candid Talk on What Women Wish Men Knew

Back in college, a close female friend and I, going through the inevitable pangs of lust that are as common to students as identity crises, used to fantasize about the guys we thought were cute. There was one in particular we both thought was exquisite—tall, blond, curly hair, very well built without looking as if he tried to be.

We also had absolutely no desire to talk to him or have any sort of relationship, because he also seemed to be a rather serious moron. All we wanted to do, we kept saying to each other but never to him, was go up to him and say, "Wanna f——?" And if he did, great. But we knew we never would, and it wasn't only for lack of self-confidence, it just didn't seem like the proper thing for a girl to do. To tell the truth, if any guy (except maybe him) had come up to either one of us and asked the same question, we would have brushed him off so fast he would have felt the breeze. I guess nobody wants to be treated solely as a sex object. At least most of the time.

We were, in short, confused. About how to proceed. Whether to proceed. What to do next. I know, for example, that I've always felt I should never seem to be the one wanting sex first. It's supposed to happen only after a guy has already put some serious moves on me. The calculus still seems to be that men gain status through sexual conquest, while women are degraded by being conquered too much, although in the last couple of decades, the equation has changed slightly so that it's become okay for women to like sex as long as it takes place within a stable relationship. That's all well and good. Though sometimes I think, just like men, that's a lot of trouble to go through just to get a little poontang.

Anyway, my friend and I, looking at the hierarchy of life's values, made a determination then and there that if it came to missing sex or missing class, class would be the one to go. Even as dim coeds we realized that either could affect our entire futures, but sex could affect our futures more. That's when we started paying attention. Still, it does seem that some men wonder if sex is important to women. Well, I'm here to tell you that it is. Here's what's in it for us.

- It means you like us, you really like us.
- It means you think we're beautiful.
- It means we're the center of the world.

P.S. And, done well, it feels marvelous, darling.

Advice from the Real Experts

I've been lucky. Most of the men I've slept with have been very skillful in bed. They've known how to touch a woman—what to approach gently and what to do when they get there. And there's no denying that it made sex really fun. But there's one man I've slept with who, technically, is not a great lover. He doesn't much bother with approximately 85 percent of my body; he doesn't even seem to be concentrating on the effect he may be having on me. But his raw energy and the pleasure he takes has an appeal of its own. It's a sort of caveman thing—and sometimes, I really want that.

"Why do you like sex?" I asked my female friends, and the answer came back immediately: because it feels good. It's true for me, too. It feels good on a purely physical level. It feels good that somebody wants to be there doing something so special with me. It feels good when someone I really like wants to be that close to me. It makes me feel that my body is being appreciated and that there's a time when I don't have to think at all (although it's taken years to let myself go that way). It feels good to trust someone to that extent. It feels fantastic to get all that attention. And, most of the time, it feels so good to have someone there in the bed with you afterward.

So here's what to keep in mind, courtesy of the "experts."

Start with foreplay. Fifteen minutes. Is that too much to ask? Just 15 minutes of foreplay. And here's the schedule.

- Zero to minute 3: Kiss me like I'm the only thing in the world that exists right now. Mute the TV and get rid of the nachos.
- Minute 3 to minute 7: Kiss me some more. But while you're doing it, begin to touch me all over, like, you know, second base. No, no. Not like that. Like this: Gently, like it's something you've never seen before. Now let me touch you.
- Minute 7 to minute 12: Very slowly take off my clothes. Start to take off yours and let me finish for you. Do not fold anything.
- Minute 12 to minute 15: Use your mouth. Everywhere. Nibble, lick, bite. A little roughly on ordinary skin; a little more gently elsewhere.

(Important note: In the future, vary the order.)

Linger along the way. I once knew a guy who was great at delaying tactics. He was great when he finally got down to it, too. But he was an incredible tease until then, and never, never, never when I indicated that I was ready. He took his time, raising foreplay to an art form, with the inevitable result that I was insane with desire by the time we finally got to the bottom line. Maybe he was doing it to keep sex interesting for him. Maybe he enjoyed seeing me so tormented. Or maybe he really wanted me to enjoy it more than I would if the timing were left to my undisciplined self. Whatever. The result was the same: It was delightful. He was all man, but he had almost a woman's sense of sex.

Almost everyone I spoke with for this article argued that women do, indeed, like sex. The reason men sometimes think women don't like sex may be that we don't enjoy sex in quite the same way. This is a simple case of misunderstanding. For example, psychologist Lonnie Barbach, Ph.D., who wrote *The Erotic Edge,* says women tend to touch men gently to show them that's how we like to be touched, while men tend to touch women a little more firmly to show us that's how they like to be touched. So, as Dr. Barbach points out, what we often have here is a failure to communicate.

In fact, says Robert Michael, Ph.D., one of the authors of the major sex study *Sex in America,* "if a man takes his perceptions of sex, of what's exciting and most appealing, and applies them to a woman, then she's likely to fail his test." Again, not because she's not turned on, but because different things turn her on.

For women, sex means fondling, touching, the formation of an intimacy that leads to wanting to give yourself over to the other person. Sex begins way before what's clinically called the genital moment, says Kim Chernin, author of *Crossing the Border: An Erotic Journey.* For many, even most, women, intercourse is the culmination, the consummation of sex—but not the whole shebang.

Joke Condoms:
No Laughing Matter

You have your "Sizzle Sticks," condoms attached to brightly colored drink mixers. And the condom-in-a-pen ("If you can't come, please write"). Then there are the condoms that look like lollipops, ones that taste like lollipops, condoms with little latex hands on the tip or a model of the Starship Enterprise ("To boldly go where no one's gone before").

All this is in the name of fun, you realize, but not necessarily in the name of safe sex. No matter how unique, novelty condoms may not prevent pregnancy or a sexually transmitted disease. In fact, some joke condoms are factory rejects that legitimate condom manufacturers have sold to novelty packagers. That has the Food and Drug Administration (FDA) worried.

"Because of their look and packaging, there's a distinct possibility people may get confused," explains FDA spokesperson Thomas Arrowsmith-Lowe. "We don't like the term 'novelty condom.' The word 'condom' implies protection. A better term would be 'sexual novelty product.' "

The FDA has sent a letter to condom manufacturers and distributors recommending that factory seconds not be sold to novelty suppliers, and that labeling clearly state when a product is meant only as a joke. Still, there's no FDA rubber stamp of approval you can look for on the package of a legitimate condom.

So, then, how can you tell the difference between condoms that can be trusted and those that can't? Use your common

"All women love sex if they can be sexual in their way," says anthropologist Peggy Reeves Sanday, Ph.D., of the University of Pennsylvania in Philadelphia. So here's how to linger with the perfect caress.

- When you touch skin—anywhere—do it as lightly as you possibly can, so lightly that there is almost air between your finger and my skin. It gives me chills; it's almost a tickle, but more tempting, teasing, erotic.

sense (would you trust your life to something that someone has stuffed inside a nut?) and follow these suggestions from the FDA.

- Read the label. Novelty condoms should say "novelty item" or "not for use" on the package. If it says "not for use," don't use it. If it's marked "novelty," take a closer look.
- Generally, don't trust condoms sold loose or packaged inside gimmicky containers such as nuts, test tubes or key chains. Real condoms are sealed in sterile cellophane or foil wrappers.
- Look for a brand name, an expiration date, a lot number or even "Made in the USA." If it's there, then the product is most likely designed for safe sex. But even that's no guarantee it's a trustworthy condom. If there is no such identification, assume it's a novelty item.
- Buy your condoms from a reputable retailer or drugstore.
- If you're confused about a product, Condomania, a chain of condom stores, operates a toll-free customer help line at 1-800-926-6366. And, what the heck, while you're on the line, order a herd of three-inch-diameter "Texas Tooltote" condoms. If nothing else, we hear they make great water balloons.

- When you touch skin more heavily and very slowly, it indicates the intensity of your desire. You let your hand almost grab me and I can feel your need. You're almost in massage territory, and we all know how good that feels.
- Work your way up to things. Start from a point somewhat distant from where you are aiming. Don't just touch my nipple, for example, ease your way over from under my arm, around the perimeter of my breast, in circles or up and down, until you hit the spot. Don't worry, this isn't rocket science; I'll let you know when you get there. Now touch that spot very delicately.
- Important note: Don't forget the face. Outline my lips and eyes, run your finger down the bridge of my nose and around my jaw—reverently, if you please. A feather-light touch on the lips causes a sort of tingling feeling. You can create a variety of sensations. Concentrate on the tips of your fingers if you want, but put your heart into it.

I still remember being 16 and spending the evening with my first boyfriend. Way back in those days, it took a long time to reach what could be called actual sex. We would sit together and he would stroke my hair, slowly, almost one strand at a time, or at least that's what it felt like. And I could feel the sensation it created all over my body, right to my crotch. Now it takes so much more to give me that feeling, but it still happens—when a man I really like kisses my neck lingeringly or bites my leg not too gently. I know you can feel that way, too, if you'll let it happen. At any rate, no one I know has ever been unhappy with the result of his or my extra efforts in this regard.

Kiss me artfully. There is one sure way to get me, and all the women I've talked to, very, very ready. It's kissing, and we can never get enough of it. How to kiss a woman on the mouth:

- Take your time at the lip stage, bite them softly or lick them

---

JUST THE FACTS

Number of different condom varieties for sale at the Los Angeles Condomania store: 314 gently; touch the corners of my mouth with your tongue; kiss me with different grades of intensity before heading inside.

- Open my mouth gently but firmly with your own. Play with my tongue. Please refrain from sticking yours all the way down my throat.
- Move your jaw a little from side to side and concentrate solely on my mouth. Don't think about what comes after. Or even what might not come after. Just that moment. And either look straight into my eyes, or close yours. Think of England, if you have to. Just don't think of optometry.

Following a relatively long hiatus from sex, I found myself one evening in a car with a friend who, you know, just happened to be male. I say that because I had never considered sleeping with him. We were just buddies. When he drove me to my apartment to drop me off, I gave him a kiss on the cheek. Then, and I know this marks me as incredibly naive, I felt so good about our evening together, I gave him another quick kiss, on the lips, though not quite intentionally. That's all it took. The next thing I knew, our mouths were open and he was pressing his against mine and playing footsie with my tongue, so to speak. I was meaning to stop at any moment, but my mouth was on his side. And after a while, so was my heart. He could have done anything to me. It felt so good all over.

As important as kissing is, I would say half the men I've been with just don't seem to want to really kiss. And yet one serious kiss from a man gets me further than 20 minutes of attention to the more obvious places. But it's risky, isn't it? There are men who see kissing as somehow a whole hell of a lot more intimate than having sex. I feel the same way, if the truth be told. There are men I would sleep with whom I wouldn't want to kiss. But these are not usually men I want to sleep with for very long.

Make me comfortable. It's one thing to get a woman into bed. It's quite another to make her feel thoroughly at ease. Here's how.

- Make sure your friends are out of your apartment first.
- If you happen to love me, and only if you love me, say it. And look me in the eye when you say it.

- Let go of some of your own inhibitions, but retain enough restrained civility that you don't overwhelm me. Otherwise, it's like being the designated driver with an out-of-control drunk in the car.

We were alone together in his apartment, and we both knew what was going to happen. It wasn't the first time. "Take off your clothes," he said, still dressed himself. So I did, without hesitation, and stood before him. "Whoa," he breathed. "Don't you feel vulnerable?" Of course I didn't. Didn't he know that sexual power has nothing to do with who's wearing the pants?

Some so-called experts say that people who fantasize freely tend not to be inhibited. I fantasize almost constantly, but in bed, I'm actually quite shy. By that I mean I'll do anything you want, but I'm still a little reticent to suggest something. Is that inhibited? Probably. It's easier to fantasize about the things I want than to ask for them.

But real life, as economists say, is a special case. There are plenty of women who wouldn't hesitate to tell a man what to do. But I can't say I'd want to be one of them. It seems too much like ordering a pizza. I think my dark urge is for a man to have plenty of dark urges. But I also want him to read my mind, so I don't have to ask for everything I want.

Make me fall. One-night stands appeal to women just as they appeal to men, though admittedly the rules of attraction are different. Here's what women see in men we don't know from jack.

- Only the good stuff—a devilish look in the eyes, the mystery, the thrill
- A chance to be intensely intimate, without being truly intimate at all
- The same thing men see: a potential headache gone tomorrow

Years ago, I was in a bar in Berlin interviewing American soldiers there for a story on the end of the Cold War. There was one soldier who not only didn't answer my questions, he made fun of the whole project. Now, women like men who are trouble, especially if we can see that deep down they're good guys. That was the situation here. But I still couldn't make the first move. I just kept talking with him (which is, it can be argued, a woman's first move, since if we weren't interested, we'd be somewhere else fast). And we danced. And then we walked out of the bar together and went straight to my hotel room.

It seems it was for only a brief time back in the 1970s that it was acceptable for everyone, male and female alike, to have one-night stands. And you know what happened then. Herpes. And then AIDS. That's what happened. It was the 1990s when I had my one-night stand, and I can't say I regret it. I mean, the sex wasn't perfect—it seldom is the first time with anyone. But it was all that's good between men and women: the flirtation, the approval, the attraction, the physical buildup, the exploration. Plus, a good-bye with no expectations.

Am I unusual for a woman? I really don't think so, because, in many ways, the first night (one-night stand or otherwise) is when we see men at their best. When you're being charming in your particular way and when you pay us the attention—throughout the entire process—that we want. Date a guy for two months and a lot of that charm disappears. But for the pleasure of doing you for the first time, he'll get down on his hands and knees and bark like a doggie, if that's what you say you want.

Make my day. You found the gun; you bit the bullet. Here's how to pull the trigger.

- Give me a C. Give me an L. Give me an I-T-O-R-I-S. What do you have? An almost sobbing, gently trembling, sometimes shouting-right-out-loud woman.
- Go gently there, boys, whether it's your finger or another part of your body. Let me find the right spot, or you take care of me, before, during or after intercourse. Preferably before. Although during is good, too. So is after, come to think of it.
- I may prefer to use my own hand while you're engaged in something else. If you can do two things at once, great. If not, get me into the act. By the way, good oral sex almost always works. But don't get sloppy: You still have to focus on the same spot.

- Some women do get there from vaginal intercourse alone. But try different positions until she tells you what works— or until it becomes obvious.
- Just pounding away roughly or endlessly does it for very few of us. And those few are faking, mostly to get a break.

I've found that my orgasms tend to last longer than a man's. In fact, as I get older, it sometimes seems that I'm like a car whose engine knocks for a while after you've turned it off. Orgasm doesn't always end the arousal. Sometimes it leads to subsequent orgasms. Sometimes to insatiability. Sometimes to unconsciousness, which is a good thing, because in many cases, once I've hit the jackpot, I just want to turn over and go to sleep. That's when I'm in touch with my masculine side. Just kidding.

As for your orgasm, well, it's true, gents, that what's often the best thing for us is if you hold off as long as you can. Hold off, even if you end up missing the boat, which can and does happen. Sex has a catch-and-release moment, to use a fishing analogy, and the release and satisfaction of orgasm is a great sensation—and sometimes you can't stand to go on one minute longer. But I'm often torn, because the buildup to it feels so fantastic.

I know one man, at least, who feels that way. As he puts it, "It's a trade-off. I can get a few seconds of pleasure or I can poke around for a couple of hours." There are times when you just want it to go on forever. Orgasms can really get in the way.

Too bad men don't understand that women don't have to have an orgasm if the sex is good enough. At the same time, as Olivia St. Claire, who has offered to the world *203 Ways to Drive a Man Wild in Bed*, notes, "women are capable of having an almost infinite number of orgasms and other ecstatic sensations that go on a long time." I don't blame you if you feel this is a bit unfair.

And, if I say so, go away. Why women say no even when you make all the right moves:

- It's not because we have a boyfriend, no matter what we say. We're just not attracted to you.
- We don't always make up our minds just like that. We need some time to consider it. "No" buys more room for maneuvering than "Maybe."

- We do make up our minds just like that. You have to assume that we mean it.

We were kissing in the street, right across from Washington Square Park. It was night. That's all I know. And we had both been drinking, but not too much. Not too much to be insensible to how his lips felt on mine, and on my neck, or to the fact that my empty apartment beckoned. Or to the fact that this man, who looked more like my childhood vision of what a man ought to look like than anyone I had yet kissed, wanted to go back with me to that apartment. He was also married. He was also quite a bit older. The alcohol hadn't washed that away, either. The presence of a cab makes a good-bye quicker, so when I said "I have to go," I didn't have to hold on to my decision through too many more kisses.

Some say that a woman's main sexual power can be reduced to the power to say yes or no—to open up or shut off the connection at any stage. Charles Darwin would say that somebody has to do this, if only to keep the species walking erect. Throughout the animal kingdom, women do most of the choosing in relationships, says Diane Ackerman, Ph.D., author of *Natural History of Love*. Women decide whether they want a flirtation to begin, whether they will go out with a man, whether they will go to bed with him, but women really don't consider this an extraordinary source of power. It's just our role.

Encourage me to go it alone. It used to be said that 90 percent of men admitted to masturbating, and the other 10 percent were lying. Well, women aren't too far behind. I know that I once went through an extremely lengthy period when I had sex with a man only twice. I did have plenty of sex, however—it's just that I was the only one in the bed.

What women want when they don't want you:

- To get rid of that unsettling buildup of sexual tension, same as men want—without all the hassle.
- Old-fashioned physical pleasure, babe—again without having to give instructions, wonder if we look fat or engage in arguments about the toilet seat.
- Someone else who is either (a) currently unknown or (b) temporarily unavailable.

• To get some rest after a long, nerve-shattering day. To me, masturbation is better than a sleeping pill, and the side effects are minimal.

We were in bed together when he asked me to touch myself while he watched. I'd never done this before, and I asked him why he wanted me to. He said that deep down he'd grown up with the idea that women didn't really want sex, and this would convince him on his deepest level that I really did.

I obliged him. Lying on my back, I reached down and put my hand between my legs, and under his gaze, with my middle finger, I did what he asked. I didn't look at him. I closed my eyes and concentrated as if I were alone. I didn't get to finish. He became extremely excited. But I couldn't help thinking—not then, but later—about what he had said about women not wanting sex. Where did he ever get such an idea? Not from me, that's for sure. And not from any woman I knew, either.

Women enjoy masturbation just as men do, but my suspicion is that women's private turn-ons and fantasies are different from men's. A case in point: The producers of the movie *Sliver* wanted Sharon Stone's big masturbation scene to be based on her looking at a photo of a gorgeous man. She told them it doesn't work that way for women. True. Just looking at a gorgeous guy can get me thinking, but it doesn't get me hot. What does get me hot is imagining that gorgeous guy making love to me. Get me? It's not just his body. It's certainly not his body parts. It's the essence of him and me together.

One last thing: In case I haven't made the point clearly enough, almost all women want sex to be fun. We don't just want to get laid, though. We want it to be good. Very good. So raise your expectations. Don't be satisfied with just getting someone into bed, because that won't satisfy us. Go for the gold.

As Larry, a man who tried to pick me up the other night, said, "Maybe men who think women don't like sex just aren't very good at it." I'm sure he thought he was. And maybe he was right. If he'd asked me out to lunch instead of directly to bed, maybe I would eventually have found out. But he didn't.

—Jen Sacks

PART 6

The Looking-Good Guide

TOP TEN

Fashion Trends
You Should Cash In On

It doesn't matter whether you're on the leading edge or bleeding edge of fashion, there are some things in life every guys needs in his closet. According to the experts, here's a list of the latest hottest-selling fashion items every man should own.

1. Band collar shirts. They dress down an outfit without being sloppy.

2. Sports jackets. Their versatility makes them an indispensable cornerstone in every wardrobe.

3. Soft khaki-colored suits. Their neutral quality makes them an office staple and a corporate classic.

4. Blue blazers. Still an eternal favorite, and not just for fraternity boys.

5. Woven sport shirts. Good everywhere, from the golf greens to the tennis courts to the board room.

6. Loose-seated, taper-legged pants. They not only look good, you won't have to think twice before bending over to pick up that pencil.

7. Flannel shirts. So you're not a lumberjack, but is there anything more comfortable?

8. Sporty vests. A nice change from wearing a jacket, they offer a stylish accent to plain shirts.

9. Hiking boots and shoes. Rugged look with the appeal of long-lasting durability.

10. Sandals. Comfy and casual, once you get over the fear of exposing your toes. Let those piggies breathe.

Smooth Operator

Stand Up and Embrace the Beauty of Baldness

Tommy Lee Jones is a damnable coward, and I'm going to tell you why. In case you missed it, his crime took place a few years ago at Oscar time, that peculiar interregnum in the year when 1.2 billion of us get to see what bizarre things actors will say when they don't work from scripts.

As we recall from this broadcast, Jones wins Best Supporting Actor for his portrayal of an FBI tough guy in *The Fugitive*. But there's a catch: Jones attends the awards with a shaved head. I mean slick-bald, except for a sort of monk-cum-Mutual of Omaha Insurance-guy tonsure around the sides.

Now, as we all know, Jones has hair. Obviously, he's bald because he's playing a bald guy in a film. Then his name is called, so Jones takes the stage, grabs his statuette, leans over to the mike and the first thing out of his mouth is: "I guess the only thing I can say now is that I'm not really bald."

A billion fans and his entire profession waiting with bated breath for his first words, and the man is worried about what people will think of his pate? It takes a special mix of cowardice and self-absorption—and a lot of it—to cover yourself with a balding joke just a couple of seconds after they've stuffed an Oscar in your mitts.

He could have squeaked by unnoticed—maybe they would've even thought it was a joke if he'd mentioned it somewhere down in his speech. But no. Jones just had to explain it, even though it was already clear why. Yeah. Big, cool, tough, award-winning Tommy Lee Jones is nothing more, and nothing less, than a balding coward.

Direction on the 'Do

So what's the meaning of this? Let me answer that by asking: Did Picasso worry about going bald? Did it stop him, basically, from painting and/or seducing bounteous, already-naked babes every single day for eight decades? In a word, no.

Picasso's body was simply his medium, the thing with which he inhabited his life. Whether there was hair on top of that head was pretty much beside the point. I mean, the cult of personal appearance was after Picasso's time, but still it's hard to imagine the old boy grinding minoxidil into his pate or spray-painting it, Strom Thurmond–style, or getting a transplant and, when that didn't take, reverting to a rug and a bunch of weird hats and eyeglasses, like Elton John.

The tortured postures, the pitifulness! The cocktail of fear and dread that so many of our brethren exhibit when it comes to their plumage! This is a deeply sad testament to our inability to carry what we have in life, or, in this case, what we have not.

This is not about not having hair. I want you to consider this a philosophical treatise about spiritual strength. Living with no hair on our heads can be an exalted way to live. I want you to think hard about that, because I want you over the next few minutes to execute a change in your lives, a sea change. I want you all, every single man who has ever scraped the hair from the shower drain, to engage in what I have come to call Power Balding.

Of Craniums and Chemistry

Let's first frame this medically: One thing it means to be a man is that you have more testosterone than women do. (This is literally true, and praise be to Allah, they have more estrogen than we do.)

One very active form of testosterone in our bodies is dihydrotestosterone, or DHT. DHT has the androgenetic power to more or less persuade some hair follicles to atrophy. Chest and pubic hair, for instance, aren't affected by DHT.

Some men have a load of DHT and some don't. Some men have the misfortune, in my view, to have been afflicted with hair. These are the boys with less DHT in their, uhhh, personalities. You know who I mean: Erik Estrada, the Nelson twins, Arnold Schwarzenegger, Donald Trump, Kenny G. All these guys have, well, hair on their heads. Hitler, Goering, Stalin, Brezhnev—all hair guys. And just look where it's gotten them.

At the risk of sounding like one of those wanky, creepy personal-service gurus, I want you to enter into a new relationship with your head. And as much as you may, in balding terms, now be striving to be like John Travolta or Bill Clinton, here's the way you do it. You wake up in the morning. You brush your teeth, you slap the razor to the face, you grab a shower, whatever. You groom yourself, so that you don't smell or look that bad.

It's that simple. What makes it easier is that it's part of the basic social contract with which you were previously engaged. Then you forget about it. Do your work, wage war, bring home the bacon. Live your life.

One critical key to this is to remember your balding forebears. Who are they? William Shakespeare. Chuck Yeager. Sir Winston Churchill. Henry Miller. Matisse. Louis Armstrong. Ken Kesey. Julius Cae-

How to Be a Power-Balding Man

Here's how you can make bald beautiful, while avoiding the embarrassing slip-ups of those hairless posers who refuse to accept they're among the coiffurely challenged.

DO:
1. Shave your head.
2. Lose ten pounds.
3. Wear seersucker.
4. Raft the Colorado.
5. Play chess.
6. Get rich, buy a 1934 BMW roadster and drive it across America and back, never using a freeway.
7. Rip out this article, make 50 copies and send them to bald relatives and friends.

NEVER:
1. Visit or join a "hair club."
2. Hold a comb or brush for more than 60 seconds.
3. Pay more than seven dollars for a trim.
4. Order hair products through the mail.
5. Allow one side to grow longer than the other side.
6. Accept balding jokes without reminding the teller of his superior estrogen levels.

sar. Now, there's a guy who had plenty of time to worry about his hair as he conquered the known world. Charles Kuralt. François Mitterand. Michael Jordan. Shaq.

I could go on, but why bother? As my father-in-law, an extremely cool bald man, would put it: Be like those guys. In other words, study their lives. Think about what they accomplished. Because, in the end, you will not be remembered for your hairline.

Which brings me to the quagmire of the putative balding "remedies." Let me quickly ask: Are we grown-ups or not? Is it really necessary for me to explain that everybody can tell? I'll do it.

Hey, you, Rudy Giuliani . . . you're the mayor of New York City, big boy, and you know, that comb-down-and-plaster combo could almost be said to work, if it just weren't for the fact that it looks like the pelt of a dead sewer rat bolted to your skull. Sam Donaldson! Your hard-hitting on-air career absolutely will not collapse if you get a crowbar and a pair of tin snips and remove that helmet. Paul Simon! Hey, man, those long-legged little spiders glued to your forehead are, like, out there, you know?

Get the drift? The point is that artifice is its own embarrassing reward—it is always legible to everybody. We do not like people, particularly men, who care too much about the way they look. They look like . . . like men who care too much about the way they look.

Before this goes any further, I must explain my own good fortune. I am deeply, genetically bald, which is to say, there are pictures in my family going back to Scotland, two centuries prior to the American immigration, that confirm that if you are not bald, then you are not a member of my family. Above all, because there is no avoiding that complete legacy, there is no contrivance that can possibly cover it. It was never thought of as anything but part of us.

Band-Aid Baldness Remedies

We now arrive at the door of what I call the panacea merchants, that slick gaggle of stylists, druggists, cosmetic surgeons and barbers who would love us to think that baldness can be cured.

The panacea merchants will sell you pig bladders, unguents, eye of newt, old car batteries, vitamin-enhanced puppy urine, a radical new surgical procedure—just any old thing—as a cure. Understand me correctly. Although literally millions of dollars of research is being done on DHT and the other chemical and genetic triggers for balding (because there are trillions to be made from dread-filled balding guys), nobody's figured anything out yet. That's because there is no cure for balding. There is no cure because there is no disease.

I can hear the whining now, all over America, of men who do not want to wake up. Some of them are even my friends, men who will never be Power Bald. I look at it this way: As they apply their topicals and gobble vitamins, as they want to look "fabulous," as they have glue attached and reattached and re-re-reattached on little circles of inflamed skin, as they stand in front of the mirror combing it this way and that, as they send their "100 percent human" pieces out for the biannual cleaning, these men are in pain. And the pain is good: It will, eventually, lead some of them to wonder what in God's name they are doing.

Make no mistake about it: I am requiring you, as a candidate for Power Baldness, to take action within your own life. But because there is no disease, becoming a Power Bald guy is often a matter of not doing something embarrassing, such as combing over, purchasing a rug or engaging in elective surgery. The trick is to get strong enough not to do it. I've also included a few rules in "How to Be a Power-Balding Man" on page 161 to get you started. And remember: It's not what's on your head. It's what's in it.

—Guy Martin

Straight Talk

The Tall Truths about Good Posture

When your parents reminded you to stand up straight, did they mention that good posture can add inches to your height, conceal a bulge in your belly and help you avoid a lifetime of back pain? Probably not, which is why you didn't listen.

Ours is a nation of men in a slump, says Phil Santiago, team chiropractor for the 1992 U.S. Olympic Team in Barcelona, Spain. But it's not entirely our fault. By nature, our center of gravity is higher than a woman's. Instead of carrying the bulk of our weight low in the hips, we carry it in our shoulders and chest. As a consequence, we're a little top-heavy to begin with. Add on a head, which few of us hold erect, and you have a tendency to slouch. Here's what better posture could give you.

No headaches and a pain-free back. For every inch your head is held in front of your shoulders, you're heaping an additional 15 pounds of strain on your neck muscles, says Carole Lewis, Ph.D., a physical therapist and posture expert in private practice in Washington, D.C. You've experienced the effects if you've ever suffered a tension headache or felt sharp pain radiate across your upper or lower back after marathon sessions at your computer. Left unchecked, these problems could eventually translate into chronic back pain.

More respect. Research suggests that posture is one of the first three things people notice about you. "Posture seems to be wrapped up in self-esteem," says Ellen Strickland, a physical therapist with the New England Medical Center in Boston. "When you slouch, you send the message that you're feeling bad about yourself." You're also hiding some of the physical power you ought to exude. In fact, shifting from an extreme slouch into military position—head back, chin tucked, shoulders pulled back, knees locked—can add as much as three inches to your stature.

A slimmer waist. Poor posture can create an exaggerated inward curve in the lower back. And what curves in on one side is destined to curve out on the other. As your lower back arches inward, your abdomen slips forward. The farther the belly hangs forward, the greater the inward bow of your back and the greater the strain on your lower back muscles and the lumbar region of the spine.

More gusto. Poor posture, which draws the shoulders forward, also collapses the chest to some degree, says Jenny Stone, a sports-medicine specialist with the U.S. Olympic Committee in Colorado Springs. This can limit your lung expansion, which means less oxygen and less energy are available to your body and your brain.

Straightening Up

These sound like some compelling arguments, but how do you determine whether a posture readjustment ought to be on your agenda? Try this test: Stand with your back to a wall and your heels about three inches from the wall. Place one hand behind your neck, with the back of the hand against the wall, and the other hand behind your lower back with the palm against the wall. If you can move your hands forward and back more than an inch, the curves in your back are exaggerated, your posture may be due for a tune-up and you may be headed toward a painful wake-up call.

But don't worry. The steps to take for better posture are easy, and they don't require you to walk around with a book balanced on your head. Here's the prescription for a taller, slimmer-looking, pain-free you.

Build up your belly. Your gut will continue to sag and your back continue to plague you until you strengthen your lower abdomen. To fortify the abs, try this easy exercise: While standing, clasp your hands together and cup them around your lower abdomen. Now use the muscles there to pull up and in, as if you were trying to tuck your belly up under your rib cage. Hold for about ten seconds and relax, repeating the procedure five times. Do this three times a day.

Find symmetry. Plenty of athletes have poor posture as a result of favoring one part of their body in training more than another. Bodybuilders, for instance, often have hunched shoulders. The reason is that their chest muscles are strong, but they've neglected their backs. The stronger muscles in the front of the body pull the shoulders forward and overstretch the muscles of the back and neck. Swimmers are likely to have the same posture problems.

The solution, for athletes as well as anyone else with taut back muscles, says Strickland, involves strengthening the muscles of the back. Here are two power moves.

• Back extensions. Lie on your stomach, a pillow under your abdomen and arms at your sides. Slowly raise your upper torso and arch your back. Hold for four seconds, then relax. Try 5 repetitions to start. Once you're comfortable with that many, increase the number of repetitions by 10, eventually working up to 40.

• Seated rows. For the upper back, consider doing rows on a weight machine. Sit at the upright rowing machine with your legs extended, keeping a slight bend at the knees. Grip the T-bar with your hands about six to eight inches apart. Straighten your back, keeping your arms extended before you. Now pull the bar to your stomach. As the bar nears your stomach, extend your chest outward, which will tighten the muscles of the upper back. Start with a weight setting that allows you to do three or four sets of 10 to 15 repetitions each.

Take time for a stretch. Working a desk job leads to tight muscles in the neck, back and legs—all of which pull your spine out of whack. There's a simple cure: While at the office or seated at home watching TV, pause every hour or so for a stretch break, using the following techniques. Hold each position for three to five seconds and complete three repetitions.

The Neck
- Tip your head to one side as if you were trying to touch your ear to your shoulder. Repeat on the other side.
- While keeping your body straight, turn your head to the side, so that you're looking over the top of your shoulder. Repeat on the opposite side.
- Tuck your chin down as if you were trying to rest it on your chest.

The Upper Back

- Extend your arms to the sides, and roll your shoulders as if you were tracing small circles in the air.
- While standing, try to touch your shoulder blades together.

The Lower Back and Hamstrings

- While seated, extend one leg forward, slowly straightening your knee. As you feel your hamstring muscles in the back of your thigh begin to stretch, tip your toes toward you and stretch your calf muscles.

Ride the desk properly. Let's say you're one of the lucky few who spends only eight hours a day behind a desk. Even so, the way you sit is critical to your posture, says Scott Minor, Ph.D., assistant professor of physical therapy at Washington University in St. Louis. Dr. Minor, who specializes in ergonomics, the science of adapting furniture, appliances and other items to accommodate the human form, offers the following advice on how to take a seat:

- Position the top of the computer screen at about eye level while sitting straight. This will allow for your eyes to fall comfortably on the screen without requiring you to tilt your head forward or back.
- Relax your shoulders and bend your elbows at about 90 degrees. You're sitting too low if you're shrugging your shoulders in order to operate the keyboard.
- If possible, rest your forearms flat on the surface of the desk, wrists relaxed. Never let your forearms rest on the desk's sharp edge or prop your elbows up on the chair's armrests; both can put too much pressure on your forearms.
- Adjust your seat height to fit the height of your desk. Your knees and hips should be bent at 90 degrees, and your feet should rest flat on the floor. Adjust your backrest so it makes contact with your lower to midback. In this position, you're almost forced to sit up straight.
- Change position frequently. Even if your chair and desk are adjusted perfectly, says Dr. Minor, you should shift your position at least every two hours to prevent muscle fatigue.

Get the right help. If your posture has extreme problems, if your back is a source of chronic discomfort or if you don't trust your own judgment, you may want to seek professional help.

Physical therapists and physiatrists (M.D.'s who specialize in physical rehabilitation) can conduct a postural assessment, which can take anywhere from 15 minutes to an hour. So can chiropractors and your family physician. Regardless of degrees, be aware of some caveats: Be certain whomever you choose has experience treating posture problems and back pain. Also, be wary of anyone who insists on taking x-rays right off the bat before assessing the results of exercise or physical therapy or who promises to improve your posture after one visit.

At best, these specialists can provide guidance. But, ultimately, the only one who can permanently improve where—and how—you stand is you. Put some time into better posture and you'll soon reap the benefits. The tension in your back muscles will ease, your gut will diminish—you'll be walking tall. You'll also prove to the world once and for all that you're no slouch.

—David Brill

Classic Whites

Expert Tips on Dress-Shirt Wear and Care

A white dress shirt is to the businessman's closet what a weedless Mepps spinner is to the bass fisherman's tackle box. It's versatile, it's simple to use and it's great to have on hand when nothing else seems to work.

That doesn't mean, however, that you can pick up any old shirt from the local department store (or worse, have your partner pick one up for you) and expect to look good in it. The shape of the collar, the cut of the body, the texture of the fabric—all play major roles in how well a shirt fits and what ties, jackets and accessories work best with it. So next time you find yourself in the men's department shopping for a classy shirt, keep these factors in mind.

Collar

Depending on the shape of your face, a shirt's collar can help hide minor flaws—or accentuate them. Make sure you pick the right one. Here's how.

- Round or broad face. Choose long, pointed collars. They're best because they create the illusion of a longer jaw, thus countering the width of your face.
- Long or narrow face. Choose rounded or spread collars. The wider spacing between the collar points offsets the narrowness of your face. Wear button-down or pointed collars only if the collars are relatively small. Very long collars will make your face appear very long, too.
- Oval face. Choose just about any type of collar. Most will work; however, avoid rounded collars, which will exaggerate the curve of your face.

Fabric

Sure, they're white and they have buttons. But beyond that, white dress shirts can feature a whole range of fabric styles, all of which work better with certain types of clothing. Here are some of the common types of fabrics and what they'll do for you.

- Broadcloth. The most common type of dress shirt, the name refers to the tight weave of the fibers. It has a soft finish and is the most versatile fabric you can choose.
- Oxford. Rougher in weave and less formal, Oxford shirts are great with wool or woven ties or for casual Fridays. But if you like slick printed silk ties and a look that's a bit dressier, you need a smoother shirt fabric.
- Linen. It wrinkles quickly, but it's also the coolest fabric

Classic Khakis: An Owner's Manual

If there's one thing every man needs, it's clothes that are forgiving. And no article of apparel fits that bill better than a good pair of chinos. Chinos go with just about anything but look particularly good with blue or white cotton shirts.

The chino's heritage is largely military. They originally were supplied by the Chinese as work trousers to American forces in the Pacific. Manufacturers used a khaki-colored material bought from English suppliers, who had used it in the British Army in the dusty, dung-colored plains of Northern India. Classic chinos are still made military-style, complete with flapped rear pockets and small fob or change pockets.

Chinos are casual, but they shouldn't look cheap. The best way to tell how well they're made is to look inside. Many trousers have taped seams, which prevent the fabric from unraveling over time. Inexpensive chinos have a single-thickness waistband that may start to curl over with wear.

Another quality check should be the pockets. Make sure the inner fabric can withstand the rigors of daily wear; otherwise it won't be long before you find your change all over the pavement. Dressier versions may have what's known as a French bearer—a fabric tab that buttons across the front behind the fly—to strengthen and support the shape of the pants.

General fit is ideally left to personal choice, but the looser, pleated styles are a bit more appropriate for office wear, and they offer a more current look. "The baggier and looser, the

going. Best for summertime wear, as long as the corporate culture isn't too starched and uptight.
- Sea Island and Egyptian. The highest-grade cottons found in dress shirts—and obviously the most expensive. Both are made of strong, silky fibers, which also make the material slightly sheer. Not for the guy who wears T-shirts underneath.

better," says designer Tommy Hilfiger. "If you have a great body, it still shows. And if you don't, it will camouflage it."

For a proper fit, the front of pleated chinos should be full enough that the pleats don't pull open when you're standing up. Cuffs can give a dressier touch to pants and can help weigh down lighter fabrics, like cotton poplin, making the leg hang more neatly. But most of what we call chinos or khakis come in heavily constructed cotton twills, which are substantial enough to hang right without cuffs.

To zip or to button? Preppie purists love the button-fly style, but these days, most chinos have zippers. Still, if you're nimble-fingered and the fabric isn't too thick, a pair of button-fronts can add an old-school aura to your wardrobe.

Khaki is still the color of choice. Its earthy, yellowish tint goes with just about any color. The fabric should be midweight (thin fabrics don't hold a press well), have a dense weave and a soft feel.

Finally, unless the tag indicates that the pants have been preshrunk, expect up to 3 percent shrinkage if you machine-dry them. If you wear them to work and want an extra-crisp crease, have them dry-cleaned. And speaking of work, given the chinos' pedigree, steer clear of pairing a pair with anything too flashy or fancy, especially at the office. Loafers look better with them than wing tips. And wear a conservative belt. That means leaving your turquoise-studded rodeo buckle back on the ranch with your Wranglers.

- Pima. A cross between Sea Island and Egyptian, this fine cotton is not as expensive, not as sheer, but still a stylish option.

Measurements and Stitching

Two more things you can't overlook when it comes to your finest whites: measuring and stitching. If a shirt comes only in small, medium or large, do not buy it for business. Unless you already know your neck and sleeve size, have the salesperson measure you, and buy exactly that size. Despite what you may have heard, one size does not fit all. If you are a size 32 sleeve, a shirt in size 32/33 might be too long and make you look like you're wearing your dad's clothes. If you can't find shirts in your exact sleeve size, don't worry; most fine department stores will shorten the sleeves for you, sometimes free of charge.

As for stitching, this is a fairly easy one: When buying a shirt, look at the stitching on the cuffs and placket (the overlap where the buttonholes are). The finer the stitches, the better the shirt will hold up. Another mark of quality is "single-needle tailoring." This refers to the single needle used to finely stitch one side of the shirt at a time; it makes for more durable seams and a better fit.

Laundering

Contrary to popular belief, most cotton dress shirts do not need to be professionally laundered. You can do it yourself at home. Here are the simple steps.

1. First, get all your grungy clothes out of there—even other white stuff. You want to wash your dress shirts separately, to prevent any color or grime from tainting them.

2. Rub a stain remover or swish a little detergent around the inside of the collar and the edges of the cuffs. Let it sit for a minute or two.

3. While the stain remover is soaking in, turn on the washing machine to cold or lukewarm. Wait until the machine fills with water, then add the detergent with or without bleach. No more than a capful or two of bleach, please—too much can actually yellow the shirts.

4. Close the machine lid and let the water and detergent mix for a minute. This helps ensure the shirts are cleaned

JUST THE FACTS

More than 13,000 miles of ties are sold for Father's Day.

evenly and protects them from bleach stains.

5. Toss the shirts in. Wait.

6. When they're done, don't throw them in the dryer—that could shrink the cotton. Instead, hang them up to dry.

7. Press them before you hang them in your closet. If you like a little starch, you can buy spray starches to use during the ironing process. They're not as stiff as the commercial kind, but they'll help the shirt keep its shape.

—Warren Christopher
and Reginald Crossfield

Fast Fixes for Looking Good

Conquer Any Image Emergency in Minutes

My boss was well-known in the industry, recognized for her elegance, her taste and her cutthroat management style. I was on the elevator. She stepped on. Her hair held a bright red bow. My hand held a bright red tissue, with which I was frantically trying to stanch the flow of blood from a razor nick.

"Don't you have one of those stick things?" she asked, wondering why an employee of hers had the impudence to be hemorrhaging in her presence.

"Uh, no," I said, trying to explain why a styptic pencil wasn't in my grooming arsenal. "This hardly ever happens to me." An excuse she'd probably heard before, in any number of contexts.

She didn't say another word. She didn't have to. The message was there, in that wicked little curl of her red-painted mouth. An impression had been made, and it wasn't a dazzling one.

The upshot is, I don't work there anymore. But if I had known the secret to sealing nicks, I might be in that corner office now: Hold a small ball of tissue firmly against the cut for about two minutes. Let it stay there by itself until you're ready to leave the house. Then apply a few drops of water to soften the paper, and slowly, gently, peel it away.

My continuous blotting did nothing to stifle the blood flow, but it was effective at stifling my career growth. Fortunately, we're here to keep you from being caught in the same situation. So here are a bunch of fast fixes to get you through even the worst of days.

Banishing Bags under the Eyes

Is there enough baggage under your eyes to fill the trunk of a 1978 Lincoln? Do you look like a "before" picture of one of the Gabor sisters? You're not old on the inside, so why should you look old on the outside? Here are quick ways to check your bags.

- Try the tea treatment. Moisten two tea bags with cold water and rest them on your closed eyes for 15 minutes. The tannin in the tea helps pull the skin taut and reduce puffiness. The cold reduces swelling.
- Go for the cuke cure. Cucumber slices can have a similar effect as the tea bags, especially if they're chilled. Added bonus: If the kids walk in and see you like this, you can scare the bejesus out of them by saying "It is time to return to the home planet, my children."

JUST THE FACTS

Number of moles the average man has on his skin: 40

Ironing Out the Wrinkles

For days when no iron is in sight (or more likely, one is, but you don't know how to use it):

- Eliminate wrinkles by hanging your duds in the bathroom near the shower. Run it hot for about 15 minutes with the bathroom door closed. The heat and steam will smooth things over.
- Get a sharper crease in your pants by turning them inside out and rubbing a little soap along the inside of the crease. Turn them back the right way and either iron them or use a rolling pin to press out the crease.
- If you tried the iron and now you have a scorch in your cotton dress shirt: If it's a white shirt, dampen the area and apply a few drops of hydrogen peroxide. Repeat every 15 minutes until the mark has faded. For nonwhite shirts, test the peroxide on an inside seam first to make sure it won't affect the color.
- Remove those little balls of wool from your sweater by lightly brushing them with a dry sponge. Lint? Use tape.

Buffing Weather-Beaten Shoes

Nothing like an expensive pair of shoes covered with the tracings of the elements. Some quick repairs:

- Erase rain or snow stains from leather shoes by rubbing a few dabs of mayonnaise into the leather.
- Mark on your suede shoes? Clean them by rubbing a piece of white bread on the offending area.

Shaving without the Cream

Forget soap. What you need isn't lather, it's lubrication. Olive oil or something similar is a perfect choice. Less perfect, because it'll gunk up your razor, is petroleum jelly or skin moisturizer. Smooth on, wait a minute, then shave.

Hiding a Bald Spot

Some of us don't have bad hair days; we have less hair days. To create the illusion of fuller hair:

- Go against the grain. After your shower, blow-dry the hair in the opposite direction from which you typically part it. That adds a little lift to those hairs underneath, says Christina Griffasi, style director at Minardi salon in New York City. When your hair's dry, comb back to its original shape and it'll look a little fuller.
- Another trick is to quickly shampoo and towel-dry the hair, but don't comb it. Instead, use your fingers to give it direction. You'll get a fuller look than if you use a comb or brush to create a part.
- Condition with vinegar. To make thin hair look thicker instantly, mix one tablespoon of white vinegar with a pint of water and massage it into your hair after shampooing. Wait a minute or two, then rinse. "It changes the chemical balance of your hair to be slightly more acidic; for some reason that makes hair appear thicker," says Harry Roth, M.D., clinical professor of dermatology at the University of California, San Francisco.

Taming Flyaway Hair

No gel on hand? Don't make the mistake of trying to plaster down a cowlick. Water will just weigh the hair down and make it look thinner. Try a dab of hair conditioner instead. Apply sparingly—no more than is necessary to keep your hair in check. If static is the problem, rub one of those fabric-softener sheets over your hair and you'll be cling-free.

Drying Out Oily Hair

Your alarm clock failed, so a shower's out of the question. Here's how to freshen up that oily mop.

- Mousse is the hair dressing of choice for oily hair. It has a drying effect, which means it can keep the oil in check until you have time to shampoo. It also helps lift the hair off the scalp a bit, making it appear fuller. Apply, then blow dry.
- Clear astringent liquids such as witch hazel (found in many products made for oily skin) will also take away excess oil. Dab a little astringent on a cotton ball and wipe gently.

Faking Out Dandruff Flakes

Flakes can usually be controlled by religious use of a dandruff shampoo, but if you've been negligent and the flakes are building up:

- Try some castor oil. You'll need time to shower with this cure, but Kenneth Battelle, owner of Kenneth's Salon at the Waldorf-Astoria hotel in New York City, swears it'll work. Take a piece of cotton and dip it in castor oil. Then rub the stuff into your scalp—it'll dissolve the dry flakes. Use it in moderation and be sure to wash it out thoroughly after five minutes.

Masking Bad Breath

You brushed. Or maybe you didn't, but there's nothing you can do about it now. If your mouth smells like something died in there, and you're facing a Certs encounter without a package of Certs, try these instant fresheners.

- Gnaw on the rind of a lemon or lime. Just rinse your mouth out afterward, since the citric acid in the rinds can harm your teeth. Sugar-free lemon drops are another good choice.
- Eat an apple. The fruit is crunchy enough to clean debris from your teeth and tangy enough to get your saliva flowing. Radishes are another crunchy breath cleanser.
- Eat a Tums. Since trapped gas in the stomach is one of the most common causes of bad breath, chewing an antacid can often clear the air, says David Halpern, D.D.S., a spokesman for the Academy of General Dentistry.

Toning Down Shiny Skin

Women powder their noses. Men must be more resourceful when it comes to dealing with oily skin. Commercial products are fine, but when there are none handy, try the following:

JUST THE FACTS

Fifty-seven percent of men surveyed say they compare their bodies to those of male models in magazines.

- Snare a wet-wipe. Most middle-brow restaurants provide them. Slip one into your pocket, excuse yourself to go to the men's room and use the towelette to eliminate shiny skin. It contains an astringent.
- Use vinegar. Dab a few drops on a tissue and gently wipe away. Be sure to rinse thoroughly with water so you don't end up smelling like a salad.

Erasing Pimples

You're no kid, and you don't want your new client to consider you one. That's why you need to lose unexpected blemishes fast. Here's how.

- Join the poison ivy league. If you feel a blemish flourishing and, oops, you stopped buying zit cream the same year you traded in your white polyester suit, apply some calamine lotion. It will absorb excess skin oil and help nip that blotch in the bud.

- Ice it. Wash your face, then put an ice cube in a washcloth and hold it against the blemish for about 60 seconds. The cold will reduce the inflammation, making the zit less noticeable.

- Try some toothpaste. Put a tiny amount directly on the zit, then rinse with water. Don't overdo it, or you risk overdrying your skin and causing a rash.

Knocking Out Body Odor

Let's say you forget the antiperspirant, or too much stress in your day caused you to sweat right through it. For some fast relief:

- A bit of strategically placed rubbing alcohol will constrict your pores and hold back sweating for several hours. Use this technique sparingly, since routine use of rubbing alcohol can cause severe drying and irritation.
- Powder yourself with baking soda. It's just as effective as deodorant is at killing odor-causing bacteria.

—Stephen Perrine with Carrie Silberman

PART 7

Man
to
Man

Recent Book Releases about Malehood

In the past few years, the publishing industry has brought us some interesting insights into the men's movement. But from Robert Bly's Iron John *on, there's been a plethora of good—and bad—books on men. Here are some of the more interesting new titles we've discovered.*

1. *How to Make Your Man Behave in 21 Days or Less Using the Secrets of Professional Dog Trainers* by Karen Salmansohn.

2. *A Man's World: How Real Is Male Privilege and How High Is its Price?* by Ellis Cose.

3. *Don't Stand Too Close to a Naked Man* by Tim Allen.

4. *The Only Boobs in the House Are Men* by Maxine Berman.

5. *Fathering the Next Generation: Men Mentoring Men* by William J. Jarema.

6. *Cats Are Better Than Men* by Beverly Guhl.

7. *What Your Mother Couldn't Tell You and Your Father Didn't Know* by John Gray, Ph.D.

8. *How Men Can Live as Long as Women: Seven Steps to a Longer and Better Life* by Ken Goldberg, M.D.

9. *In a Time of Fallen Heroes: The Re-creation of Masculinity* by R. William Betcher and William S. Pollack.

10. *Masculinity Reconstructed: Changing the Rules of Manhood at Work, in Relationships and in Family Life* by Ronald F. Levant, Ed.D., with Gini Kopecky.

Talking to Dad

Making the Most of Father-Son Relationships

Let's say it's a quiet Sunday afternoon in Pleasantville. The kids are in the yard and the dog is sleeping on the porch. Suddenly, there's a knock at the door. In our little scenario, that's the bad news. The good news is, you get to choose who's there. But the other bad news is, whoever it is, he's going to stay for the weekend. Is it:

a. A modern poet?
b. An aluminum-siding salesman?
c. Your old man?
d. My old man?

Of course, my dad's always been a pretty popular fellow, but that's not the point, is it? No, the point is that for many of us, dealing with Dad is part of the background noise of everybody's life.

The Padre Principle

I wouldn't have thought much about father-son relationships if I hadn't gotten a call from a friend—a man of the Catholic cloth, as it happens—who was asking for my advice on how he could pass a weekend with his father, whom he was supposed to meet in New York City.

Now, there's a bit of irony. A man called "father" as part of his job ought to be able to work out his own padre problem without much help from the laity, don't you think? But, in fact, fathers are mysterious figures for all of us. They're big mythic characters. For years, they were the voice of safety, the growl of danger, the man in charge. They've spent their whole lives toting all the baggage of personal paternalism.

181

It's all very complicated, of course. The cleric, for example, couldn't quite get to the source of his problem, so we went back to basics. "Is he a nice guy?" I asked. A pretty simple question, but it took him aback.

"I don't know," he said. "I never thought of it that way."

There it is, my dear chaps. The shank of the Dad dilemma: Fathers aren't guys. The hardware-store guy is a guy. Cousins are guys all the way. Anybody you feel comfortable calling by his first name is a guy. But dads are guys the way the Pope is a guy.

Cleaving Ward Cleaver's Curtain

Between you and your dad is this odd curtain of impenetrable angst and expectation. Respect and solicitude don't work, and neither does subservience or condescension. The fact is, you can't hang out with Dad unless you can first make him into one of the guys.

But you have to do a complete guy conversion on the old feller. Nothing else will enhance his overall "hangoutability." Here's how you rig it.

Look for his secret life. Fathers have an existence that parallels the one we see—sort of the same way dogs and houseplants have secret lives.

It is there, in that hidden world, where pops all live life like guys. Every dad's guy world is different, so you sort of have to test for it, the same way you do for allergies. Now, lots of men shed their father follicles in the presence of strange women. Put a pop in a room with an attractive woman of a certain age, and he goes guy right away, reaches down deep and comes up with great lines and funny war anecdotes, instead of his usual advice on how to straighten out your individual retirement account.

Sometimes you have to settle for the symptoms of hidden-life guyness, instead of the real thing. For example, you stop by the old homestead one Sunday and there's a dark-haired stranger inhabiting your father's body. Turns out, according to Mom, he went out and OD'd on Grecian Formula. Dads with late-life vanity are practically pure guy.

Adopt a dad. When I was in college, I flunked a course called Coed Golf. The only time I showed up was to take the final exam on the last day of class—don't you agree that attending or not attending a course called Coed Golf is nitpicking?—in which I was expected to take a nine-iron and chip a Wiffle ball over some cinder blocks and into a wicker basket.

So there I was, shooting the breeze with another guy, waiting my turn, when the instructor interrupted to tell me he'd run into my father at a grocery store. "Listen," he said, "your dad's a heck of a nice guy."

I think what put me off my game that day—in addition to not knowing how to hold a golf club—was the sudden appearance of a surprise witness who gave credence to one of those really simple ideas, the kind of thing that makes you slap yourself on the forehead and say "Why didn't I think of that?"

I just never thought of it before, but there it was: Dad was a nice guy. I mentioned it when I got home, but it didn't take. Dad thought I was pretty stupid for flunking golf, though.

The point here is that everybody's dad is just another guy to everybody else. So adopt him. Pretend he's somebody else's pop, and a pretty nice guy, to boot.

Get his jokes. The first sign of anybody's nice-guy congeniality is usually his sense of humor. As the Commissar of Law and Order in the household gulag, dads often don't engender big belly laughs in sons. That doesn't mean he wasn't cracking wise. It only means you weren't getting the jokes.

You thought he was dour and humorless. He thought you were mind-numbingly intense. A friend of mine, Mr. F., Jr., found himself at his mom and dad's house for a weekend. Short on good ideas and desperate for distraction, he volunteered to accompany his old man to the golf course. Junior F teed off on a ball and sent it at a right angle deep into the rough. F., Sr., lined one down the fairway.

As they were walking away from the tee, F the elder said, "If you can't hit it as far as the ladies' tee, son, you ought to drop your pants and walk that little thing right through the course naked."

JUST THE FACTS

The safest day for driving is Tuesday.

The neo-F almost seized up. Why? First, because he'd never heard his old man make a ribald wisecrack before, and his knee-jerk reaction was that it was unseemly. Second, the last guy in the world you want to make small-penis talk with is Pops, who, assuming a certain sexual orthodoxy on your part, is the only other guy on the planet who knows your equipment almost as well as you do. Third, it was, for the time and place, "a really funny thing to say," according to small F.

By the time they were on the back nine, F., Jr., had figured out that his old man was actually a pretty funny guy, and by the time he broke 100, young F was telling jokes of his own. Some of them were funny—one or two of them even funny enough to make the old F laugh.

Talk his talk. On another level, playing Dad's game means hanging out on Dad's terms instead of yours. Maybe you have a cosmic bone to pick with the old man, and you think the best way to tackle it is to sit and talk, man to man. That might be what you want, but that's the kind of thing that makes most men's skin crawl. Almost all guys like to talk to each other while they're doing something else, so if you want your dad to talk to you, find out what he likes doing, and do it. He'll talk. It may be about the horses at the track or the old spark plugs he's changing or the pictures in the museum, but talk's talk, and eventually it'll turn into guy talk, and, given enough time, it'll also turn into the conversation you want.

Warning: If you feel like the conversation has to be wrenched around to what you want to talk about, you're missing the point here. If you want to know the real story on why Pop left you and Mom and the farm and ran off with the preacher's wife, you stand a much better chance of finding out by talking about agriculture and religion than you do trying to meet the subject head-on. Men talk around important subjects. Just pay attention and you'll get what you came for.

Walk his walk. Lately, dad bashing has become a booming boomer industry. Every man worth an ounce of self-absorption will chatter on endlessly about how little he got from his old man, how badly he screwed and how much more involved he is as a father.

What that really means is that our dads never sat around the kitchen table talking about how much they loved everybody. Instead, all they did was work, work, work, while Mom stayed home and mopped up. Today, we know better, and to demonstrate our deep involvement, we pick up Junior from day care on Mondays, Wednesdays and Fridays and tell him we love him all the way to his mother and stepfather's house, where we drop him off until the next alternating weekend.

What also makes it tough for us to fill Pop's boots is that by almost any measure, the world is a dumber, more hostile, more dangerous, less civilized place today than it was on the old man's watch. We make less and know less and spend more and talk lots more, mostly about ourselves. All this makes it difficult for us to enjoy good hang time with Dad, as there's always the chance he'll say, "Idiot. I told you so." Fortunately, most dads are nice guys and keep all this to themselves. You gotta like a guy like that.

Let bygones be bygones. If much of your life is devoted to conducting a private Nuremberg for your old man, you're the one making the big mistakes in life, not him. One chap bristles every time his father innocently asks whether it's time for a haircut, because, he says, "I still remember the time he dragged me to his barber and made him cut off my Beatles bangs." Now, of course, he wears his hair just like Dad's.

Let him help out. This guy conversion project may seem a bit daunting, but once you get into it, it gets progressively easier. Besides, your old man will chip in and do half the work, once he sees what you're up to. First of all, to him, sons aren't guys, either. And second, he's already been through all this once with the guy he called Pop.

—*Denis Boyles*

A State of Perfection

It's Easier to Achieve Than You Think

We live in an age of imperfection. Need evidence? Check out the alternatives to Barbie on the market: Good-bye, statuesque, wasp-waisted, 11-inch piece of perfection. Howdy, dowdy, plump, bepimpled mirror of all human shortcomings.

Soon, it'll be good-bye to Ken, too. At the moment, the perfect mate for the perfect doll is a bronzed boygod dressed like a male figure skater playing Vegas lounges. The new, imperfect Ken, no doubt, will look like G.I. Joe without the G.I. benefits.

Why are we selling ourselves short? Perfection is there for the taking if a man only knows what to look for. Hence, this handy guide to a do-it-yourself perfect life, complete with a perfect mate, a perfect job, perfect health and, yes, perfect manners. You want perfection? Read this, do that, then look in the mirror. You're perfect.

The Perfect Mate

Nothing dresses up the bachelor-trashed hovel of a man's life like the scenic, aesthetic and intellectual accessory of a lifetime—the perfect mate. There's one for everybody, and enough to go around.

But finding true love isn't as easy as it looks in the movies. Before you say "I do," here's how to tell if the one you choose is perfect for you.

The Ingredients

A perfect mate:

• Knows you as well as you know yourself

- Agrees with you about important things, such as friendship, religion and the virtue of red, spiked heels
- Gives the relationship priority
- Can turn you on just by asking what time it is

The Recipe

If love were real estate, we'd all be speculators: Even attractive, peaceful parcels can hide fault lines and toxic waste. Still, there are ways to recognize a good deal when you see it, and to make the most of your investment once you've committed. For example, you can predict ahead of time whether a relationship will succeed or fail, says David Olson, Ph.D., professor in family social sciences at the University of Minnesota in Minneapolis. How?

Make a reality check. Start telling your partner what you really think about your relationship before you set up house. Though partners start out expecting mostly lovey-dovey stuff from each other, if you wait until you've both signed the mortgage to say how much you dislike her taste in interior design, you have more than a design problem. You have a marriage problem.

Make a background check. What beliefs does this person hold dear? Relationships last longer when both partners really share basic beliefs in such matters as sex, parenting, friends, religion, leisure time and division of household labor—factors that Dr. Olson's research has identified as crucial to the success of relationships. To help couples sneak a crystal-ball look into the future of their relationships, Dr. Olson has devised a 125-item questionnaire called Prepare that, when interpreted, predicts divorce with 80 to 85 percent accuracy. The questionnaire is administered by trained counselors and clergy. For a list of people trained to give this test near you, write: Prepare/Enrich, P.O. Box 190, Minneapolis, MN 55440.

Make a bed check. Take a good look at the person you love. Imagine the two of you together 50 years from now and say to yourself "This is the last person with whom I will ever have sex." Think about it. If you're ready, you'll know it.

Make a maintenance check. Even a mechanical dunce can tell if all the parts are working right in a marriage. Bad communication is the most obvious sign of a breakdown; most divorcing couples cite factors such as incompatibility and volatility—both communication problems—as factors leading to marital woes. Women often accuse men of stonewalling in relationships, but walls don't just fly up; they're constructed slowly, brick by brick, through mutual effort. Can you talk to each other, or is your conversation a series of accusations? In general:

- Avoid criticism. Say: "I'd like to get out more." Don't say: "You never want to go anywhere."
- Avoid defensiveness. This includes matching your partner's complaints with more of your own, denying that you're in any way to blame or claiming that circumstances beyond your control make you act a certain way. Treat your partner's words as information, not attacks. If you're genuinely open to what's expressed, the other person is less likely to become critical.
- Stay calm. Men are particularly prone to let arguments make their blood boil. The experts call this flooding. Stress hormones soar, blood pressure climbs, the stomach constricts, and next thing you know, you have a shouting match. Keep arguments from getting out of control—make a habit of letting her know what's on your mind.

Working the Perfect Job

Work, work, work. What does it get you? Money, power, satisfaction, identity, free insurance, servants to do your bidding, a gold watch. As a man, you'll invest a lot in your career. The downside: You'll eventually die, and if you've devoted all your time to your lousy job and not to your family, it will all mean nothing. The upside: You'll get all the payoffs before you croak—if you do everything absolutely, completely, 100 percent perfectly!

The Ingredients

How to tell if your career is perfect? It's jake if it:

- Starts before you know it
- Has a straight-line trajectory
- Isn't built exclusively on monetary rewards
- Ends when you want it to end

The Recipe

Get smart. First things first. Stay in school. Graduate work will never be more convenient or cost-effective than it is now. And don't just study the trade you're in; if you're a business major and you don't know beans about Shakespeare or Socrates, you may be well-trained, but you're still dumb. Many corporations are sending their MBA-clad management candidates back to school for a dose of liberal arts. Business is finding that men and women with some understanding of philosophy, literature and art make better decisions and have better judgment.

Get a map. When gates open before us, we tend to go through them automatically, says Stanley Teitelbaum, Ph.D., clinical psychologist at the Postgraduate Center for Mental Health in New York City. Better to look ahead first. Before you make a move:

- Find out what guys who once had the job you're considering are up to now. If they're not doing anything that appeals to you, steer clear.
- Think happy, not rich. Don't be blinded by an attractive salary offer if the work doesn't turn you on. You'll soon feel like you're paying yourself to be miserable.
- Broaden your scope. Be alert for opportunities in jobs that seem beneath you or unrelated to your field: A no-brainer job can be a good initial move if it takes you where the action is. Ask any waiter in Manhattan.

Get a promotion. Getting a job is like taking the Normandy beaches on D-Day: Once you've done it, you still need to take France. To be a Patton, career-wise:

- Work for your boss, not the company. "It took me years to learn this," says Karin Ireland, author of *The Job Survival Instruction Book*. "I thought the main thing was to perform my job description well; if the boss wanted something that got in the way, I resisted it." Doing your job well won't count at review time if your boss doesn't feel you're in his corner.
- Be a leader. "The higher you go, the less bosses care about your grasp of technical details, and the more they care about

whether people will rally behind you," says Washington, D.C.–based organizational counselor Peter Wylie, Ph.D. If you're vying for high corporate positions, you'll need to demonstrate people power before hitting age 30. To do it, you need first and foremost to build trust. Others will follow you if you keep your word and don't shift position with every change of the wind. Another key leadership trait is being aware of the personal needs of the people who report to you. Learn what they do in their spare time, the names of their kids, their professional history.

- Get feedback. Even if you get good job reviews, it's not always easy to know where you stand with the boss or colleagues. Problem: You need reliable intelligence, but not through the regular channels. Solution: Ask the boss's assistant. "Secretaries see everything," Dr. Wylie says. "They're virtually the only people in a position to tell you things like 'The way you speak up in staff meetings really annoys Mr. Johnson.'"

Make yourself fireproof. Corporations are so accustomed to ruthlessly thinning the ranks for a quick lift to the bottom line, they don't even feel guilty about it anymore, says Karen Kerkstra Harty, co-author of *Finding a Job after Fifty.*

Usually, the ax falls on the over-50 crowd, who earn the most money and are sometimes viewed (however unfairly) as less sharp than younger turks. To protect yourself, keep your finger in the wind. "People often don't have a clue that layoffs are coming," Harty says. Warnings include an unrecovered drop in the company's stock value, the firing of the chief executive officer or a failure of the company to meet projected earnings. Also, appraise yourself honestly. Are there other people in the company doing the same things you do? If so, you're a possible target. What to do?

- Adopt the attitude of a consultant. "Consultants look for problems and solve them, with a constant eye on what they bring to the table," says Harty. If you act that way as an employee, you'll be way ahead of more complacent peers when the winnowing begins.

• Keep up with the times. If you're still using your favorite old Royal while others are zipping down the information super-highway, it may be time to update. Ask yourself: When was the last time you did anything to improve your job skills? Then get on it.

Get out alive. Jumping ship becomes an issue in your forties, when you've realized a lot of the professional goals you set for yourself 20 years ago and are wondering what else life has in store. It's a time of opportunity—and also of rash, regrettable mistakes. "Men can be overly dazzled by new opportunities," says Mark Gerzon, author of *Coming into Our Own.*

• When facing a seemingly bright prospect, you'll keep the sun out of your eyes if you ask yourself what your best friend would say. An objective person will ask questions. Why are you doing this? What makes you think it's the right thing? If you have a nagging feeling that you're acting rashly, that's your experience talking, and you probably are.

• Then actually ask the friend. Check your own judgments with those of someone you respect, especially someone your own age or older. If your views and theirs are fundamentally at odds, you may need to reconsider.

Being a Perfect Gentleman

Perfection can earn you a whole catalog of benefits. For example, good-looking and charming men enjoy decided advantages, and not just with women. Men who look great also earn 14 percent more money on average than men whose appearance leaves something to be desired, according to research from the University of Texas at Austin and Michigan State University in East Lansing. So if your life is one long bad-hair day, and if your last suit came with its own white belt, you have some work to do.

The Ingredients

A perfect gent:

- Looks good
- Acts good
- Is good—and not just to dogs and old ladies

The Recipe

Pay attention to details. The extras can pull your whole image together—or destroy it. Three major ways to improve your fine points:

- Keep shoes shined. "You can have a terrific suit, but worn-looking shoes will ruin the whole effect," says New York City clothing expert Warren Christopher, style adviser for *Men's Health* magazine.
- Buy interesting socks. Don't get anything too loud, but do try muted patterns with colors that tie in with your suit.
- Replace worn shirts. If collars are stained, colors have faded, whites have yellowed or cuffs have frayed, relegate shirts to yard duty.

Learn some etiquette. If your family ate dinner around a table where sleeves were napkins, then you have to go out and get some manners. Why? Because nothing communicates perfection like proper etiquette—the old-fashioned, get-up-and-hold-the-door, don't-interrupt, chew-with-your-mouth-closed variety.

Adjust your attitude. When handling livestock, attitude adjustments are made with a two-by-four. It makes a rowdy bull a sweet one almost instantly. If you've managed to get through your first few decades with a sneer and a slide, then get ready to get adjusted. Perfect men are nice men with pleasant attitudes toward strangers and friends alike. Sullen coolness and aloof rudeness are signs of a deeply imperfect yahoo. If you can't figure out how to shake hands and smile like a man, hit yourself with a board until you get it right, because without charm, you're doomed to imperfect failure.

Enjoying Perfect Health

Health is an either/or proposition. Either you're healthy or you're unhealthy. Sometimes you get to choose; sometimes you don't. The trick is to maximize the number of times you get to do the choosing and minimize the number of times fate does it for you.

The Ingredients

Looking for signs of perfect health? You're in the pink if you:

• Avoid needlessly maiming yourself and others
• Treat your body like a delicate machine, and not like a fat-whacker
• Read the idiot lights on life's dashboard

The Recipe

One false move and you're dead. A great deal of our lifetime is spent on an eight-inch I-beam 90 floors up, figuratively speaking, where one single misstep means the end of life as we know it. We put ourselves in these predicaments by choice, yet often we don't even know we're in danger until it's too late. Need proof?

Gentlemen, start your engines. Until men reach their midforties, the thing most likely to maim or kill them is a good old-fashioned motor-vehicle accident. In fact, we have accidents at an average rate of one every ten years. Do other guys cause all the problems? Yeah, sure. But bear in mind that 76 percent of drivers say they're safer than average. Since that can't actually be true, some of us could use more improvement than we think. In the interests of helping you drive defensively, Leonard Evans, General Motors safety researcher and author of *Traffic Safety and the Driver*, recommends the following:

• Control your braking. Instead of barreling up to traffic lights, then braking hard, let up on the gas as soon as you see the light change to red and coast the rest of the way. Doing so makes you more noticeable to other drivers, decreases your risk of being slammed from behind and also saves gas and time. If you're at all lucky, it'll also mean you're still moving when you get the green.

• Don't drive in formation. One obvious difference between you and the Blue Angels is that you're in a Chevy Cavalier and they're not. It's more dangerous to be adjacent to another car than either behind or ahead of it. The safety tip: When passing, pass. Don't hang out next to the guy and watch to see if he picks his nose.

Keep a potbelly at bay. It's visible evidence that you're at risk for heart disease, as well as other problems such as stroke and diabetes. Between ages 30 and 55, it's common to gain a pound a year, says James Brand, M.D., assistant professor of family medicine at the University of Oklahoma College of Medicine in Oklahoma City. The culprits: a metabolism that slows, an appetite that doesn't and a sharp decline in physical activity. If you're not exercising regularly by your midthirties, you should be.

Bolster your back. As you begin to lose flexibility and muscle tone with age, you also lose support of the spine, making lower-back problems increasingly common after age 30.

Here's a simple way to prevent back pain for the chairbound. Sitting in a chair, cross your left ankle over your right knee. Twist your torso to the left, hooking your right arm over your raised knee and pulling on it gently. Continue turning slowly to the left, drawing your chest toward your knee until you feel a stretch in the left buttock. Hold for 15 seconds and repeat on the other side.

Stop heart disease. As many as three out of four men die of it, with heart attacks starting as early as the forties. "I've never seen a heart attack patient who didn't have a warning days, weeks or months ahead of time," says Noel H. Ballentine, M.D., assistant professor of medicine at the Milton S. Hershey Medical Center of the Pennsylvania State University in Hershey. Sometimes it's chest pain, but sometimes it's a tight band of pressure around your chest, as if someone were laying a weight on you. This is angina, a temporary clot in a blood vessel that quickly clears and leaves you feeling fine. A lot of guys mistake it for heartburn. Then one day the clot doesn't go away and there's big trouble. "The whole thing is very treatable, and you don't want to miss your chance," Dr. Ballentine says. If your chest tightens or hurts, especially when you're doing something physical, see a doctor immediately.

Check for prostate cancer. Prostate cancer claims more men than any other type except lung cancer. The message is get screened annually. Screening consists of two parts: a digital-rectal exam, which can be done quickly in your doctor's office, and a prostate-specific antigen blood test, which measures a protein the prostate produces when there's trouble. Neither test is perfect, but getting both together is better than getting either one alone.

Check for testicular cancer. It's the most common type of tumor diagnosed in men between ages 20 and 35. There's no known way to prevent the disease, but if it's noticed early, it has one of the highest cure rates of all cancers—95 percent. So, examine yourself monthly. The testicular self-exam is quick, easy and effective—and hardly anybody does it.

While the testicles are relaxed and loose (following a shower is a good time), take each testicle one at a time and roll it between your thumb and forefinger. It should be smooth and firm, but not hard. If you feel lumps or areas of hardness, experience pain or notice one testicle is larger than the other, see a doctor immediately.

Being a Perfect Dad

The last ten years have been tough on dads. Not on us, mind you. We are the perfect generation, so for us every decade is the "us decade." But it's been a rough ten years on our dads, the unfeeling, insensitive, withdrawn creatures who made our lives miserable by not telling us they loved us often enough.

The Ingredients

But as dads, we have this nagging doubt. Are we perfect enough? Are we:

• Accessible?
• Dependable?
• Responsible?

Yes to all three? Then we're perfect.
Yes, but only sometimes? Imperfect.
No wonder. "We have increased demands to be very proficient both in our careers and at home as engaged fathers," says Nolan Brohaugh, senior associate at the Menninger Management Insti-

tute in Topeka, Kansas. That's not all bad. One study shows that being more successful on the home front makes men less stressed in general.

The Recipe

Be a visible dad. Success as a father depends on three basic things, says Wade Horn, Ph.D., director of the National Fatherhood Initiative in Lancaster, Pennsylvania.

- Give kids time. "Reject the idea of 'quality time,'" Dr. Horn says. "Coming home and saying 'I have five minutes, let's make it good' won't work." Doing and saying a lot together isn't the issue; being together a lot is.
- Make and keep commitments. When you promise you'll take them to the playground or make it to the school recital, you're telling your kids they're important. When you actually show up, you're proving it. Forgetting to show for the show means exactly what they think it means.
- Accept responsibility for their well-being. This entails both bringing home the bacon and, say, eating it with them while they talk about their troubles. It also entails a couple of life's really, really difficult chores: keeping the relationship with Mom on an even keel. That's one. And demonstrating religious and moral convictions. That's two.

Be a dad with his foresight intact. Buy enough life insurance. "It sounds surprising, but 75 to 80 percent of us are underinsured," says David Chilton, financial adviser and author of *The Wealthy Barber*, a guide to wise investing. Plan to have enough coverage to pay off your mortgage, all your current debts and your kids' college educations. Add to that an adequate monthly income for your spouse and family until they get back on their feet. Don't price policies until you first figure out how much insurance you'll need to cover everything. Start by checking term policies, which

JUST THE FACTS

Number of eye injuries caused each year by auto-battery explosions, primarily triggered by jump-starting cars: 6,000

can be surprisingly affordable. Whole-life policies with a savings plan are a better buy over the course of a typical lifetime, but fewer than 3 percent of policyholders keep these plans in place for 20 years.

Find a way to pay for college. Don't be paralyzed by grim statistics about the fortunes you'll need to save for education. Some pointers courtesy of Kalman A. Chany, co-author of *The Princeton Review Student Access Guide to Paying for College*:

- Keep money in your name. It's generally a bad idea to sock your money away in your child's name to take advantage of Junior's lower tax bracket. The hundreds you save can cost you thousands when applying for financial aid, in which formulas for determining need assess a child's money at a rate almost seven times higher than a parent's money.
- Sell stocks two years before college bills are due. Financial aid need is assessed from a period starting January 1 of the student's junior year in high school. Get out of the stock market or mutual funds before that, or the rise in income due to capital gains will reduce your aid eligibility.
- Avoid prepayment plans. With these, you lock in today's tuition rate by giving the college your money years ahead of time. The deal has its risks—most of them yours. Your child might not be accepted, the college's reputation might go down the tubes, or it might not offer the right programs. You'd get back your principal and in some cases interest, but you'd generally do better investing elsewhere.

Being a Perfect Son

What a drag. So much easier to be a shortchanged son than a perfect one. Get over it, because someday you'll be an orphan, perfect or not.

The Ingredients

A perfect son:
- Loves his mom and dad
- Doesn't whine
- Takes care of family business

The Recipe

Be forgiving. Aside from you, nobody's perfect. What kids often forget is that their parents forgave them for being household flotsam for two decades. Parents deserve to be paid back: "What parents look for later in life is a sense of being appreciated and forgiven for their flaws and imperfections," says Brad Sachs, Ph.D., director of the Father Center in Columbia, Maryland. Expressions of love and forgiveness rarely come in words, and they don't need to. "Active attempts at connecting are the most profound way of saying they're valuable to you," Dr. Sachs says.

And as for those disputes that aren't going to get resolved? "It's important to get beyond these things," Dr. Sachs says. "Focus on the things that do work well between you."

Be prepared. Yes, yes. You love them. They love you. But what about the details? A good son ought to ask his parents to put in writing how they would like to be cared for if they become incapacitated and can't issue directives for themselves. These are the docs you need before your folks need a doc.

• A decent insurance policy. Prepare for infirmity. As chronic health problems make them more dependent, you may have to step in to ensure your parents are properly cared for. Mothers are especially unlikely to have health insurance from pension plans to supplement Medicare. Both parents will need it to cover long-term hospital and nursing care. Consider enrolling your parents in the plan offered by the American Association of Retired Persons (AARP), which offers competitive rates on insurance for members. Write: AARP, 601 E Street NW, Washington, DC 20049.

• A living will directing doctors to abstain from extraordinary treatment—the kind of treatment, for instance, that makes Dad a houseplant by leaving the ticker going even though the lights have long since burned out. Along with this, it's a good idea to get a power-of-attorney document, which broadens your authority to make health-care decisions on behalf of your parents if they can't do it for themselves. Ask the admissions office at any hospital for information, which they're required by law to provide.

• Burial instructions. Don't bring this up in the middle of a round of golf, but since Mom and Pop's funeral is their last shout, make sure the party goes the way they want, including an under-taker-in-a-cake, if necessary.

Having a Perfect Retirement

Until you're about 45, getting old is the last thing on your mind. But once it is on your mind, it's virtually the only thing on your mind, except women. That means, of course, finding the fine line between being a dirty old man and a perfect old man.

The Ingredients

Count yourself in the perfect category if you're:

* Independent
* Busy
* Older than you look

The Recipe

Save a bunch of money. The way to do it?

* Start saving early. The problem with getting old is that you're always so busy being the age you are, it's hard to plan for the age you aren't—yet. "The biggest financial blunder I see is procrastination with savings," says Chilton. "The longer you wait, the more you lose the value of compounding," in which you earn interest on your interest.

   For example, if you sink $1,000 a year into a stock mutual fund at 15 percent interest starting at age 35, you'll have $500,000 at age 65, according to newspaper and radio financial commentator James Jorgensen, author of *It's Never Too Late to Get Rich.* If you do the same at 40, your savings plummet to $250,000. "Every five years you wait cuts your nest egg in half," Jorgensen says. "But every five years you invest, your nest egg doubles. In the end, 80 to 90 percent of your retirement money is money you never saved in the first place—it's the return on the 10 to 20 percent you invested."

* Invest aggressively. The younger you are, the more money you can afford to put into stock-based mutual funds, which are riskier than, say, bond funds or certificates of deposit. The reason is that even if the bottom drops out of the market tomorrow, stocks will eventually bounce back and in the

long haul perform much better. "Historically, if you stick with stocks five years or longer, there's virtually no risk," Jorgensen says. His formula for how much of your money to put into stocks: 100 minus your age. For example, subtracting age 35 from 100 gives you 65 percent of your savings dollars in stock mutual funds.

• Avoid panic. Keep track of your funds and invest for the long haul, not just today, says financial adviser Richard Kraner, partner at Ernst and Young in St. Louis. Ideally, your fund's performance shouldn't fall below that of the S&P 500, but don't judge harshly if it deviates from time to time. "There's actually a very select list that outperforms the S&P consistently. Don't worry about moving your money unless your fund is significantly different from the market as a whole for more than one or two years," he says.

Keep busy until the hearse rolls up. "Most of what people plan to do in retirement can be accomplished in the first 90 days," says Monica Brown, assistant manager of work-force education for the AARP. Make life beyond that more fulfilling.

• Be a volunteer. "Ideally, you should retire from something to something," says Brown. Volunteer opportunities are ideally suited to older people, who feel it's time to give something back. Get involved in churches, politics or senior centers.

• Get training. The AARP has chapters nationwide that offer training in a variety of services. "Some of our volunteers have found second careers through the training we offer," Brown says. To contact your local office, call 1-800-424-3410.

• Avoid isolation. Suddenly stopping work after more than 40 years' employment is one of life's biggest challenges. We risk becoming disconnected from the world and, as a result, well, bored. For some of us, it's a mistake to move to a retirement zone. Before you head south, ask yourself two things: Do you have any family or friends there? and what are you going to do there? A general rule of thumb: "Don't move any place you've only visited in February," says Brohaugh.

Finding Perfect Balance

Okay. You have your perfect mate, your perfect job, your perfect health, your perfect kids, your manners and your perfect parents. But something's still wrong: You're close to perfect, but you're not quite there. What's missing?

Balance. You're only almost perfect until you get all this stuff in perfect equilibrium. If you slough off the good-manners part, for example, because you're too busy working on being the perfect dad part, you're screwed, perfection-wise. You have to get it all perfect, all right. But you also have to get it all perfectly balanced. That's why nobody's perfect. Yet.

—Richard Laliberte

What Men Really Want

Forget Sex: Here's a Real-Life Wish List

Sometimes, when he least expects it, a man can be struck by a fleeting glimpse of clarity, a sudden realization that what he wants—what he really wants—isn't what he's been working for. What he really wants isn't that next promotion (more responsibility and less gratitude) or that big house (1,001 nagging new improvement projects) or that woman over in finance with the lips like candied fruit (same boat, different anchor).

What he wants—what he really wants—is something else. Might be something that changes life as we know it. Or it might be something so insignificant that its meaning escapes everyone but him. Either way, sharing our innermost desires with others isn't something that comes easily to men; that's why we always get ties for Father's Day instead of, well, what we really want.

So we decided to find out what was truly going on in the minds of American men. We polled our friends with surveys and asked them to poll theirs. We cruised the Internet and solicited responses from cyberspace. And we strong-armed the men we work with and the guys in our neighborhoods. And somehow, we got them to open up. Some of their desires strike universal themes; others are as unique and distinctive as they themselves. Either way, consider this the ultimate eavesdropper's checklist, a compendium of what's really going on inside the heads of your fellow men.

I want my father alive again for one day.

—Writer, 44

I want to know why women shouldn't be taught to leave the toilet seat up.

—Media buyer, 41

I'd like to be able to take stairs two at a time, like I did when I was a teenager. Back then I was always going fast, even though I had no place in particular to go. Now I have twice as much to do but I move half as quickly as I used to.

—Manager, 52

I want my hair back. To tell you the truth, I'd settle for getting half of it back.

—Tax accountant, 31

I'd like to have the kinds of friendships I had in high school and college.

—Journalist, 31

I want back the child my wife and I chose to abort ten years ago. At the time, I thought I wasn't financially or emotionally ready to have children. But the fact is, you're never ready. You just have the baby and cope the best you can.

—No occupation or age given

I want to be able to relax for a minute. I'm a husband, a father, an employee, a citizen, a coach, a volunteer and too many other things. I wish I had time to sit back and be me for a minute.

—Junior-high-school teacher, 35

I wish my children could have the kind of childhood I had. On summer days my pals and I would head for the woods, where we'd make these little bows and arrows out of saplings for hunting rabbits and birds. We'd fish and swim in the creek that ran along the south side of town. And sometimes our parents would let us sleep out in the field beneath the stars. They didn't have to worry, because it was safe. Everyone knew everyone in our little town. I couldn't imagine letting my kids do that these days. And I think they're really missing out on something precious. It's an innocence, a freedom from fear that's totally vanished from our country. And that's a real shame.

—Director of personnel, 45

I wish my parents were healthy and financially secure. They're at the point where they need my help, but with a mortgage, a three-year-old son, a wife who doesn't work outside the home and another baby on the way, I'm totally strapped.

—Grocery store manager, 37

The chance to remake two decisions that I made earlier in my life. One involved a woman—really a choice between two women—and the other was a business opportunity I didn't take. Hardly a day goes by when I don't wonder what my life would have been like if I'd made different decisions back then.

—Automobile salesman, 61

I'd like to stand up in church and argue a few points.

—Chemical engineer, 52

I'd love it if young women would stop calling me "sir."
—Electrician, 34

James Bond movies as good as the old Sean Connery ones.
—Editor, 40

I wish I could raise children. One thing about being a gay man is that there's a lot of free time that gets wasted because there's no family to share it with. I wish that it were easier for gay men to raise children, and that we could raise them to respect people's differences.
—Attorney, 30

I want to do a really good deed—save a life or something—and, the selfish part, get recognized for it.
—Agricultural researcher, 44

How about someone to believe in. That's what I want. It seems like every hero I've ever had has later been exposed by some writer as a monster or a fraud or a pervert. And every politician I've ever voted for seems to turn into a spineless, poll-obsessed weasel. I'm afraid I've become too cynical, but there's not a lot of evidence lately that I'm wrong.
—No occupation or age given

I'd like my son and I to get through his fast-approaching teenage years better than my father and I got through mine. I would give anything to stay close to my son for life.
—No occupation or age given

I'd like my girlfriends to take charge once in a while and plan what's happening on our dates. I'd especially like it if they initiated sex instead of leaving the first moves up to me.
—Financial planner, 29

I'd like my kids to miss me when they grow up and leave the house. But even if they don't miss me, I want them to grow up and leave the house.
—Salesman, 39

I want to look as young as I feel, or at least I'd like the two to be closer together. I feel like I'm about 25 or so, but when I look in the mirror, I see this fleshy, middle-age guy. I'm really beginning to hate mirrors and photos of myself.

—Bank vice-president, 42

My wife lost a breast to cancer three years ago. I don't want the breast back; I want her back. She hasn't felt the same about herself since.

—Orthodontist, 50

I want to look like a million bucks in casual clothes. You can always tell when a man is rich and successful because he just seems to look great in a pair of slacks and a polo shirt. I want to have that look.

—Disc jockey, 39

I want to travel faster. Airplanes still take at least a half a day to get from point A to point B. I want it to be instantaneous, like on Star Trek.

—No occupation given, 23

I want my wife not to have to work. I'm as liberated as the next guy, but I'd like to feel I can support my family the way my father did.

—Furniture wholesaler, 33

I want to know where I stand at all times. I want to know who my friends are, who I can trust and who I have to worry about.

—Chief financial officer, 46

To have the power to make it illegal for the children of movie stars to become movie stars.

—Career counselor, 36

I want my clothes to coordinate without having to think about it. And I want to tie my ties perfectly the first time, every day.

—Manager, 31

I'd like women to appreciate the genius of the Three Stooges. If I can sit through The Piano *without complaining, you'd think there would be a woman out there who wouldn't call me a moron for laughing at Moe, Larry and Curly hitting each other with pickaxes.*

—Postal clerk, 24

I'd like cool dogs available for weekend rental to walk through the park. Someone would deliver Rover on Saturday morning and pick him up again on Sunday night.

—Media planner, 24

I'd like women to ask me to open jars once in a while. It makes me feel good (except when I can't open the darned things).

—Men's clothing buyer, 34

I'd like a clause in my marriage vows that allows me to be single one week a year.

—Physical therapist, 32

I want not to be the one who handles everything. I'm the one who has to haggle with salesmen, keep after repairmen and mechanics, arrange to get things fixed when they break. Why is this the man's job?

—Physical therapist, no age given

I would like to hear about a near-death experience where the person is headed for hell; just to hear something different from the usual going-toward-the-beautiful-light vision. Basically, I'd like to know what really happens when you die.

—Photographer, 49

I want women never again to ask me the following questions: "Do I look fat?" "Where do you see us in three years?" "Why didn't you call?" "What would you say if I were to tell you I was pregnant?"

—Graduate student, 24

I'd like to be able to say one really witty thing every day. It seems that men who can tell jokes well are universally popular.

—No occupation or age given

I want immortality, which is really the power to take chances, make mistakes and never feel like time is closing in on you.

—Architect, 41

50-Day
Epiphany

Go on Extended Leave and the World Changes

Fifty days off. If you're like most overworked men, these words probably excite you more than Claudia Schiffer. But who can swing it? Even though you may get three or four weeks of paid vacation yearly, to take even five consecutive days is nearly impossible.

But what if . . . ?

A career shift recently enabled me to live the dream and escape work for seven weeks. Like other new "retirees," I'm proud to say that my sidewalk is perfectly edged, my garage floor swept dinnerplate clean and my lawn clipped to crew-cut length. All the other guys in my neighborhood hate me.

But beyond life's landscaping, I did some serious mental yard work, too. This "near-retirement experience" enlightened me in several ways that don't typically happen during one- or even twoweek getaways. Here's what I found (and what you might expect to find) when the labor ends.

I started dreaming again. I never used to remember sleeping. I'd pass out after a hard day, then wake up six or eight hours later feeling crusty and kind of dazed. Occasionally, I'd dream about Mona, the secretary, or being swept away by an in-box tsunami, but most of my downtime was black—blank.

Then, after a few days away, I started having these incredible dreams. It was as if Spielberg, Hitchcock and Coppola were directing my subconscious. What's amazing is that all the activity was somehow very restful. I awoke feeling fresh and alive—sort of the same "whoa, now I'm ready to go" exhilaration you get after riding a roller coaster.

Robert Van de Castle, Ph.D., author of *Our Dreaming Mind*, says that no one ever really stops dreaming—the average is 100 minutes per night. "It's just that in your hurly-burly world you weren't giving yourself the opportunity to lie in bed and recall your dreams. They were off with the sheets because your mind was pre-occupied."

The longer you doze, adds Dr. Van de Castle, the longer your dream-rich periods last. With no morning deadline, I was sleeping later, dreaming more and waking up better rested.

I lost track of time. I used to marvel when my five-year-old would ask what day it was or puzzle over the necessity for a watch. But during my hiatus, Monday morning lost its dread and Friday afternoon all its unproductive wishfulness. I had no reason to clock-watch or even look at a calendar. And guess what? Time finally slowed down. It was like being a kid in mid-July again. After years of feeling as if my life were speeding by, the brake lights came on and living became luxuriously unmeasured again.

I walked the mile to the grocery store. I stopped in to get my hair cut without an appointment. I nearly bought a hammock. And I learned to enjoy driving 55—especially at rush hour.

My memory returned. Harvard psychologists have demonstrated that the mere expectation of memory loss with age seems to encourage that fate. While there's much to be said for the power of positive thinking, I'm also convinced that today's man is becoming increasingly forgetful because of "information saturation."

Say there's an important remembrance—your wedding day, to choose a crucial example—that you want to retain. But as more passengers board the ol' brain bus, it gets pushed further and further back, until the driver—that's you—can only make out vague bits and tux colors.

Nowadays, we're bombarded with more daily intelligence than

JUST THE FACTS

One in seven women wishes she'd been born a man.

J. Edgar Hoover ever was—through newspapers, magazines, television, e-mail and that annoying Larry King. But when the shelling subsides, even for a short time, you'll be surprised at what's still standing.

"Why, how silly of you, dear. They were gray Pierre Cardin tuxedos, of course."

I became thoughtful. When I was working, I never read anything; I scanned. I didn't listen; I heard. And I didn't see; I glanced.

The result was a harried, superficial existence—the information saturation thing again, dumbing us down. What I realized during my time off is that you have to chew your food if you want to digest it properly. I also discovered that it's better and more healthful for the mind to know a few things well than a great many things slightly.

I got taller. No kidding. Two different people said I actually looked like I'd grown. The worries and responsibilities of my old job must have been hunchbacking me. Quick, measure yourself.

My hair got fuller and the gray disappeared. Sorry, my mistake. That was a dream.

I stopped yelling at my kids. It's not that they were any less devilish, it's just that I hadn't previously been pushed to the brink of tolerance by the nine-to-five office equivalent of spilled Spaghetti-Os, unflushed "boom-booms" and Legos chattering through the heating ducts. I learned that I have more patience with children when I'm not dealing with their grown-up counterparts all day. What a relief: I'm not an ogre after all.

All my energy went into my life. Imagine that your life is your job, your career, and that you're working exclusively toward its success. Fifty, sixty hours a week are spent solidifying the assets, balancing the books and otherwise perfecting the product. What a business life would be!

When you no longer have to devote so much time and energy to someone else's bottom line, it's amazing what you can accomplish. I painted my entire house. I bicycled at least 20 miles every day. I analyzed and restructured my investments. I cleaned out my T-shirt drawer. And, yes, I went to Disney World.

I noticed my wife. You hang a new painting on the wall—a true work of art—and for the first few months you admire it daily. But as the years pass, it becomes just another part of the room—no less beautiful, just less appreciated. My wife of ten years has soft sienna eyes framed by matching brown hair, and there's a dimple on her left cheek. When she's daydreaming, she'll touch the tip of her tongue to her upper lip. And she looks best in red—no, make that crimson.

I started having incredible sex. The two biggest obstacles to the sex lives of most working men are (1) not enough time and (2) fatigue. Since I suddenly had all the time in the world and was never really tired, my libido returned from Toledo.

I gained perspective. Funny how the closer you get to something, the less of it you see. In my previous strife, er, life, I was the editor of a bicycle magazine. For eight years, the job and the sport consumed me. Then I quit, and realized that cycling is—forgive me, God LeMond—just a game. For that matter, accounting is only playing with numbers, banking is a lot like Monopoly and even complex urban planning is just a real-life version of SimCity.

After all the career noise had subsided, I realized that very few jobs carry any life-or-death consequences except your own. And, hey, I'll never be remembered eternally. And I'll never do the twist with Uma Thurman. And isn't work really just something you do for eight hours a day so you can afford more toys?

I realized the value of doing nothing. To hell with all those articles and experts that tell you how to make your free time more productive. I say it's productive to be unproductive sometimes. Channel-surf until your eyes swim. Lie in the grass and stare at the sky until large squawking crows circle overhead. Linger in bed until your wife gets nervous and feels for a pulse. Drool.

Don't feel guilty about occasionally doing nothing. It's calming. It's rejuvenating. This is your mind. This is your mind in neutral. Any questions?

Now, it's only fair to point out that not all the side effects from this time away were positive and fun. Although it was a life-altering experience to have my dry-cleaning bills dwindle to nothing, there were some troublesome wrinkles that developed.

I lost a bit of my self-worth. While it's every man's fantasy to retire young and live large, I got a taste of what can humble, and eventually even defeat, some older men. The message light on my phone stopped blinking. My circle of friends condensed. And my old job continued without me.

You don't have to be a social psychologist to know that a man becomes his career. It is his identity, his pocket square, his reason for being. Standing at the school-bus stop without mine, however temporary, left me feeling undefined. Imagine hesitating, searching, when someone asks what you do for a living. Why is it so painful if the answer is "nothing"?

Soon I started looking forward to going back to work. Somewhere into the sixth week, after the kids had returned to school and I had painted even the bathroom vent pipes, I got this twang, this gentle mind nudge, this almost-evolutionary urge that maybe it was time to "go back." It had something to do with boredom, I'm sure, and a bit more with ego and re-proving myself professionally. But a large part stemmed from being satisfied that I had completed one job and was ready to move on to the next. I had siphoned off the stress, gotten reacquainted with my family, read a few books, gotten into respectable shape and made the house presentably suburban again. I had proven to myself that I could control my life and be relatively content.

But most important, I had realized that I was still here. That fun person my wife had fallen in love with . . . that carefree father who used to play weekday Wiffle ball with his kids . . . that positive, energetic journalist who gave every story his all . . . that guy I used to like.

The realization that I hadn't changed significantly and that I was still alive down deep inside made a huge difference in how I felt about myself. Although I'm certain the afterglow from this time off will fade and that I'll eventually forget a lot of its lessons, I know now that everything isn't inevitable. It's just a matter of how you handle it.

Oh, and one more thing . . . I ran out of cash. And that was when I knew I'd really better go back.

—Joe Kita

PART 8

Men at Work

Real-Life Résumé Goof-Ups

Whether you're looking to break in, move around or move up, the résumé is your ticket to success in corporate America. It can also be your ticket to slinging hash at Ma's Restaurant for the rest of your life. These guys should get their aprons on, because here are some royal résumé foul-ups that job recruiters have recently come across.

1. Employer references: None. I have left a path of destruction behind me.

2. I have become completely paranoid, trusting completely nothing and absolutely no one.

3. If you should choose to hire me, kindly work through my lawyer to have an agreement drawn.

4. Work experience: Dealing with customers' conflicts that arouse.

5. Proven ability to track down and correct erors.

6. Fired because I fought for lower pay.

7. Work history: Unsuccessfully searched for a job, incompletion of graduate program, took bar exam and failed.

8. Suspected to graduate early next year.

9. I procrastinate—especially when the task is unpleasant.

10. Instrumental in ruining entire operation for a Midwest chain store.

Sexual Harassment

What You Need to Know

Remember those great old flicks from the 1930s and 1940s—the ones in which some secretary to a private eye would sashay into her boss's room, plant herself atop his desk and proceed to flash a stretch of thigh as smooth as polished marble? Well, dream on, fella; thanks to the changing law of sexual harassment in the workplace, about the closest you're going to want to get to a scene like that is on late-night TV.

To say that things are different now is a severe understatement. Time was when a kiss was indeed just a kiss, a sigh just a sigh and suave men in fedoras would tip their hats to good-looking women and whistle as they passed. But no more, at least not in the workplace—unless you want to risk winding up before the Equal Employment Opportunity Commission (EEOC) on a charge of violating Title Seven of the 1964 Civil Rights Act.

In the wake of Clarence Thomas and Bob Packwood, sexual harassment cases have been multiplying like bacteria. In 1990 alone, the EEOC handled 6,127 such complaints. By 1993, the annual total had nearly doubled to 11,908. No one has yet been found guilty of sexual harassment for a tip of the hat, but charges are certainly being filed on increasingly flimsy grounds. And it's the charges themselves you want to avoid. As with the two schoolmistresses in Lillian Hellman's *The Children's Hour* who saw their lives destroyed on a false charge of lesbianism, the taint of suspicion lingers even if the facts themselves are disproved.

"In my experience as a labor lawyer, I have not come across any-thing as harmful as a sexual harassment allegation," says Frank Harty of Des Moines, Iowa, who represents employees and employ-ers accused of harassment in the workplace. "It can be a career-end-ing experience for both the accuser and the accused."

The legal headaches alone can be monumental. Take the case of Richard Glanton, a prominent lawyer in Philadelphia, who was ac-cused in 1992 of sexually harassing a female associate after she al-legedly ended a brief office affair.

Glanton denied all charges and further denied that he had ever been romantically or sexually involved with the woman in any way. A five-week trial followed, with the jury finding in Glanton's favor. But that wasn't the end of the story, for by that time Glan-ton had gotten so incensed at what had been happening to him that he had openly accused the woman of being an "extortionist" and "disturbed." Result? The jury slapped Glanton with $125,000 in damages, not for sexual harassment but for defamation. Both sides are now appealing in what has already developed into a pro-tracted and hugely expensive legal battle all around.

Harassment's Coming-of-Age

How did all this sexual harassment business get started in the first place? For an answer we return to Title Seven of the Civil Rights Act of 1964, which banned discrimination in hiring and employment on the basis of race, creed, sex, religion or country of origin. Essentially, Congress left it up to the EEOC to figure out what the commandment "Thou shalt not discriminate on the basis of sex" actually meant.

As the 1960s gave way to the 1970s, Title Seven got swept up in the activist enthusiasms of sexual politicians like Bella Abzug and Betty Friedan, and the long march toward the extremist goal of outlawing flirtation had begun.

Ironically, the feminists of three decades ago seem to have had nothing of the sort in mind. "Whatever anyone says about them, they certainly weren't set on banning all references to their own sexuality," says Lisa Schiffren, the conservative former speech writer for Dan Quayle who penned his famous Murphy Brown speech. "After all," she says, "these were the women who championed bra-burning as a pro-female political statement. For them, sexual liberation and feminism were two sides of the same coin."

But then came 1980s-era thinkers like Catherine McKinnon, who gave a legal framework to the notion that references to the female anatomy were nothing less than sexual assaults with words instead of body parts. In short, as McKinnon argued in a 1979 treatise titled "Sexual Harassment of Working Women," speech alone could create the kind of "hostile environment" that by its nature degraded and violated women. With that, the floodgates of politically correct thinking were flung open.

Is there a need to expose behavior that's genuinely offensive and ugly? Of course. After all, the increase in sexual harassment complaints has been accompanied by an astonishing decline in general civility. Bad manners are everywhere, and even though sexual harassment laws can't do much to change that, they can at least make sure that fair play and one of the most revered of all manly traits—respect for women—is observed while society seeks to rewrite the rules of etiquette and gender relations.

But when rudeness reaches the level of oppression, the crass fellow involved ought to be held liable. That's what happened not long ago to a thoroughgoing slob who fired a female employee because she refused to play strip poker with him. The boss admitted to the behavior, and the employee collected $1 million in damages. What's more, the dirty old man was prevented from laying the cost off on his insurance company, which successfully argued that the policy it had written did not cover harassment that was willful and intentional.

Now compare that case with that of Ewart Yearwood, a student at p.c.-crazed Swarthmore College in Pennsylvania, who was accused of sexual harassment for "stalking" a female dormitory mate, Alexis Clinansmith. Two separate hearings by a campus tribunal were held, and both found that Yearwood hadn't stalked or harassed anyone. Nonetheless, the university asked him to transfer to another school, mainly, it seems, because he unintentionally violated a tribunal order to stay at least 40 feet away from Clinansmith at all times—a near impossibility considering the fact that both lived in the same dorm, ate in the same cafeteria and attended many of the same campus functions.

Yearwood's first choice was to transfer to Columbia. But when news of his plans reached the *New York Post*, it unfurled a banner headline announcing "Columbia Gets Accused Sex Harasser," while the campus itself erupted in a storm of protest. Understandably, Yearwood began looking elsewhere. He is now at Boston University, where, ironically enough, Swarthmore is actually paying his tuition—anything necessary, it would seem, to keep him away from Swarthmore. Says Yearwood's lawyer, Harvey Silverglate, "I guess sexual harassment has gotten so serious that even innocence is no defense!"

In fact, the law of sexual harassment has become an amorphous, ever-expanding body of case and statute law that varies from state to state and from one federal court district to the next. In some jurisdictions, people are governed by the "reasonable man" standard: "Man," in this case, means person; in order to establish guilt, the plaintiff needs to prove that a reasonable person would take offense. But in other jurisdictions, the "reasonable woman" prevails— essentially a legal guideline that decrees that women have a different sensibility than men, and one that makes it much easier for a woman to prove harassment. Under EEOC guidelines on the matter, great weight is given to what the alleged victim seems to think, as opposed to what the defendant apparently intended. As attorney Harty sums the situation up, "The law is a mess."

The only consistent trend is the expansion of the alleged victim's rights over those of the accused. In the view of Hans Bader, who studies sexual harassment issues, the problem boils down to "the power politics of numbers."

Says Bader, "Seventy-eight percent of American colleges and universities today have codes of conduct outlawing sexual harassment. By contrast, only about a third have similar codes banning racial discrimination. Why? Because there are vastly more women than blacks and other minorities on college campuses."

It's the same in society as a whole. Thus, Bader points to a 1992 Supreme Court case—*R.A.V. v. St. Paul*—that held that the burning of a cross in front of a black person's home was "protected speech" under the First Amendment. Yet the same court held last autumn, in the widely commented-upon case of *Harris v. Forklift Systems*, that far less menacing "speech"—when sexual in nature and directed at women—could create a "hostile or abusive" environment in the workplace. Moreover, said the court, to recover damages, a plaintiff did not have to show actual financial or economic loss, just that the hostile work environment existed.

And even if you're careful not to say anything vaguely sexual to a woman, you haven't necessarily avoided liability for sexual harassment. Last year, a court in Minnesota held that an offensive utterance doesn't have to be directed specifically toward the plaintiff; an off-color joke or phrase repeated between two men in the workplace can create a hostile environment if the wrong woman overhears it. In Florida a court found that the placement of girlie pictures in the workplace would create the same environment. That case is now under appeal.

Staying Clear of Court

Just how tender can the sensibilities be of those claiming to be offended? J. Donald Silva, a highly regarded professor at the University of New Hampshire in Durham, learned the answer to that question the hard way. The university suspended Silva for a full year, without pay, for having had the audacity during one of his lectures to compare the act of writing to sex. In another class, he paraphrased a belly dancer who described her art as being "like Jell-O on a plate, with a vibrator under the plate."

Add it all up and this nearly 30-year trend now imperils companies and their employees alike. All face the threat of being hauled into court on sexual harassment charges for behavior that was accepted and even celebrated in movies less than a generation ago. Nor is it just male employees who are potentially at risk. Sure, it's relatively rare for a male to

bring charges of harassment against a female co-worker. The un-
likelihood is underscored by a *Men's Health* magazine survey that
shows only 4.6 percent of men have ever been harassed at work.

Sexual politics in the workplace are often not only about sex itself
but about power as well. According to a survey titled "Sexual Harassment in Medical Training," reported in the *New England Journal of Medicine*, "it is much more likely that the person with more
power will harass the person with less." It's the person in charge, regardless of gender, who's likely to face harassment charges. Today,
far fewer women than men hold middle- and upper-management
positions in American corporations, but as the numbers even out
(which they're expected to do by the year 2000), more and more female executives and supervisors will begin to learn the dark side of
what feminist extremism has unleashed in the workplace.

In the meantime, here are some pointers, based on advice from
legal experts along with a cautionary reading of the EEOC guidelines, to help you stay out of court on sexual harassment charges.

Remember the ultimate sin. The EEOC guidelines define sexual overtures accompanied by *quid pro quo* offers of such things as
promotions, salary raises and so on as the very embodiment of sexual harassment in action. Most of us would have to agree: That
kind of behavior by a few bad eggs is what gives all men a lousy
reputation. But just because you don't say the words "promotion"
and "sex" in the same sentence, that doesn't mean you're safe. If you
enter a relationship with a co-worker, and there's even the hint that
some benefit other than mutual satisfaction might be involved—
even if that wasn't your intention—you could be at risk.

Don't flirt at the office. Especially with subordinates, and most
particularly with lithesome young things fresh into the workplace.
"Even if you're only 25 years of age, you'll never be able to convince
a jury you aren't a dirty old man," says attorney Harty. "There are
plenty of places for sexual conquests, but the office isn't one of
them any longer. Any other attitude and you're asking for trouble."

Don't touch, ever! "I've handled several cases in which the
meaning of allegedly harassing language attributed to a defendant
was ambiguous, and not necessarily harmful," reports Harty. "But
then came testimony that the defendant had actually touched the

plaintiff. And juries take touching very seriously. In one case the defendant was accused of harassment because he patted the plaintiff on the back and she claimed he had actually been feeling for her bra strap." Thus if it involves more than shaking hands, don't do it.

Don't refer to body parts. Your female colleague might have a terrific figure, but as the *New England Journal of Medicine* pointed out regarding medical students, "If a male resident tells a female student in front of the medical team that he likes it when she wears skirts because she has great legs, she may feel angry and humiliated, even though he genuinely intended his remark as a compliment." Thus, this rule: If you wouldn't say it to a guy, don't say it to a girl, either—at least not at the office.

Don't joke around with sexual humor. There's nothing quite so unfunny as an unfunny off-color joke—unless it's an unfunny joke that keeps getting repeated in front of people who didn't laugh the first time. Like the nerdy character on "Saturday Night Live" who hangs around the copy machine and wears out his welcome with every new person who comes in the room, a sex-happy jokester can indeed cast a pall over the office. Don't be the jerk who doesn't get the hint—and winds up in court as the price of his obtuseness.

Take a minor complaint seriously. If a female employee objects to something in the workplace environment, take action—no matter how innocuous you think the offense is. If she complains about a picture of Marilyn Monroe in a guy's office, make him take it down. Your goal is to preclude a "hostile environment" suit. Showing concern for, and acting on, complaints is the best defense.

Such rules may seem almost Victorian in their primness, especially in light of what takes place in the rest of American life every day of the week. But as Walter Cronkite used to say, that's the way it is. Anyway, if the thought of buttoned-up rectitude at the office is just too grim for you to bear, you can always drop by a video store and bring home a couple of those Golden Oldies from, oh, say, Hollywood in the 1940s, when guys were guys, gals were gals and a wolf whistle in the street was guaranteed to get the girl in the silk stockings to turn back and smile.

—*Chris Byron*

Success in the Sales Game

A Guide to Winning as Buyer and Seller

In these disputatious, fractious, ill-spirited times, we know there are a million ways of dividing the planet in two. There's the North-South thing, for starters. There are haves and have-nots, men and women, owners and players, First World and Third World. Finally, you have what we can call buyers and sellers. That's where life on earth gets tricky—and expensive. We're buyers some of the time. We're sellers some of the time. And a man needs to be mindful of which is which.

Virtually every meeting between a buyer and a seller leaves behind a residue of resentment. Who knows why? It's not that sellers are carnivores in a world of vegan buyers, or that those with money have bludgeoned those with goods. The real problem is that very few people know how to sell anything, and too many people will buy anything. In the course of this modest lesson, I will explain how I came by this information. But for now, just trust me.

Being a Winning Seller

When salesmen go to sales school, they learn that every sale has just four ingredients: discovery, presentation, close and follow-through. Discovery is when you listen to what the customer wants. Presentation is when you offer to supply what the guy says he needs. The close is when you shake on it. And the follow-through is when you call the next week to see how everything's going.

When we want to sell something, most of us have almost no interest in the discovery and follow-through parts, because we know what we want to sell, and we don't particularly care how it works out later. So we go crazy on the presentation and the close. Case in point: Watch some chap in full courtship mode. He meets a woman, says hello, but can barely bring himself to listen to her name before he starts playing the endless tape of his life. The presentation part of his sale goes on forever. He's thinking that if he can just pitch the product the right way, the close will take care of itself.

Follow-through? Yeah. Sure. He'll call in the morning. Most of us sell cars, houses, garage junk all the same way.

Ears are a salesman's best tool. Ever notice how some guys can sell anything? We like to think that guys who can sell anything do their work by talking fast and slick. But that's not how it works at all. Guys who are great salesmen use their ears, not their jaws, because of all four parts of a sale, it's listening that counts most. A good salesman listens to as much as the buyer wants to tell him. For example, let's say you're the manager of your local hardware emporium and some suburban gentleman walks in looking for a snowblower. If you're any good, you'll spend the first few minutes listening, maybe asking a few questions: Gas or electric? Hilly lot or level? Paved driveway or gravel? Because you know if you sell the guy the new Desert Storm snowblower when what he really needs is the turbo-charged Sno-Sluice Deluxe, you'll have made an enemy. Buyers want guidance and help, not shortcuts.

Besides, there are added benefits to listening. Two, to be exact: First, it makes the buyer want you to succeed in selling him, since you seem to be on the same side, and everybody loves a good listener. Second, it makes the buyer do the heavy-lifting part of the sale. Get the buyer to talk to you long enough, and he'll tell you what he needs, why he needs it and how much. You, the salesman, just have to sit back and write up the order. (A side tip: To get a compulsive talker to clam up, start talking about yourself. Works every time, usually within three minutes.)

Being a Winning Buyer

There are no schools for buyers as there are for sellers. But if there were, they'd teach the same routine, starting with the importance of listening. If you listen to the salesman, you'll better understand what he's selling and why, and you can make a better deal. Here are some of the principles.

Find out what's in it for him. The more the salesman needs the sale, the more likely he'll give you a better price. One guy, Sean, told me that when he went into a car dealership, he knew he was in the right place when he saw the sales chart showing his salesman was only one sale away from beating out all the other salesmen. "Go on the last day of the selling period," he said. At many dealerships, that's the last day of the month, a time when there's bound to be at least one salesman eager to do whatever it takes to win himself that set of steak knives.

Be ready to walk. If the salesman has really listened to you talk about what you want, why you want it and how you plan to use it, he knows whether or not he's got a sale. It's what happens next that counts. Some salesmen won't try to sell you something you've already said you don't need. But most will. The chance that you'll leave angry is one many salesmen are willing to take. After all, once you're out the door, what difference does it make?

"Car dealerships often see a sale in terms of conflict rather than cooperation," a car salesman told me. A salesman who's willing to work with you, instead of against you, is the kind of guy who sees

---

JUST THE FACTS

Forty-eight percent of business executives would become self-employed if only the start-up capital were available.

his customers as long-term investments, rather than short-term hustles.

Listen to yourself. If you expect the salesman to listen to you, you ought to expect the same of yourself. If what you hear is a slight murmur of ambivalence, duck out of the deal until you've had time to think it over. By the way, if a salesman tries to tell you the deal is now-or-never, it's always never. Always.

Make the salesman talk. Just as the salesman gains an edge by listening, the buyer can gain an edge by refusing to talk. One guy described this as the Zen-sounding Trick of Silence. You don't volunteer information, you don't explain conflicting data, you just follow the admonition once given by the smartest man in the world, the late rare-book expert George Leinwall, to a rookie bibliophile attending his first book auction: "Keep your hands in your pockets and your mouth shut."

Now, that doesn't mean you lie, exactly. It just means that you make the seller come to you. You say, "How much?" The salesman says, "Twelve-fifty." And you say nothing. Eventually, the salesman will say either, "Twelve" or "So long."

The Trick of Silence works because, just as nature abhors a vacuum, so do natural-born talkers feel compelled to fill any silence. The result is that you get to listen to a lot more than the salesman really intended to tell you. Another example: You say, "How's that car runnin'?" The salesman says, "Fine." You say nothing. Eventually, he'll say, "There was a minor accident, but don't you worry. We've repaired the crack in the frame." Keep not talking, and eventually, you'll learn about the bubble in the tires, the rust on the muffler and the stains on the backseat. Then price is up to you.

Don't buy the salesman. If a salesman does listen, it's only for purposes of obtaining information. I once went to a car lot to buy a used car. The dealer had only women selling cars—a nice touch, I thought. I got into an Olds with a strange woman and drove away to no place in particular. There we were, out on the open road, just me, her, the car and America. The wind blew through her hair. She was talking to me, asking me all about myself, sharing her dreams for the future. She complimented me on the baldness pattern I was developing, and she patted my arm whenever I cracked a joke. It was like a great first date—until we got back to the lot and I said the price was out of my range. Before I finished the sentence, she was across the floor and back at her little cubicle talking on the phone to somebody named Marcie.

In fact, this is how I came by this small chunk of wisdom. Once, during a previous incarnation, I woke up to find that I was the proprietor of a small business. I ran the place for five years or so, and in the course of that demi-decade, I occasionally had to hire salesmen. Rather, salespeople: I hired two saleswomen because I was single at the time and they just looked great, okay? Plus, they were crazy. But I also hired a couple of guys and a woman because I thought that they were the nicest people I ever met. Unhappily, they were all terrible at selling things—except for that one make-or-break deal, when they sold themselves to me. After all, I couldn't say no to these worthies. How could anybody else? Turns out I just wasn't listening. Goes to show.

—Denis Boyles

Workplace
Wisdom

Advice on Surviving Office Life

Office life is fraught with pitfalls, trapdoors and strange, wild beasts ready to pounce on you and rend your career into the job equivalent of hamburger meat.

But the workplace isn't just a jungle out there—it can be a veritable Garden of Paradise, if you know your way around. We've compiled a list of workplace wisdom so you don't have to enroll in the School of Hard Knocks to earn an advanced degree in Corporate Ladder Climbing.

Why You Almost Got That Job

The interview process can make even the staunchest candidate feel like a steer waiting in line for slaughter. We asked Roger Cameron, president of the Dallas recruiting firm Cameron-Brooks, to describe the three deadliest mistakes applicants make and how to avoid them.

1. Not listening. "Don't presume you know where an interviewer is going and step on his questions," Cameron says. "It'll sound like you have your own agenda when the point is to convey how you'll help with their needs."
2. Holding back. Maybe you want to seem all poise and control, but the guy across the table wants to see enthusiasm bursting out all over the place. "He'll listen for it in your voice and look for it in your posture," Cameron says. When you speak, lean forward slightly to create a sense of dynamism.
3. Rambling. You're nervous and you want to talk just to fill up any dead air. Bad idea. "A lot of people don't know when to shut up," Cameron says. Answer questions directly, using as many specifics as you can about your past performance, but don't digress or get mired in minutiae.

Achievers Go the Distance

Steady success in your career won't just put money in the bank; it also gives you more years to enjoy it. So concludes a study that tracked nearly 500 men, most of them professional or managerial types, for over 40 years. "We found that certain career patterns made a difference in how long these men lived," says researcher Eliza K. Pavalko, Ph.D., assistant professor of sociology at Indiana University in Bloomington, one of the study's leaders. Men who kept advancing in their jobs tended to live longer than the men who jumped around to unrelated jobs or who didn't advance throughout their careers. An onward and upward career means continual intellectual challenge and growth and more control over your working life—both of which have been linked to health and well-being, explains Dr. Pavalko.

Ten Deadliest Office Sins

You know all the right career moves: getting in early, meeting deadlines, taking on tasks the boss wants off his desk, staying late. But doing everything else right won't help when you really foul something up. From *Never Read a Newspaper at Your Desk,* by Richard Stiegele, here are ten of the worst office mistakes you can make.

1. Promise what your boss can't deliver. In the end, you make your boss the scapegoat.
2. Use "stressed out" or "burned out" as excuses. Learn to adjust to chaotic times. It's never going to get any easier.
3. Brown-nose to the point it requires radical surgery to remove you.
4. Outdrink others at office parties. If you're the boss, nurse your drink and leave early so the party can start. And always drink soda at "martini lunches." You never know who's going to be waiting for you when you get back to the office.
5. Underevaluate or overevaluate your contributions.
6. Play favorites or get involved in co-workers' lives, particularly if they report to you.
7. Talk loosely in the rest room; it can damage your career if the boss is reading a newspaper behind the closed door.
8. Leave time bombs for your boss when you go on vacation.
9. Broadcast derogatory or confidential information that can hurt the corporation.
10. Forget to sell yourself. Remember, nobody else will. But promote your talents, not your ego.

It's All in the Wrist

When we hurt, we like to blame it on something tough-sounding like an old football injury. But often it's those simple daily movements that give us problems. Like typing on a computer keyboard. "People don't realize that typing for hours at a time is an athletic activity, and just like tennis, it can cause an overuse injury," says Emil Pascarelli, M.D., co-author with Deborah Quilter of *Repetitive Strain Injury: A Computer User's Guide.* To reduce pain and heal overworked wrist muscles, Dr. Pascarelli prescribes two flexed forearm stretches prior to every typing session.

1. Hold your left arm straight out in front of you, keeping it parallel to the floor and palm down. Place your right hand over your left-hand knuckles and gently press that hand down. Hold for a count of ten. Repeat with your other hand.
2. Next, with your left arm straight out again, grab its palm with your right hand and gently pull it upward and toward you. Hold for a count of ten. Repeat with your other hand.

Don't Die in the Graveyard Shift

More than seven million Americans work at night and sleep during the day. Most have trouble getting enough sleep. "Even permanent shift workers have a hard time resynchronizing their internal clocks," says Robert Sack, M.D., director of the Sleep Disorder Service at Oregon Health Sciences University School of Medicine in Portland. But there are tricks that can help. In a landmark 1990 study, Charles Czeisler, M.D., director of the Laboratory for Circadian and Sleep Disorders Medicine at Boston's Brigham and Women's Hospital, showed that exposure to bright light at night and darkness during the day can help night workers get restful sleep. Here's what you can do to stay alive while working the night beat.

• Replace the light in your office with a bright, daylight bulb, or lobby your employer to install brighter lighting if necessary.

JUST THE FACTS

Getting a lot of mental exercise on the job may protect you from Alzheimer's disease. Researchers at Columbia University in New York City have found that people who spent their lives in intellectually demanding occupations had half the risk of developing Alzheimer's as those in less-stimulating jobs.

- On the drive home from work, shield your eyes with dark, wraparound glasses if the sun is up, so the light won't stimulate you just before you go to bed.
- Sleep in a private room in a quiet part of the house.
- Make that room as dark as you can. Put black plastic over the windows, if necessary, or wear sleep shields over your eyes.

Making an Impression

If you want to seem brainy, you have to meet occupational standards. What seems smart in one job may appear downright foolish in another. Here's how the categories break down.

Social Occupations

If you're a:

- Teacher
- Social worker
- Counselor
- Doctor
- Psychologist
- Nurse

Do this:

- Come up with an especially acute analysis of another person's problems—the more intensely personal, the better.
- Don't worry if your analysis leads to a solution of the problem or not.
- Go heavy on the jargon. The perception of perceptiveness is critical here for convincing others you are smart, so an extensive, unnecessarily vague vocabulary is a definite plus here.

Scientific Occupations

If you're a:

- Biologist
- Researcher
- Physicist
- Mathematician

Do this:

- Use a stilted and jargon-loaded vocabulary.
- Mock "laymen" who ask dumb questions.
- Offer opinions on very obscure topics. If you risk being easily understood, you also risk being thought to be unintelligent.

Impressing a Computer with Your Résumé

You loaded your résumé with power verbs and printed it on classy-looking gray linen stock. So how is it the big companies haven't come calling? Probably because you never got past their computers.

Up to 80 percent of medium- to large-size companies will use computers to process résumés by the end of the century—and computers don't care about your fancy linen paper. (That's why so many companies ask applicants to fax résumés; those faxes go right into a database.) To make your résumé stand out to a computer, you need to know what the scanning software is looking for, says Joyce Lain Kennedy, a syndicated columnist and senior author of *Electronic Résumé Revolution*. Here's a primer on the new rules.

List companies, titles and jargon. Action verbs such as "managed," "developed" or "instituted" don't score with computers searching for job-specific nouns such as "MBA" and "engineer" or key phrases like "will relocate."

Use white paper and simple, high-contrast printing. Colors, including gray, inhibit letter-background contrast, making it harder for the computer to read. For the same reason, don't get fancy with typefaces, boxes and graphics.

Be detailed. More information means more potential keywords. Don't worry about exceeding one page—computers don't care.

Use the right type. Use 10- to 14-point type, nothing smaller or larger.

Don't fold. Cramming your résumé into a business envelope creates creases that make scanning difficult.

Get free advice. Resumix, a company that sells résumé-scanning systems, offers a free pamphlet on preparing computer-scanned résumés. Send a self-addressed, stamped envelope to Resumix Pamphlet Offer, 2953 Bunker Hill Lane, Santa Clara, CA 95054.

Artistic Occupations

If you're a:

- Painter
- Entertainer
- Musician
- Writer

Do this:

- Come up with anything unusual, regardless of its intrinsic value.
- Ridicule any accepted wisdom.
- Put esoteric, obtuse theories ahead of conventional practice. Practicality is not an issue when it comes to defining an artistic person as "smart." In fact, the more impractical or obscure the device or design, the smarter you'll seem to your peers.

Enterprising Occupations

If you're a:

- Lawyer
- Politician
- Salesman
- Stockbroker

Do this:

- Subordinate common sense to manipulation and persuasion.
- Define all contests on your own terms.
- Stick to a strategy.
- Above all, nurture your credibility.

Exacting Occupations

If you're a:

- Mechanic
- Engineer
- Carpenter
- Police officer

Do this:

- Make few mistakes and solve problems on your own without asking others for help.
- Develop a reputation as somebody to whom people can turn for help in resolving dilemmas. Do this enough and you'll become the go-to man at your place of work.

Mathematical Occupations

If you're an:

- Accountant
- Computer programmer
- Tax auditor

Do this:

- Allow for few variations to accepted rules.
- Cite regulations whenever possible—the more obscure, the better.
- Foster an air of aloofness, removed from petty human emotions. Nobody goes to an accountant for emotional support.

Your Travel Companion

Smart Advice for Road Warriors

Business travel no longer is reserved for top corporate brass, who sip free scotch-and-sodas in the extra-wide seats of the first-class flier set. Today, even the lowliest of worker bees may be called upon to take flight for the corporate hive. And all that travel—whether it's globe-trotting to Taiwan or just a one-day flight to the coast—can make your head feel abuzz.

Here's a compendium of miscellaneous travel tips we've compiled from insiders and experts alike. They'll keep you pointed in the right direction before you pack your bags or pop open that complimentary pack of peanuts.

Averting Travel Theft

"Anyone who looks successful today is likely to be victimized," says Tim Larkin, vice-president of Direct Action Security Corporation in Phoenix. "And a man away on business is just too easy a target for a criminal to pass up. You have a cellular phone, a portable fax—maybe an expensive laptop, too."

His point: You're not living in Mayberry, and a man is being realistic (read: not paranoid) to plan for the worst. "We spend most of our lives in a defensive posture, but that makes us easy marks for the bad guys," he says. Larkin has made a name for himself among high-profile types for his aggressive approach to self-defense. He teaches courses in how to strip a criminal of his weapons and how to prevent carjackings and kidnappings. We asked him about safety precautions travelers should be taking.

Q What's the biggest mistake business travelers usually make?

A Failing to get the lay of the land before they go. The worst thing you can do is drive to an unfamiliar city and hit a bad part of town where you look out of place. One client came to me after being carjacked while walking to his Porsche in downtown Los Angeles. Now, this guy owned a Toyota, too. If he'd only checked out where he was going beforehand, he could have taken the less noticeable car instead.

Q How can you find out if tomorrow's business meeting happens to also be in carjacking territory?

A Call a top hotel in the area and talk to the concierge. Tell him you'll be arriving in a few days and ask about the neighborhood. If this is not a good place to walk around after dark, a good concierge will tell you. If you're rolling into downtown Los Angeles, or Times Square for that matter, you'll know to leave the Porsche behind. And the Rolex, too.

Q Your clinics teach businessmen to convey an aggressive attitude in public places. Doesn't that tactic fail if someone calls your bluff?

A Criminals, like water, take the path of least resistance. They look for easy marks—so make yourself a tough one. That doesn't necessarily mean being physically imposing. Sometimes just visual contact—letting a bad guy know you know he's there—is enough. He wants someone who is confused, flustered, pissed off, distracted. Drop the wide-eyed tourist gaze. Be focused and walk with confidence. The key is awareness.

Q Where are you most vulnerable?

A Getting in and out of cars. This is where most attacks occur, because it's where we're unaware. See, the guy who lost his Porsche had his arms full and was fumbling for his keys and staring into space. But if you're alert, you'll spot the potential crook ahead of time. For instance, if you are parked on the street and someone is near the driver's door, get in on the passenger side. This puts the car between you and him. Another car tip: Remove any papers or stickers that indicate you're driving a rental. These scream "tourist."

Q How about the hotel room? What if you're carrying some pretty expensive stuff?

A Most people hide valuables under the nightstand, the bed or mattress. All obvious places. There's no law saying you have to use your hotel room. Use the hotel safe. And always put the chain on the door—someone, after all, has a master key. It also pays to buy a portable motion sensor. You can get one cheap at any electronics store.

Q What about crowded areas like airport terminals?

A Conceal. Having a laptop doesn't mean you should advertise. Put it in a briefcase—something of lesser value. Never put it down in a busy place. That's an easy snatch and run.

Getting a Shot in the Arm

If you're heading south of the equator in the summer, consider getting a flu shot. While it's summer where you live, it's winter in the Southern Hemisphere and, thus, flu season. In most cases the only government-required inoculation is for yellow fever, but you may want to consider getting a hepatitis A shot, a meningitis vaccination and a polio booster, depending upon where you're traveling, says James H. Runnels, M.D., of the Travel Medicine Service at Baylor College of Medicine in Houston. Check with a doctor well-versed in travel medicine before embarking on a trip abroad.

Taming Tummy Trouble

Vacationing in the Caribbean? On many islands, drinking the tap water may give you stomach trouble. Here's where you shouldn't drink the water unless it's bottled, according to an excellent resource, *Traveler's Health: How to Stay Healthy All over the World*, by Richard Dawood, M.D.: Anguilla, Antigua, Bahamas, Bonaire, Dominica, Dominican Republic, Grenada, Guadeloupe, Haiti, St. Vincent, St. Kitts, St. Barts and throughout the U.S. Virgin Islands.

Sleeping through the Ride

A portable device called NoiseBuster might help you sleep on a plane. The small electronic box emits not white noise but *anti*-noise through regular headphones. That's a special sound wave that cancels out low-frequency sounds like those made by jet engines, but it allows you to hear human speech. For information, call 1-800-278-3526.

Outfoxing the Trots

Traveler's diarrhea can leave you dehydrated faster than you can say *huevos rancheros*. Here's a homemade rehydration drink that replaces lost water and salts, from *The Travel Health Clinic Pocket Guide to Healthy Travel*, by Lawrence Bryson, M.D.: Pour eight ounces of orange juice or apple juice in a glass and mix in one-half teaspoon of honey and a pinch of salt. In a separate glass, mix one-quarter teaspoon of baking soda with eight ounces purified water or carbonated bottled water. Drink alternately from each glass.

Finding Fare Game

You'll be better off purchasing plane tickets on weekdays. Often, airlines will increase fares on weekends, as a test to see if other carriers will follow suit. If competing companies do not match the increase, the airline will almost always bring the ticket price down on the next business day.

Avoiding Bottlenecks

Don't pack your prescription medicines in plastic bags for your trip. Without the original container, you won't be able to get an emergency refill if you need it, and you might also get hassled by customs agents who take a dim view of suspicious-looking, unmarked capsules.

Dining Defensively

To limit your risk of having stomach trouble or contracting the dangerous liver disease hepatitis A on a trip into less developed areas of the world, avoid:

- Ice cubes and any drink made from tap water (drink only boiled or bottled waters)
- Milk (drink only canned milk)
- Uncooked vegetables (fruits, nuts and vegetables with thick skins or shells are safer)
- Cold meat platters, buffets and foods sold by street vendors
- Meats and fish cooked rare (order everything well-done and be sure it's served steaming hot)

JUST THE FACTS

Ninety-one percent of Fortune 1,000 presidents start reading the morning paper on the john.

Finding Fun in New Frontiers

You're in a new city to entertain clients, but you haven't had a chance to hunt for a good restaurant and theater tickets. Where do you stay, where should you eat, what's there to do? By calling (310) 372-4474, you can order up-to-date, city-specific travel information that's delivered via fax. Fielding's Cityfax service offers guides to more than 30 domestic and foreign cities 24 hours a day. If you travel with a laptop, try Taxi, a software program that displays maps, hotel locations and Zagat restaurant reviews for New York, Chicago, Los Angeles, San Francisco, Washington, D.C., and ten other cities nationwide. For information, call 1-800-439-8294.

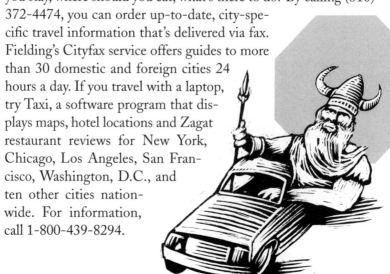

PART 9

Men at Play

TOP TEN

The Most Popular Sporting Pastimes for Men

Ever wonder what other guys like to do on the weekends? Wonder no more. The National Sporting Goods Association has come to the rescue. They asked 15,000 people ages seven and up about their participation in 26 sports. Here are the top ten activities, as listed by the men ages 18 to 64, starting with their most favorite.

1. Freshwater fishing

2. Exercise walking

3. Hunting

4. Exercising with equipment

5. Bowling

6. Camping

7. Golfing

8. Playing basketball

9. Running/jogging

10. Playing volleyball

Getting Out Alive

Survival Tips for Every Occasion

Maybe this has happened to you: It's a dark and stormy night. You're alone in a strange city, walking down a dark alley in a nasty part of town. Suddenly, rats scurry, cats screech, and out jumps a wild-eyed divorce lawyer! He clocks you in the noggin, steals your wallet, breaks your heart and leaves you to die, alone and busted.

The streets are mean and the times are perilous for most of us. Anybody who thinks it's still a man's world has spent a little too much time watching *Wild Kingdom* through rose-colored specs, because that limping, lonely antelope is us, and that pack of jackals at his heels is modern life.

So think of this chapter as Marlin Perkins with a sense of justice. For while life is chock-full of narrow escapes and close calls, we've seen 'em all coming, and we know what it takes to get out alive.

Hounding a Bad Dog

You're jogging along and you hear the barking and scratchy paw steps of an angry dog behind you. Grade Z horror movies from the 1970s spring to mind as you picture your vitals being torn out by a hellhound.

The Basics

1. Animals are not humane.
2. If you panic, they panic.
3. If they panic, they bite.

The Details

Don't head for the hills. Nearly two million people annually are bitten by dogs. To make sure you don't join them, the best strategy is to overcome your urge to outrun the animal (you won't) and stop in your tracks, says veterinarian Michael W. Fox, D.V.M., Ph.D., vice-president of the Humane Society of the United States. "Most of the time, you've entered the dog's territory and he's putting on a big bluff—lots of bark and no bite," he says.

Humor him. Stand still, turn and face the dog. Play it cool, don't stare in a threatening way and don't make any quick movements.

"Talk in a quiet voice—'Hi there, nice doggy. Go home now.' Show him you're not a threat," says Dr. Fox. "He'll probably circle you, maybe even urinate on you, then leave you alone."

After the dog has calmed down, back away slowly, keeping your eyes on the animal.

Throw the dog a bone. Got a snack in your pocket? Share it. Dogs really are less likely to bite the hand that feeds them.

Go for mad-dog options. If the dog doesn't calm down, the best bet is to try to intimidate him, according to Randall Lockwood, Ph.D., another Humane Society vice-president and animal behaviorist. Face him down, make yourself as big as you can be, scream and stare him right in the eye. While you're shouting, take off your jacket and wrap it around your fist. If the dog lunges, feed him your padded hand. Back away until you can get to safety, then sacrifice the garment.

If you are cornered by a powerful dog like a Doberman, pit bull or Rottweiler and can't fight it off, as a last resort, drop to your knees and curl into a ball with your hands laced over your head.

"You'll get bites on your shoulders and buttocks, but you'll be protecting your throat and genitals," says Dr. Fox.

Enduring a Storm-Tossed Sea

There's an old joke about being seasick: First you're afraid you're going to die, then you're afraid you're not.

Anyone who's ever chummed the whales gets it: While that Great Blue is out there blowing water, you're below decks blowing lunch. Here's the root of the problem: From the time we learn to walk, we develop a strong subconscious connection to terra firma. We just love the ground we walk on. A rocking boat throws this delicate balance system out of whack.

The Basics
1. Go with the motion of the ocean.
2. Don't eat grease.
3. Stay in the middle of the boat.

The Details
Deny everything. Don't worry about getting seasick, and there's a good chance you won't get ill. "The placebo effect is extremely strong," says Charles Mazel, Ph.D., an ocean engineer and author of the appetizingly named *Heave Ho! My Little Green Book of Seasickness.*

"If you think eggs keep you from getting seasick, don't get on a boat without having eggs."

Mind your input. In general, however, it's best to eat moderately—soda crackers and the like—and to avoid alcohol. Drink lots of water to stay hydrated.

Never go below. Down in the bowels of the ship, you're more likely to get seasick because your eyes will tell you that you're standing still when your inner ears tell you that you're moving.

Suck ginger. "There's something about ginger that soothes, ginger in any form—gingersnaps, ginger tablets, ginger ale, watching Ginger Rogers movies," says Dr. Mazel.

Do drugs early. For over-the-counter medical help, try dimenhydrinate (Dramamine). Take them an hour or two before getting on the boat, since they won't do you any good once you get seasick. Or ask your doctor about prescribing scopolamine patches, which are worn behind the ear and release a steady stream of the drug into your blood through the skin.

Negotiating with a Grizzly
Bears are like you and me. They hate to be surprised by unannounced visitors when they're lying around the house or in the middle of dinner. Not only is it rude, but bears find it threatening

and they tend to express themselves with razor-sharp claws.

The good news is that bears will give you the right of way if you just let them know you're coming ahead of time. You do that by making noise—singing, proclaiming, shouting, keeping that bell on your boots. Many bear confrontations occur along good fishing streams where the rushing water masks the noise of approaching hikers and where seafood-eating bears can be startled by Boy Scouts, Sierra Clubbers and other nearly hairless bears.

The Basics

1. Never scare a bear.
2. The closer you are to running water, the louder you should yodel.
3. Bears need glasses.

The Details

In the event that you do confront a bear, "don't ever run," says Sterling Miller, Ph.D., a bear research biologist with the Alaska Department of Fish and Game in Anchorage. "Grizzlies can run at 40 miles per hour."

Besides, running may trigger his natural predatory reaction to give chase. Instead, do this.

Stand your ground. If you're in a group, stand shoulder to shoulder, shout and wave your arms to give the appearance that you are some ungodly animal with multiple appendages that is much bigger than he is. Or he might think you're Shelley Winters. Or the House of Representatives. The thing is, when bears encounter something big and loud and weird, they run.

Stroll away. Don't turn, but walk off slowly at an angle, keeping your eyes on the bear.

Know your bears. Brown bears, including grizzlies, don't climb very well; they need thick low branches to support their weight. So if you are right next to a tree with thin branches and think you can climb fast and high, go for it. Black bears can climb trees, branches or no branches, so don't bother.

Play dead. If a brown bear is ready to attack, dive into a bush and play dead. Black bears, on the other hand, eat dead things. Don't be one.

Emerging from a Bar Fight

There's a right time and a wrong time for everything. And there's right bar and a wrong bar for everybody. Put two wrongs together and you have a right ugly fix.

The Basics

1. Escape.
2. Apologize, but don't explain.
3. Keep your back to a wall.

The Details

Look for "Keep Out" signs. As a rule, you can spot a wrong bar with no difficulty. A saloon with a 50-yard line of Harleys parked out front and nothing but women in leather inside may be the wrong bar at any time. Or maybe not.

Know the opposition. The most important thing to realize about barroom confrontations is that you're dealing with drunks, which is like dealing with infants who weigh 200 pounds and want to fight. Drunks are more likely to misconstrue ordinary gestures as threatening, according to Roland D. Maiuro, Ph.D., director of Harborview Anger Management and Domestic Violence Program at the Harborview Medical Center in Seattle.

Talk smooth. Let's say you accidentally knock over a guy's beer. What do you do? Act normal. Apologize, but don't treat the accident as if it were anything other than that. Don't buy into the premise that it was something you intended to do. Be polite. Volunteer to buy the guy another beer, but don't let it become a big deal.

Keep a safe distance. If, as it often happens, the guy has been waiting all night for somebody to dump his beer just so he can exercise his knuckles, stand back. Rule: Keep the approximate height of whomever you're facing between you.

Fly. "Sometimes," says Dr. Maiuro, "your feet are your best weapon." For running, that is, not for kicking.

Surviving a Heart Attack

Heart attacks are big killers, but you can survive an assault on the ticker by simply beating the clock. If you get help before Mr. Death comes knocking, you win.

The Basics

1. Take the warning symptoms seriously.
2. Dial 911.
3. Yell "Medic!"

The Details

Know what to look for. Knowing what to expect is half the battle. Here are the common symptoms of ticker trouble.

- A feeling of fullness, pressure or squeezing pain in the center of the chest
- Pain spreading to the shoulders, neck or arms
- Dizziness, fainting, sweating, nausea or shortness of breath

If you recognize any of these symptoms, contact someone nearby for help. Then try these other steps immediately.

Cough vigorously. That's all that may be needed to kick an irregular heartbeat back to normal and give you time to reach a phone, says Carl E. Bartecchi, M.D., author of *Emergency Cardiac Maneuvers.*

Call the ambulance. Don't drive yourself to the emergency room. You'll get faster attention by arriving in an ambulance with the lights a-flashin'. Besides, you wouldn't want to black out behind the wheel and crash your car on the way to the hospital.

Take an aspirin. Aspirin helps prevent the blood clot from becoming complete. Chew the tablet to speed the medicine to your bloodstream.

Call your family doctor or cardiologist. Your normal doctors know you best, so they can help familiarize emergency room doctors with your medical history.

Escaping a Towering Inferno

Irwin Allen's disaster epics were fun to watch. What isn't fun is starring in your own. When you're as close to God as modern architecture allows and suddenly it turns hotter than hell, you're in a high-rise of trouble.

The Basics

1. Stay out of elevators.
2. Keep a low profile.
3. Close the door against fire.

The Details

The following tips were developed by the National Fire Protection Association:

Plan your getaway. In any building—your own office building or a new hotel—know where the fire escapes are and mentally map out at least two escape routes. If you're in a hotel, count the doors between your room and the fire exits in case you have to escape in the dark.

Step lively. Get out of the building as quickly as possible using smoke-free stairwells. Never use the elevator.

Limbo. If the room is full of smoke, crawl on your hands and knees. The best air and visibility are found 12 to 24 inches off the floor. If possible, put a wet handkerchief over your mouth and nose as an improvised filter.

Fortify your defenses. If you're trapped in your hotel room, first call the fire department and tell them where you are. If the phones are out, use a flashlight or hang a light-colored towel or sheet out the window to signal below for help. Fill the bathtub with water— liquid gold in a situation like this—for soaking towels and dousing flaming clothing. Next, seal door cracks and vents with wet towels. Shut off fans and air conditioners.

Supporting Friends Who Divorce

They loved each other. You loved them both. Now they hate each other. But you don't.

Remember the scene in *The Ten Commandments* where Charlton Heston leads a crowd of Hollywood extras through the Red Sea? Remember what happened to the Pharaoh's chariots hot on his heels? You get to choose: You can be Moses. Or you can be the chariots.

The Basics

1. See no evil.
2. Hear no evil.
3. Speak no evil.

The Details

Stay out of the crossfire. When two people start shooting and you're in the middle, they may survive, but you won't. According to

Frank Pittman, M.D., an Atlanta-based psychiatrist and family therapist, "Peacemakers are the first casualties" when a divorce breaks out.

Keep value judgments to yourself. Hold back on advice, too, unless one of the warring parties demands it. Even then, realize you're taking a great risk. What your friends want from you is concern and support, says Dr. Pittman.

Think Swiss. Be absolutely neutral, always. If you can't maintain your neutrality, resign yourself to choosing sides—and losing a friend.

Take a hike. If you have vacation time coming, take it now. Getting away from the heat will make it easier for everyone, since eventually the whole ugly situation will cool down.

Surviving a Fight with Your Wife

Here it is, in writing: You're right. She's wrong. But somehow, by the time the dust clears, who's right and who's wrong is beside the point.

Arguments carry a cost, and anything that carries a cost is subject to cost analysis. If the cost of the argument is worth the point you want to make, then the argument's a good deal. Some arguments, after all, help clear the air and open all those communications sinuses.

But most arguments aren't worth the cost. That doesn't mean you won't have them. It just means you have to find a way to pay for them.

The Basics

1. You can be right and still be wrong.
2. Women are almost always right.
3. Men are almost always fair.

The Details

It's history. Before you can patch up a war-torn marriage, you have to stop the fighting. So put the argument in perspective. Lessen your personal investment in it by placing it in the context of your marriage. Then figure out what the argument really was about: Most people argue about something other than the thing that's really bothering them. She's yelling at you for not doing the dishes, and you're yelling back that you already work two jobs. But the thing that really set her off is how little she sees of you. It is in this fog of conflict that we see the real psycho-differences between men and women.

Understand how women fight. According to Judith Siegel, Ph.D., a marriage counselor and professor at the New York University School of Social Work in New York City, women want to analyze the problem thoroughly.

"Men typically try to fix things," Dr. Siegel says. "They feel overly responsible for problems." This, she says, makes them feel that if they could only get to a resolution and skip all the middle stuff, everything would be fixed. But the middle stuff is important. By talking things through instead of going for the bottom line, you learn how to avoid arguments in the future.

Listen closely and talk turkey. Once you decipher what the fighting is really all about, talk about it the way you would to any other friend. That means you have to let her talk, too: "Don't be defensive," says Dr. Siegel. "Don't explain, don't rationalize. Just listen."

Finish it. Don't be afraid to direct the conversation a little, though. Women may resolve arguments by wading through the process, but that doesn't invalidate a guy's need to bring the whole epic ordeal to a logical conclusion so that he comes away with something resembling a resolution for him, too.

Enduring a Tax Audit

The IRS works for all of us. That's okay—somebody has to collect the bills we run up guarding the coasts, collecting the tariffs and supporting performance artists everywhere. What's not okay is when the IRS turns from working for us to working on us.

If it's your misfortune to be one of the more than one million taxpayers who will endure IRS audits this year, calm down, put on a nice suit and take along these insider tips.

The Basics

1. The auditor is not interested in making a new friend.
2. It's fair play to protect yourself.
3. Don't give a foot when an inch will do.

The Details

The following tips are from Jack Warren Wade, Jr., a former IRS revenue officer and author of *When You Owe the IRS*:

Postpone the audit a month. That'll allow time for you to get all of your documentation in order and for your return to fester awhile on the auditor's desk while other, perhaps more pressing, problems close in on him. When you finally come in, he may be likely to breeze through it, just to lighten his workload.

Schedule the audit late in the day. Schedule it on Friday, if possible. An auditor's human; provided he also has a real life, he won't stay past 5:00 to nitpick.

Keep politics out of it. Forget your harangue about politicians or bureaucracy. "Don't attack the government or bring up the president's taxes," says Wade. "That'll only antagonize the auditor."

Don't volunteer more information than you need to. Answer only when questioned and be as well-mannered and forthright as you can. "People tend to tell too much and bury themselves," says Wade.

Bring some paid brains. If you're called in for anything more complicated than justifying a simple charitable deduction, have the professional who prepared your return come to the audit with you. Or pay a lawyer, certified public accountant or enrolled agent—someone who has passed an IRS exam—to represent you. Their expertise can save you a lot of trouble.

Throw the dog a bone. Most auditors feel it isn't a tax return if there isn't something they can find wrong with it. If there is some way you can guide him toward a minor glitch that he can discover on his own and you can defend as an honest mistake, do so; he may be satisfied and quit probing.

Swimming with Sharks

According to *The Waterlover's Guide to Marine Medicine*, by Paul G. Gill, Jr., M.D., only 50 to 100 shark attacks are reported worldwide each year. That means your chances of being attacked by a shark are about 1 in 75 million. So the odds are better that Daryl Hannah will show up at your motel room door with a bag of pretzels and a party hat.

Of course, knowing that won't get you far when you're taking a dip and there's a fin in the water. Here's what you need to know to keep Jaws at bay.

The Basics
1. Don't act like bait.
2. Punch an attacking shark in the nose.
3. Sharks are dumber than pit bulls. Meaner, too.

The Details
Don't panic or splash. You'll only look like a wounded seal. Instead, swim away with slow, even strokes.

Go deep. If you are scuba diving, move to the bottom against a rock so you are protected from the rear. You might also scare the shark away by sending a stream of bubbles his way from your regulator.

Duke it out. If the shark attacks, punch it or poke it sharply in the snout, eyes or gills. Sharks, like many other animals, are sensitive around the schnozz, and a good punch in the nose makes you too much trouble to be dinner.

Dress down. Don't wear brightly colored swim trunks or flashy silver chains.

Hold it in. No matter how scared you are, don't pee in the water. Sharks love that stuff.

Getting Out of White Water Alive

There are many important things everybody should know about white water by now. For instance, you can't tell by looking how deep it runs or how fast it goes. Not only that, but once you're neck-deep in it, you can't see where it'll take you, mostly because the really big trouble is beneath the surface.

The Basics

1. Keep your mouth shut.
2. Get to high ground as soon as possible.
3. Stay afloat at all costs.

The Details

Like a Boy Scout—be prepared. According to Michael Weber, a writer and former commercial river guide, the problem is one of unpredictability. When things go wrong, they go from bad to worse in a hurry.

"It's like a car accident," says Weber. "Things happen so quickly you don't have time to do anything but get yourself in a position to avoid injury." So be prepared as much as possible. Also keep these tips in mind.

Get away from the boat. If you're rafting or boating in white water and you flip, your boat can turn into a lethal weapon, pounding you on the head or smashing you into rocks.

Sacrifice. Forget trying to save anything—boat, binoculars, tuna sandwiches—except your life.

Point your legs downstream. "You're usually better off using them as a kind of bumper," Weber says. Float on your back with your head up so you can see oncoming trouble, and as soon as you can, paddle your way to the bank.

Swimming with Lawyers

You're staring down the double-barrel shotgun of a lawsuit. What's your move? Try these tips from attorney Wesley J. Smith, a consumer advocate and co-author with Ralph Nader of the book *The Mega Lawyers*.

The Basics

1. Let your insurance company settle it.
2. Settle it yourself.
3. Settle for a lawyer.

The Details

Use someone else's dime. If you are sued, your first step should be to see if your insurance company will cover the cost of your defense.

Let the dust settle. If insurance won't cover it, "it doesn't hurt to first try to settle the suit on your own, without lawyers, since that can save you a whole bunch of money," says Smith. "You have to analyze whether you want to go through the time, expense and uncertainty of litigation." Or whether a thousand bucks will make your problem go away.

Hunt for a specialist. If you choose to hire counsel, get the right lawyer for your specific problem. Interview three highly recommended lawyers who offer free initial consultations.

Decide on fight-or-flight. You're right; they're wrong. Now you have to decide if seeking justice is worth the cost. Only you can tell.

Escaping a Swarm of Killer Bees

Africanized honeybees, the so-called killer bees moving slowly northward from Texas and New Mexico, got their nasty reputation from their defensive nature. They don't go out and hunt down humans, but they are a bit, well, oversensitive. For instance, if you disturb them—play your radio too loud, knock their house down, beat at them with swatters and bug-bombs—they'll swarm on you, hundreds, thousands of them, stinging you on your arms, your face and your back.

They just don't care. They're killer bees. Fair play means nothing to them. They laugh their little bee laugh at your cries for mercy. Killer bees take no prisoners. They hate you, and if you mess with them, they'll try to kill you.

The Basics
1. Run like crazy.
2. Keep your shirt on.
3. Jump in a lake.

The Details
Scram. "Run like the devil," says Roger Morse, Ph.D., professor of beekeeping at Cornell University in Ithaca, New York. Get into a house or a car "or run into a dark area, like dense woods, since stinging insects typically fly over woods."

Button up. Shirt, pants and especially lips. Bees fly into the mouths of people screaming for help. "They can sting the back of the throat," says Richard F. Clark, M.D., a killer-bee expert and medical director of the San Diego Regional Poison Center. When that happens, the airway can swell shut, and no amount of Heimlich maneuvering is going to open it up again.

Dive! Dive! Jump into water to confuse the swarm. The bees aren't following you per se, "they're homing in on an alarm odor left by the first stings you received," says Morse. Water washes it off.

Bee aware. A few notes on what to do when you tangle with the killer bees' wimpier cousins: Avoid the temptation to smash a yellow jacket that's buzzing around your beer can.

Squashing a yellow jacket's venom sac releases a chemical that incites its brethren to seek revenge, which is bad news, since yellow jackets can sting repeatedly.

When a honeybee attacks, on the other hand, it's a suicide mission, since its barbed stinger remains embedded in your skin, killing the bugger. If you get stung by a honeybee, remove the stinger as soon as possible. Use your fingernail or a credit card to gently scrape the skin under the stinger until it pops out. Be careful not to squeeze the stinger or the attached venom sac, or you'll release more poison into your system. Next, wash the sting site with soap and water.

Stopping Yourself from Choking

Choking on a piece of steak is a cruel way for a man to die, especially if he's a vegetarian. But it's the sort of thing that happens all the time. If something becomes lodged in your windpipe, don't wait around for someone to rescue you. What a horrible way to learn your friends never liked you. Besides, saving your own life is always a swell do-it-yourself project.

Luckily, there's only one detail you need to know: the Heimlich maneuver. Clench a fist and place the thumb side against your upper abdomen, just below your rib cage. Grasp the fist with your other hand and thrust hard inward and upward a few times.

If that doesn't work, lean over the back of a chair so the edge sticks into your abdomen. Push yourself quickly downward, forcing air out of your diaphragm until you're shooting little steak bullets across the table.

Living through Airplane Accidents

When your favorite jumbo explodes at 35,000 feet, survival isn't an option. But in almost all aviation mishaps, it's usually not the crash but the fire and toxic smoke that kill. So think of a plane wreck as if it were a marriage proposal made on a bad night with a cheap drunk: Your best bet for survival is knowing how to make a speedy and panic-free evacuation.

The Basics

1. Know where the emergency exit is.
2. Know how to open it.
3. Exit.

The Details

Eye the exit. Every type of plane has a different layout of emergency exits. Know where the exits are, and plan two escape routes in case one is blocked.

Make a map. When you first take your seat on a plane, "imagine trying to get out blindfolded," says Alan Pollock, spokesman for the National Transportation Safety Board. "Count the number of rows between your seat and the nearest exits." That way, you can feel your way to safety if the cabin is filled with smoke.

Get down. In an airplane fire, your vision can be obscured by dense black smoke. Your only chance is to go low and follow the little lights on the floor to an exit.

No smoking. Look outside the windows before you open side exits. If the wing or fuselage is on fire, you could let flames inside. Other passengers just hate that.

Travel light. Obviously, leave your luggage behind.

Avoid hijack high jinks. If the nature of your airline misadventure is caused not by gravity but by hijackers, Frank McGuire, editor of *Security Intelligence Report*, offers some suggestions.

- Be as inconspicuous as possible. Be quiet, stay seated, read a book. Hijackers tend to leave people alone who don't appear threatening to them.
- Cooperate when approached. Being noncommunicative depersonalizes you and could increase your risk.

Overcoming an Office Screwup

Nothing quite disappoints the boss like losing one of those billion-dollar accounts many people worked hard on to lock down.

Imagine the boss's melancholy if the reason the account was lost is that you blew it (or, worse, that your boss blew it but needs to make you responsible). Imagine the meeting in his office. Imagine the pink slip on your desk. Imagine the new friends you'll make at Unemployment. Better yet, imagine a way out of this pickle.

The Basics

1. Clean up after yourself.
2. Honesty pays.
3. Emotionalism doesn't.

The Details

Mix good news with the bad. According to Marilyn Moats Kennedy, managing partner at Career Strategies, a Wilmette, Illinois, management consulting firm, most men can survive a first-class screwup if they do a little first-class damage control fast.

At the initial sign of a fiasco, says Kennedy, "go directly to your boss and say 'Here's what I did wrong and here's what I've done to correct it.'" Bosses hate hearing about problems. They love hearing about solutions.

Keep your chin off the office carpet. Don't go into the boss with a direct apology, Kennedy advises. Begging forgiveness and throwing yourself on the mercy of the brute only puts an added burden on your boss—who not only has to hear about your screwup but has to summon absolution for it as well. It also makes the situation look even more grim. Simply state facts. Value judgments will come on their own.

Keep the excuses to a minimum. Once a situation is screwed up, the reasons it got that way will have to wait. Solve the problem first.

JUST THE FACTS

Percentage increase in number of restaurant meals office workers ate at their desks over the past decade: 29

Avoiding a Car Accident

If there's one guy in the world you don't want to run into, it's the guy piloting that pickup across the center divider. Head-ons kill 5,000 people in the United States every year. So if you want to avoid being the deer in somebody else's headlights:

The Basics

1. Quick! Swerve right!
2. Rear-ends are better than head-ons.
3. Buckle up.

The Details

Light up. Drive with your headlights on during the day, says Charles Butler, director of driver safety services for the American Automobile Association. That cuts daytime two-vehicle collisions by 30 percent. Eventually, all new American cars will have daytime driving lights that come on automatically when you turn on the ignition.

No skidding. Take your foot off the brake and steer away from trouble. At speeds above 30 miles per hour, it takes longer to stop a car than to successfully steer around something. "The average driver is a much better steerer than braker," says Butler.

Do the right stuff. Generally, it's safer to veer to the right to avoid a collision. Your odds are better that way, since the other guy's more likely to steer to his right.

Go straight ahead. If you must hit another car, hit one that is moving in the same direction as yours is. The crash will be far less messy.

Ricochet. If you have to hit something stationary, like a tree, try to hit it with a glancing blow rather than head-on.

Buckle up. Wearing your seat belt is one of the best ways to prevent a crash be-

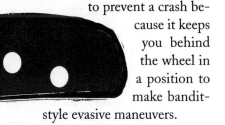

cause it keeps you behind the wheel in a position to make bandit-style evasive maneuvers.

Give yourself a brake. If your brakes give out, try these safety precautions.

- Pump the brakes once or twice to see if you have any braking power.
- If you don't have any brakes, put the car in neutral and gradually slow yourself with the parking brake, keeping your attention on the road ahead.
- Don't lock the brakes up, which will send the car into a dangerous skid. Keeping your finger on the brake-release button (on a center console parking brake), ease the brake lever up. On a foot-pedal parking brake, keep your left hand on the release lever as you press down with your foot.
- If that doesn't work, steer into an open field or let your tires rub up against a curb to slow you down.

—Jeffrey Csatari with Josh Adams and David Zinczenko

Instant IQ

How to Supercharge Your Brain

There are two things wrong with smart. First, it hurts your head. Heads are products of their times, and these aren't the brightest of days. Think too much with a modern head and you can blow the sucker right up. A hundred years ago, when kids had to know Latin just to get into high school, heads were made of cast iron. Today, we get a polyresin job, and that's if we're lucky.

Second, smart doesn't just happen. You can't just go to the beach, look at butts, eat sno-cones and come home smarter than when you left. To get smart, you have to get out there, catch it and stick it behind your eyes so you can find it later, in case you need it.

That's where we come in. We must have 300 different things to make you smarter than you are right this minute. But we're only going to give you 50 or so. That way, you'll come back for more. We're not stupid, you know.

Thinking Better

You think you're thinking fine? Think again. Here are the secrets to buff mental muscle.

Keep on running. Senator Strom Thurmond is in his early nineties and a member of the Senate Judiciary Committee, which means he's smart enough to sit around and talk about Clarence Thomas's sex life with guys like Joe Biden and Ted Kennedy. Want smarter? Thurmond has been running for the Senate every six years since 1954, and he's won every race. That's brain endurance. How does he do it? Exercise, of course.

"To keep your brain working well, you have to exercise to keep the arteries that take blood to the brain clear for nutrients, and to help push the blood there with your muscles," says Thurmond, who swims a half-mile twice a week and does 10 minutes of stretching, 20 minutes of calisthenics and 20 minutes of stationary cycling every morning. "If you can do that, there aren't many things you won't be able to do."

Other smart guys agree. One study at Scripps College in Claremont, California, found that people who exercise routinely think better, remember more and react faster than people who don't exercise at all. And a University of Illinois study found that subjects who exercised scored 30 percent higher on auditory and visual tests than sedentary subjects. "The brain is a physical organ, and its fitness is dependent upon the fitness of the body in which it resides," says Michael J. Kushner, M.D., a very smart neurologist at the Wilson Neurology Center in North Carolina.

JUST THE FACTS

Number of cellular telephone subscribers in 1994: 19 million
Estimated number in 1998: 33.7 million

Vitamin	Daily Minimum	Optimum
Thiamin	1.5 mg.	10 mg.
Riboflavin	1.7 mg.	10 mg.
Niacin	20 mg.	100 mg.
B_6	2 mg.	20 mg.
Folic acid	400 mcg.	400 mcg.
B_{12}	6 mcg.	30 mcg.
Biotin	—	200 mcg.
Pantothenic acid	10 mg.	20 mg.

Eat your way smart. When you eat, your body devours the proteins, carbohydrates, fats, vitamins and minerals in the chow, then converts them into chemicals your brain will use to learn, think, feel and remember. Here's the line on smart foods.

• Take your Bs. The buzz in brain functioning comes from B vitamins—especially B_6—found in oats, tuna, chicken, whole wheat and bananas. Smart researchers in Holland figured this out by giving a bunch of healthy 70-year-old guys 20 milligrams of B_6 every day for 12 weeks. They found the B_6 men did better on tests of long-term memory than a group who had been given a placebo.

Other B vitamins—specifically thiamin, riboflavin, niacin and number 12—boost mental energy, too. Vitamin B_{12}, in fact, actually helps in the manufacture and repair of brain tissues—a big help to guys who ride Harleys without helmets. Vernon Mark, M.D., a retired neurosurgeon and president of Boston's Center for Memory Impairment and Neuro-Behavior Disorders, recommends getting the levels of each of the B vitamins listed in the above table.

• Hold back on carbohydrates. Carbohydrates are what you need to eat if you're a guy who wants to lift heavy objects. Carbohydrates are what you need to avoid, however, if you want to be the guy smart enough to decide which heavy objects the carbo-eaters ought to lift. A meal that's overly loaded with carbohydrates can mean trouble for the brain. In fact, in a Harvard study, people who ate sherbet, which is almost pure carbohydrate, had up to twice the difficulty concentrating and performing mental tasks as those who had eaten turkey, which is practically carbo-less.

So, if you want to stay smart all the way through lunch, eat the protein food before you eat the carbo food. "If you're at a business luncheon and you want to keep your mental edge, it's a mistake to fill up on rolls while waiting for your entrée," says Judith Wurtman, Ph.D., a nutrition researcher in the Department of Brain and Cognitive Science at Massachusetts Institute of Technology in Boston and the author of *Managing Your Mind and Mood through Food.*

• Eat less, think more. Graze, don't feast. Feasting causes a drop in energy because it shunts blood to the digestive tract, instead of your brain. Try to eat several small clever meals a day, instead of three big stupid ones.

Smell smart. Certain fragrances might make it easier for you to think more clearly and cut down on mistakes. "You can change brain frequencies with smell," says Alan Hirsch, M.D., a neurologist who heads the aromatically named Smell and Taste Treatment and Research Foundation in Chicago.

Japanese researchers discovered that air scented with a lemon spray decreased errors among workers by 54 percent. Jasmine cut goofs by 33 percent. Lavender? 20 percent. According to Dr. Hirsch, lavender induces a more relaxed state so you can think more clearly. Jasmine has the ability to excite—even in concentrations so low you wouldn't know it's there—resulting in quicker thinking. And other odors, such as baby powder, can trigger good memories of childhood, bringing forth feelings of happiness and security.

Meanwhile, researchers at the Monell Chemical Senses Center in Philadelphia discovered that customers stay at store counters longer—increasing sales potential—when there's an aroma of fresh flowers in the air.

Use your head. Your brain is like that other use-it-or-lose-it organ. If you neglect it, it gets permanently soft. Smart guys solve crosswords, read theology or talk to their wives about money just to give the old noodle a workout.

Hard thinking causes neural circuits to flash into action. Suddenly, capillaries expand, neurotransmitters zip back and forth and blood flow increases. The result? A brain that stays younger longer, says Nancy Wadsworth Denney, Ph.D., professor of psychology at the University of Wisconsin at Madison. And your ability to handle complex issues—things that involve both reasoning and remembering—can remain strong years longer than if you weren't mentally active.

Curious researchers at the University of California, Los Angeles, Brain Research Institute, examining the brains of 20 dead adults, found that gray matter from college grads who remained mentally stimulated throughout life had significantly longer dendrites—the branchlike parts of nerve cells that bring in information and help promote sophisticated processing—than the brains of people who had less than a high-school education.

Here are some things you can do to beef up the brainpower.

• Make new connections. Longer dendrites mean a greater surface for synaptic connections. The longer your dendrites, the more possibilities open for you. Also with longer dendrites, you get glial cells, which nourish and support neurons and are known to increase in number with learning and experience. Smart guys can make their noggins into big, lush, wet glial plantations—with dendrites like wild capellini—by doing something they've never done before, brain-wise, such as learning Portuguese or figuring out what it is that women want.

• Hang out with Einsteins. Get this: In the early 1980s, University of California, Berkeley, researchers looking into the egghead of well-known thinkperson Albert Einstein discovered the goofy-haired genius had longer dendrites in his brain than normal, less relativistic guys. You can lengthen your dendrites, the scientists concluded. The number one fertilizer, they say, is hanging out with guys smarter than yourself.

Watch the clock. If you want to use your smarts, use them while they're hot. For most of us, that means midmorning meetings and early lunches. Every day, you wake up dumb, then get smarter and smarter until around noon. Then it's downhill to dumb again, which strikes most of us sometime in the late afternoon. Then you make a slight intellectual recovery. But around 10:00 or so, you're on the slippery slope to idiocy again, until you slide into the nightly coma and end the ride.

Improving Your Memory

Having a supercharged brain is better than having a super-charged laptop. You can play games with it and use it to balance your checkbook, plus it impresses women. Like a computer, though, your brain is worthless without memory. Here's what to do about that.

Dream on. Dreaming helps you hold onto new information, say researchers at the Israel Weizmann Institute of Science. The best sleep for learning is uninterrupted sleep. Research shows that people won't remember very well a task they learned if they're awakened during REM sleep, a period of deep sleep characterized by intense dreaming and brain activity.

Remember what you learn. Simply relaxing can significantly enhance your ability to learn something, report researchers at Stanford University School of Medicine. In a small study, when members of one group were taught to relax every muscle in their bodies from head to toe before a three-hour memory-training course, they were able to remember 25 percent more than the groups that had not been trained to relax.

Remembering Names

Sometimes when you meet people, you're so busy trying to impress them or struggling to keep the conversation that their name breezes right by you. The key to remembering a name?
- Concentrate on the person you're meeting.
- Play around with the name for a moment in your mind.
- Say it at least once to yourself.

You need to rehearse the name in what's called a distributed fashion, says Douglas J. Herrmann, Ph.D., a memory expert at the University of Maryland University College in College Park and author of *Supermemory* and *Memory from a Broader Perspective.* To do this, repeat the name to yourself a few times, waiting an extra second each time you repeat it, until there's four or five seconds between repetitions. "If you say a name quickly, it never enters your conscious mind," Dr. Herrmann says. Example: You're introduced to Jim Bozo. Say "Bozo" softly to yourself until you have it.

Remembering Important Events

Memories aren't always carbon copies of events, says Elizabeth Loftus, Ph.D., author of *The Myth of Repressed Memory* and a researcher at the University of Washington in Seattle who has studied eyewitness accounts of everything from murder to revolution. In fact, your mind is in a constant editing mode, changing the original memory so that it reflects newly acquired facts. "This is why one person's view of a particular incident may be quite different from someone else's, even if it happened just seconds ago," says Dr. Loftus.

To ensure you remember something exactly as it happened, Dr. Loftus suggests writing it down in detail immediately afterward. Then review it—aloud, if necessary. This records the memory while it's fresh, reinforces the memory by freezing it in place, and provides you with an opportunity to review what really happened so the original memory doesn't fade or get distorted.

Remembering What You Read

Remember the last time you read a book? Remember how five minutes after you put it down you couldn't remember anything in it? You have a recall problem bigger than General Motors's worst nightmare. Here are ways to retain what you read.

Get the big picture. Use the table of contents to map the book and quickly find what you want to read. Skim through the index and look for things you already know a little something about, and flip to the parts of the book where they're discussed. Read the introduction or preface.

Skip it. Feel perfectly comfortable skipping the parts that don't really look interesting. Your interest is dictated by what you need to know. If it doesn't intrigue you, you don't need to learn it.

Reduce the book or article to about six key terms. Try to visualize the key players and events, and analyze the relationships among them. Ask yourself questions about what's in the article. In a novel, imagine yourself in the scene as one of the characters, dealing with the problems before him.

Write it down. "What you write down isn't as important as the act of writing," says Dr. Herrmann. "You can throw notes away or never refer to them again and you'll still be much better off than if you didn't write them at all."

Thinking More Effectively

The brain is capable of doing a lot more than we ask of it. Here are some ways to shift your noggin into higher gear.

Learn to do two things at once. There is no Jerry Ford clinic. If there were, it would be devoted to helping guys do two things at once. One of the easiest ways to learn how to do so without dividing your attention, Dr. Herrmann says, is to put two TVs next to each other, tune them to different channels and try to listen to both at once. "See how much information you can absorb from each, and try not to miss a thing," he says.

Once you're able to do this well, you can use the TVs to learn how to resist distractions. For this, instead of trying to take in everything from both TVs, concentrate on one program and ignore the other. It'll be hard at first, but stay with it. When you think you've mastered it, try lowering the volume on the set you're watching and raising it on the one you're not. If it doesn't drive you crazy first, this technique is guaranteed to teach you how to pay attention effectively. The downside is that you have two TV sets going and nothing worth watching on either one.

Become an expert. If you want to prove yourself invaluable, try to become an expert on something. Keep it in the ballpark, though. If you're working in shipping, don't try to study neurosurgery at home in your spare time.

A little expertise is a great thing. "What guys should know is that people in their office who are really on top of the facts on the job or other pursuits, like sports, go home and study," says Dr. Herrmann. "They wouldn't admit it, but they do."

If you want to be at the front of the pack, do your homework. Spend a half-hour going over some aspect of your job—or, if you're angling for a move, someone else's job. It takes very little effort to get a leg up on other guys who don't take the time to increase their worth as an employee.

Try home school. You can give yourself a tremendously wide liberal arts education by focusing on the one thing that interests you most—say, sex or canoeing—and slowly but tirelessly learning everything there is to know about the subject. The history of the world can be told in canoes or in fellatio. One thing leads to another, and if you follow each and every lead, pretty soon you'll know all there is to know.

"Once you get a good grasp, knowledge builds. What you already know helps you take the next step. At the foundation, the main areas must be history, English, math and science. Once you understand them pretty well, everything builds on itself and comes together," says E. D. Hirsch, Jr., compiler of *The Dictionary of Cultural Literacy*.

Write right. To get your point across better on paper, have a conversation with yourself. Read everything you write out loud. Does it sound natural and unforced? Are there a lot of little pet ideas and cute phrases that you've allowed to get in the way of the main idea?

Writing is speaking in slow motion. You have plenty of time to get it right. If you read aloud what you write, not only will your level of erudition improve, but your sentences and paragraphs will be better formed—and so will your ideas.

Speed read. Most of us read at a snail's pace, according to speed-reading expert Kim Johnson, coordinator for Evelyn Wood Reading Dynamics Programs. "Most people read 254 words per minute—about one-fifth of our potential. If you remember a few important tips, you can get yourself to between 1,000 and 1,500 words per minute within four weeks," says Johnson. "It's just a matter of conditioning." Here's how.

- Preview what you're going to read. Look at the titles, sub-heads or anything that's in italic or boldface. "Authors do this because they want you to remember," says Johnson. "It helps you subconsciously pick up on ideas, concepts and other important information."
- Use your hand as a pacer to underline what you're reading and to keep you moving rapidly through the material. "It's a concentration tool," says Johnson. "It keeps you focused on what you're reading, which means you'll retain more."
- Read groups of words. Words are meant to trigger thoughts. Hearing everything in your head—as opposed to just seeing it—can actually slow your thinking. "We're taught that in order to comprehend what we read we have to read every-thing word for word," says Johnson. "It's not necessary. You can read groups of words and get just as much out of it, in less time, without sacrificing tone or style." Start reading words in groups of twos and threes, and increase the num-ber as your skill improves.
- Read vertically. Left-to-right eye movement wastes a lot of time and causes you to read everything, most of which isn't all that important. By keeping your left-to-right eye move-ment at a minimum as you go down the page, your eye can take in swaths of up to 3,500 words a minute.

Spot a good idea. Ideas come and go all the time. Even the least imaginative among us has more good ideas than he can use. How to spot a good one? Easy. All ideas are good ideas, at least to some-body. The difference between a good idea and a bad idea to you, however, is that you know it's a good idea if you can believe in it so thoroughly that you can make others believe in it, too.

Capture fleeting ideas. Creative people are always receptive to fleeting ideas, and that may be the only difference between us and them. As the poet Amy Lowell wrote of the urgency with which she captured new ideas: "Whatever I am doing, I lay it aside and attend to the arriving poem." A poem for Lowell, a marketing plan for you. Either way, with a pocket computer, a napkin or a note on the back of your hand—just get it down.

But don't force it. Sometimes, you have to coax an idea into reality. That takes a lot of time. "A blinding flash of light doesn't hit me and I just sit down and write great stuff," says humor columnist Dave Barry. "I think what makes my writing funny is that I distill it. I'll interrupt myself a hundred times a day to eat, clip my toenails and pick my teeth."

If things aren't working, put off your writing for another day: "It's amazing how much easier things are the next morning," says Barry.

Take the sound track to smart. Researchers at the University of California, Irvine, plugged 36 college students into a recording of Mozart's "Sonata for Two Pianos," then gave them an IQ test measuring abstract reasoning. Results: The students scored eight or nine points higher than those who listened to nothing.

According to Frances H. Rauscher, Ph.D., a research psychologist in Irvine, California, who specializes in the effects of music on intelligence, "Listening to a complex and highly patterned piece of music acts as a 'warm-up' for the mind, which could be good for high-level mathematics, navigation, architecture or playing Tetris."

—David Zinczenko

Higher
Education

A Guide to Learning the Unexpected

You've heard it before: Never stop learning. But education should be fun, and sometimes the best lessons learned are the ones that get your heart beating the hardest.

So wake up your body and mind by enrolling in one or more of the camps and workshops that are listed below. You can "study" everything from windsurfing to creative writing, from umpiring to aerial dogfighting. There are even courses in beer drinking and machine gunning (although it's illegal to double major).

We've spoken to every one of the featured camps, and unless otherwise noted, the prices given are per person and don't include transportation. Free brochures are available from all the organizers upon request. And here's the kicker: Little or no experience is required for most of them.

Hard to believe someone would let you—Mr. Thumbs—race a $25,000 Indy car at 100 miles per hour, but that's the joy of liability insurance. Have fun!

Acting

Okay, so you've mastered acting stupid and you want to move on to bigger things. The International Film and Television Workshops in Rockport, Maine, offer a $500 one-week course in acting for corporate videos, commercials and feature films. Go get 'em, Humphrey. Call (207) 236-8581.

Auto Racing

Here's how to do everything you've ever wanted on your commute to work. Except you'll have detailed instruction, a safer environment, plenty more horsepower to horse around and no police to give you a speeding ticket. Try Bertil Roos Grand Prix Racing School in Blakeslee, Pennsylvania, 1-800-722-3669. Others include Buck Baker Racing Schools in North Carolina, Georgia and Virginia, (704) 366-6224, with one- to three-day instruction in Winston Cup stock cars; Skip Barber Racing School, based near Lime Rock Park, Connecticut, with 20 locations nationwide offering courses in competition or performance driving, (203) 435-1300; and Pitaressi ProDrive in Portland, Oregon, (503) 285-4449.

Bagpiping

There aren't too many occasions for which a man needs to don a skirt, but you won't want to miss this opportunity. Here's just the ticket when you get the urge: North American Academy of Piping, with summer sessions in North Carolina and Maryland, (803) 884-5155. Also Balmoral Schools of Piping and Drumming, with classes in Pennsylvania, Kentucky and Washington State, (412) 323-2707.

Barefoot Waterskiing

Finally, a way to get rid of those damned corns. One day for $100 and one week for $450 for beginner workshops offered by Walkin' on Water in West Palm Beach, Florida, (407) 762-0955.

Beer Drinking

The cure for what ales you. Sample 200 varieties of beer and participate in brewing seminars at the Oldenberg Brewery in Fort Mitchell, Kentucky. The $395 weekend is capped by a beer banquet in which all the food is prepared with suds. Leave with a T-shirt and your own personal beer gut. Call (606) 341-2802.

Bike Repairing

Learn, once and for all, how to adjust the doohickey with a thingamabob. A one-week fundamentals class costs $475 from the Barnett Bicycle Institute in Colorado, (719) 632-5173.

Birding

Go in search of the Giant Coua, a member of the cuckoo family. Or sneak up on the Wonga Pigeon and pray that it uncovers its underwing. Field Guides offers nearly 80 birding trips, from $445 weekends in Maine to $8,000 Antarctic cruises. Call 1-800-728-4953.

Captaining a Ship

Take the tiller of a diesel-powered Lockmaster and guide it through the Erie Canal in New York or the Okeechobee Waterway in Florida. But watch out for that giant carp! One-week rentals range from $1,200 to $2,000. Boat sleeps four. Mid-Lakes Navigation Company, 1-800-545-4318.

Cattle Driving

Sleep under the stars, eat out of a chuck wagon, relive the famous campfire scene from *Blazing Saddles*. Cost: $1,200. High Island Ranch and Cattle Company in Wyoming, (205) 383-0000 September through May; (307) 867-2374 June, July and August.

Caving

Seven days of spectacular spelunking in Kentucky's Mammoth Cave National Park. Workshops from $290 through Western Kentucky University, Center for Cave and Karst Studies, (502) 745-0111, ext. 3252.

Creative Writing

Whether you're a would-be poet, playwright or novelist, the annual Summer Writing Festival at the University of Iowa in Iowa City is considered the mecca of wordsmithery. Tons of weekend ($150) and weeklong ($335 to $360) workshops featuring professional writers. No experience necessary; call (319) 335-2534.

Dinosaur Hunting

Become part of a scientific research team excavating a Jurassic watering hole at Rabbit Valley near Grand Junction, Colorado. Five days of amateur paleontology for $775. Other dino digs in Wyoming, Indonesia, Argentina, England, California and Mexico. Dinamation's Dinosaur Discovery Expeditions, 1-800-344-3466.

Dogfighting

We're not talking pit bulls here, either. These are military T-34A fighter-trainer aircraft equipped with laser machine guns that can make smoke pour realistically from an opponent's plane. A safety instructor helps you take the controls regardless of flying experience. Cost: $695 for a half-day mission over Atlanta with Sky Warriors, 1-800-759-2160.

Doing Just about Everything

If you're indecisive, here's the perfect trip. Road biking, indoor rock climbing, swimming, sailboarding, sea kayaking, in-line skating, tandem biking, hiking, playing tennis, trail running, urban walking, stretching, weight training, doing aerobics, mountain biking, doing isometrics, water biking and practicing yoga. That's Backroads' five-day, $1,600 "Go Active Sports Sampler," held in the San Francisco Bay area. Call 1-800-462-2848.

Filmmaking

If you saw any of the Ernest movies, you know how little talent it takes to be a successful filmmaker. Maine Workshops' $1,100 weeklong course on the 16mm film camera will teach you the basics of zooming, panning, directing, editing and, perhaps (but don't get your hopes up), appreciating Oliver Stone. Call (207) 236-8581.

Fly Fishing

Doesn't matter if they're biting. It's just as fun. Orvis Fly Fishing Schools in Vermont and Colorado, 1-800-548-9548. Others include L. L. Bean, with introductory, parent/child, intermediate and saltwater programs in Maine, 1-800-341-4341, ext. 6666; the Complete Fly Fisher in Montana, (406) 832-3175; and Wulff School of Fly Fishing in New York City, (914) 439-4060.

Four-Wheeling

Rush hour on the interstate will seem like child's play once you've driven the Vermont woods in a Land Rover. One- to three-day courses from Rover North Off-Road, (802) 879-0032, start at $310. Hey! Did you see that bear just cut me off? Others include Rod Hall's Off-Road Driving School in Nevada, (702) 331-4800.

Golfing

Stop puttering around and learn how to play golf without losing a carton of balls and yelling "Fore!" till you're hoarse. Golf Digest Schools has three-day, $2,795 lessons at premier courses across the country that combine half-days of instruction with 54 holes with a pro; call 1-800-243-6121. Others include Arnold Palmer Golf Academy near Tampa, Florida, (813) 973-1111, ext. 4653; Ben Sutton Golf School in Sun City Center, Florida, 1-800-225-6923; and Chuck Hogan Golf Schools, 1-800-532-7686.

Hang Gliding

If you're too scared to do it yourself, then fly tandem with a pro. A weekend beginner package costs $199 at Lookout Mountain Flight Park in Georgia, 1-800-688-5637. Another school is Mission Soaring Center in Milpitas, California, (408) 262-1055.

JUST THE FACTS

Ninety-eight percent of the nation's one million volunteer municipal firefighters are male.

Kayaking

They say you don't ride a kayak, you wear it. Find out for yourself at these adventurous places: Riversport in Confluence, Pennsylvania, (814) 395-5744. Others include Otter Bar Lodge in Forks of Salmon, California, (916) 462-4772; Nantahala Outdoor Center in North Carolina, (704) 488-6737, with race training camps; Aqua Adventures in San Diego, (619) 695-1500; Kayak and Canoe Institute in Duluth, Minnesota, (218) 726-6533; and Sea Trek in Sausalito, California, offering ocean kayaking and moonlight paddles, (415) 488-1000.

Mountaineering

Master the fundamentals of alpine climbing with a six-day, $680 course on Washington's Mount Baker. If it really piques your interest, work toward the $64,000 Everest expedition. Call Alpine Ascents International, (206) 788-1951. Others include REI Adventures, with a seven-day Mount Rainier Climbing Seminar from $850, 1-800-622-2236; Exum Mountain Guides in Wyoming, (307) 733-2297; and Rainier Mountaineering, (206) 627-6242.

Pioneering

Yeehaw! GiddayuplildogieImchafing. Head west through Wyoming's beautiful Targhee National Forest with an authentic covered wagon train. Three-night treks for $595 from Bar-T-Five, 1-800-772-5386. Also Wagons West in Wyoming, 1-800-447-4711.

Playing Baseball

If you have the money ($1,700 plus), you can rub pinstripes for a week with the likes of Brooks Robinson and Rollie Fingers in a variety of "Dream Camps" licensed by major-league ball clubs. Major Sport Fantasies, 1-800-226-7794, organizes a number of them, or call your favorite team. If you can't afford to go, just pretend you're at strike camp.

JUST THE FACTS

Number of miles running shoes generally last: 600

Playing Basketball

Become a weekend warrior at Don Nelson's Fantasy Basketball Camp. Instructors include coaches and players from the Golden State Warriors of California. Four days for $2,095 in northern California, 1-800-433-6060.

Playing Football

Take a handoff from Bart Starr, lead a power sweep with Jerry Kramer, get a pat on the butt from Fuzzy Thurston. It's all part of the Green Bay Experience, a $3,295 fantasy camp held at Lambeau Field, where fans can relive the Pack's glory days. The only thing missing is Vince Lombardi screaming at you. Call 1-800-945-7102.

Playing Tennis

John Newcombe's Tennis Ranch in the hill country of Texas serves up two-, three- and five-day camps for $200 to $875. Ace instructors will have you serving better than a Four Seasons waiter. Call 1-800-444-6204. Others include Harry Hopman Tennis Academy in Wesley Chapel, Florida, 1-800-729-8383; Naples Bath and Tennis Academy in Florida, 1-800-225-9692; and Swarthmore Adult Tennis Camp in Pennsylvania, (212) 879-0225.

Road Biking

Olympic gold medalist Connie Carpenter and Tour de France stage winner Davis Phinney promise to turn you into a big wheel. Five days of coaching at Carpenter-Phinney Bike Camp in Colorado costs $1,133, including lodging and meals, (303) 442-2371. Others include John Howard's School of Champions, (619) 944-3787; and Walden School of Cycling, (810) 652-0511.

Rock Climbing

If you have yet to find a career toehold, there's still hope. Go to Red Rock, Nevada (just 20 minutes from Vegas), and scale some "desert-varnished Aztec sandstone." Beginners' weekends from $180. Sky's the Limit, (702) 363-4533. Others include International Mountain Climbing School, (603) 356-7013; and Jackson Hole Mountain Guides and Climbing School, (307) 733-4979.

Rodeo Riding

This is no mechanical barroom bronc. This is a living, breathing, angry animal with a kick more devastating than a Colt .45. But you'll learn to ride 'em—at least for a millisecond. Monty Henson Rodeo Schools in New Mexico and Louisiana. About $300 for three days; call (505) 862-8704.

Sailing

Become a sailor in one weekend for $225. The country's oldest and largest sailing academy in Annapolis, Maryland, guarantees it. Black wool turtlenecks and pipes optional. Annapolis Sailing School, 1-800-638-9192. Others include J World the Performance Sailing School, 1-800-343-2255.

Scuba Diving

Swim with the fishes in the world's very own aquarium. Try Dive In! on St. Thomas, 1-800-524-2090. Or for a free list of dive centers and resorts in a particular area, call the Professional Association of Diving Instructors, 1-800-729-7234. Others include Southpoint Divers in Key West, Florida, 1-800-824-6811.

Shooting

How about a gift certificate to Gun Camp? Pick from courses such as General Pistol, General Rifle, Tactical Shotgun or, our favorite, Submachine Gun. Most last 5½ days and cost $700. Proof of good character required. Gunsite Training Center in Paulden, Arizona, (602) 636-4565.

Skydiving

Chute yourself for $125 at the Horizon Skydiving School in Kansas City, Missouri, (816) 923-7006. Others include Skydive Monroe in Georgia, (404) 207-9164; and Skydive Dallas, (903) 364-5103.

JUST THE FACTS

Percentage of men surveyed who say they love their cars more than their women: 38

Speaking Foreign Languages

Forget about that nasty episode of high school Latin with Sister Cigarlips. Here's a fast, fun way to learn a language. Overseas "immersion classes" in Spain, Italy, France, Germany, Russia, Switzerland and Japan start at around $627 for two weeks. Eurocentres, 1-800-648-4809.

Stuffing Dead Animals

Now, wouldn't a stuffed beaver look good on that end table? If you agree, get on over to Storey's School of Taxidermy in Spencer, Iowa. In one week ($700, including dead animal and accommodations), they'll teach you how to bring him back to life—or a reasonable facsimile thereof. Two-week courses for fish; six weeks if you want to make a living doing this. Call (712) 262-6441.

Surviving

Learn primitive skills such as food gathering and fire- and tool-making, then go solo in the Utah desert. We're talking serious character building. Seven-day "Walkabouts" cost $575 with Boulder Outdoor Survival School, (602) 779-6000.

Taking Pictures

Picture yourself on a hunt for tufted puffins, polar bears, bald eagles, wild wolves or even tigers. Joseph Van Os Photo Safaris teams you with a pro photographer in some of the world's most exotic landscapes. If your shutter tends to flutter, stay in California and shoot trained animals like the MGM lion during a five-day, $2,700 Wildlife Models Photo Shoot, (206) 463-5383. Others include Voyagers International, (607) 257-3091, with 15-day photo safaris in East Africa; and Maine Photographic Workshops, (207) 236-8581.

Umpiring

For some strange reason, nothing is more satisfying than bending your knees, twisting your hips, crooking your thumb and screaming, at the top of your lungs, "Yer out!" Try it. Ron Luciano Umpire Camp, $950 for one week at various U.S. locations, 1-800-226-7794.

Windsurfing

Skitter across the ocean at one of the best places for windsurfing in the world, Maui's Kanaha Beach Park. Package rates from $220 through Hawaiian Sailboarding Techniques, (808) 871-5423. Another good one: the Sailboard Center School in Florida, 1-800-253-6573.

—Joe Kita

PART 10

Ask *Men's* Health

TOP TEN

Male-Related Topics on Recent Talk-Show TV

For sheer lurid entertainment, it's hard to beat daytime talk shows. There's not much talk on them anymore, but there's plenty of screaming. And laughing. And crying. And finger-pointing. Here's our list of trendy, kinky and just plain bizarre male-oriented topics that—believe it or not—actually made it onto the airwaves.

1. "Secret Admirers"—Jenny Jones

2. "I Love Someone I Can't Have"—Jerry Springer

3. "Women Who Are Turned On by Blue-Collar Men"—Ricki Lake

4. "Why Men Marry Prostitutes"—Geraldo Rivera

5. "Women Bikers"—Montel Williams

6. "Men Who Won't Commit to Women"—Geraldo Rivera

7. "Men Who Can't Pick Up Women"—Ricki Lake

8. "Lascivious Teen Dancers"—Bertice Berry

9. "Men Who Promise to Call and Don't"—Bertice Berry

10. "Women Who Married Men in the Mafia"—Geraldo Rivera

Ask Men's Health

Answers to Your Top 20 Questions

Banishing Unsightly Ear Hair

Q I'm embarrassed to say this, but I'm starting to sprout hair out of my ears. I want to get rid of it, but have heard that trimming only makes it worse. True?

—*R. J., West Lafayette, Indiana*

A Not true. "It will grow back, but it absolutely will not grow back thicker," says John Romano, M.D., a dermatologist with New York Hospital–Cornell Medical Center in New York City.

To take care of unwanted ear hair simply add a small procedure to your shaving ritual. Just moisten the ear when you're shaving and gently work your way around the earlobe. Do not try to snip off the hair with scissors. "Most people who use scissors end up cutting themselves," says Dr. Romano.

Another option is electrolysis, a procedure that'll run you about $50. A certified electrologist will destroy the hair roots by zapping them with a series of electric currents. While this does rid you of unwanted hair for good, it's painful and can leave scars.

Eating and Exercising

Q If you're trying to lose weight, is it better to eat before or after you exercise?

—*J. H., Enfield, Connecticut*

A It depends on the type of exercise you're doing to shed the pounds. If you prefer light-to-moderate activity, such as walking or recreational cycling, it's probably better to eat before. Ten percent of the calories you eat are burned simply through the process of digestion—that's called the thermic effect of food. "By exercising within the first half-hour after a meal, you can actually boost that thermic effect and burn 15 percent more calories," says Bryant Stamford, Ph.D., director of the Health Promotion and Wellness Center at the University of Louisville School of Medicine.

Eating first isn't a good strategy, though, if you lift weights, run or do another type of training that calls for greater exertion. Strenuous exercise requires extra blood flow to your extremities, while digestion requires extra blood flow to your innards. Your circulatory system's equipped for only one or the other. Do both and you'll get nauseated—a self-defense tactic the body uses to prevent strain on the heart. At this point, either you're going to stop exercising, or you're going to stop digesting. We'd suggest the former.

Taming Trash Talk

Q Three days a week I play touch football at the local YMCA. Problem is, one of the men I often play against uses verbal jabs to get under my skin and take me out of my game. I try to talk trash back, but frankly, this guy's just plain better at it. Is there anything else I can do to rid myself of this menace? He knows the tactic's working, so I doubt he'll quit any time soon.

—*J. I., Princeton, New Jersey*

A Next time your nemesis starts razzing you about your dropped pass or questioning the sexual proclivities of your ancestors, don't try to match wits with him. That's playing into his hands. Instead, take some tips from U.S. Olympic Committee sports psychologist Sean McCann, Ph.D.

• Visualize the problem ahead of time. Take a minute before the game to imagine your opponent saying things you know would tick you off. If you can picture yourself performing well during the heckling, you're more likely to do so when you get on the field.

• Use a cue to regain control. Lots of pro athletes use this technique. When the ribbing starts, snap your fingers, touch your belt buckle, tug your ear—create some physical cue to remind yourself to focus on your game.

• Stick to your game plan. When somebody ticks you off, you'll naturally want to show him up. That can make you start trying to do too much—and ignoring the fundamentals. The result: dropped passes and fumbles. Instead, concentrate on, say, catching the ball with your hands and tucking it away just like they taught in Pop Warner.

Finally, remember that in a sense, he's giving you the edge. If he's spending time thinking up jokes about your relatives, he doesn't have as much time to concentrate on his game, says Dr. McCann. "If you don't fall into his trap and respond, it will start negatively affecting his game, and he'll be easier to beat."

Walking versus Running

Q I was pretty much out of shape and decided to take up running, which I used to do ten years ago. My girlfriend says speed walking is just as good but easier on the body. What's the deal?

—E. O., Dallas

A We'll go with your girlfriend's advice, particularly since you told us you're just getting back into training. Speed walking—by which we mean walking as briskly as possible without breaking into a jog—offers a couple of advantages over running. The most important of these is that it's less demanding. Half the battle in starting or restarting a shape-up plan is simply hanging on for the first four weeks when exercise doesn't feel very good. That's not always easy. "Too many people push themselves too hard out of the starting gate and end up quitting their programs," says Wayne Westcott, Ph.D., *Men's Health* magazine adviser and the YMCA's national strength-training consultant. In this critical early period, 25 percent of people get discouraged and hang up their sneakers for good.

We understand wanting to run; it burns calories at approximately 1½ times the rate of speed walking, but speed walking (eschew the 1980s term *powerwalking,* by the way) does burn calories faster than regular walking—about 50 percent faster.

An additional benefit of speed walking accrues to the knees. During a run, the precious joint absorbs roughly three to four times a person's body weight with each step. "With speed walking, you never have both feet off the ground," says Dr. Westcott.

A note on form: You should land on your heel, roll on the outside edges of your foot and push off with your toes. Keep your elbows bent so your movements are fluid. We know what you're thinking, but you won't look like a duck if you concentrate on proper form and don't exaggerate your upper body movements. In the meantime, you might want to practice after dark.

Helping Your Wife Climax

QRecently my wife of six years admitted to me that she has never had an orgasm during intercourse. She climaxes in other types of sex, and says she enjoys intercourse even though she doesn't reach orgasm. But I can't help feeling I'm doing something wrong.

—*T. A., Knoxville, Tennessee*

AYour situation is not as unusual as you may think. According to sex researchers Masters and Johnson, one out of every five women has never reached orgasm during intercourse. In some cases the underlying problem is anatomical or psychological. But if your wife is already experiencing orgasm during other forms of sex, chances are high that the same can be achieved during intercourse. The only missing ingredient is some rather precise communication about the hows, whats and wheres.

"The only way you're going to know what works is by having her tell you," says Judith Seifer, R.N., Ph.D., president of the American Association of Sex Educators, Counselors and Therapists. "You can't know by yourself, since everyone's needs are different."

The fact that she's already opened up to you about not having an orgasm during intercourse is the first and, some say, the toughest step. The next step, as unspontaneous as it may sound, is to rendezvous outside of the bedroom and discuss what she'd like to do differently. If talking about it is uncomfortable, pick up a good sex manual and let her point to what looks about right.

Then stop worrying. It's her body, her orgasm. Ultimately this is not a reflection on your manhood, even though that's probably what you're thinking. You can do no more than offer to be of assistance.

Avoiding Overtraining

Q I've been working out quite regularly, and lately my muscles have been getting sore. Is this because my workouts are working or because I'm overtraining?

—*N. L., Windsor, Ontario*

A Muscle soreness comes in different varieties. There's the mild burning sensation you get after a workout that is your body's way of saying "Roger on the lactic-acid buildup and muscle fatigue. Job well-done." But if your soreness consistently comes in the boy-do-I-ache-for-two-days-after variety, you're probably overdoing it.

"Soreness that lingers for more than a day or two indicates excessive damage to the muscle," says Priscilla Clarkson, Ph.D., professor of exercise science at the University of Massachusetts in Amherst. She explains that while some strain on the muscle fibers is necessary to muscle growth, overdoing it will actually impede your progress. "If you are going back into the gym still sore from the last workout, you aren't giving your muscles the recuperative time they need to rebuild and grow."

Other telltale warning signs of overtraining include general fatigue, loss of appetite, depression or a "plateauing" in your workouts—meaning you can't add any more weight or repetitions. Constant pain coupled with any of these signs is a sure cue to scale back your routine to something slightly less than superhuman.

Preventing Thinning Hair

Q Is there anything I can do to keep my hair from thinning? I have a full head of hair now, but I want to take some preventive measures to make sure it doesn't happen later.

—*C. H., Asheville, North Carolina*

A When Thomas Jefferson wrote that all men are created equal, he was probably wearing a wig. Today, with no indication of a powdered-hairpiece revival on the horizon, our genetic weaknesses aren't as easily hidden. You're either going to wind up a bald guy or you're not, and there's very little you can do about it, says Philip Kingsley, founder of the Philip Kingsley Trichological Center in New York City and author of _The Complete Hair Book_.

The good news: Make it to 35 without signs of thinning and you have a pretty good shot of going to your grave with a decent head of hair. According to experts, the most profound thinning of hair starts when you're in your twenties. If relatives on both sides of your family kept their hair late into life, that's another good sign.

While there's nothing we can do to prevent hair from falling out, here are a few tactics that may help your situation.

• Wash your hair every day. Contrary to popular belief, washing won't speed the fallout. Feel free to lather up.

• Give yourself a scalp massage every day. Kneading your scalp with the pads of your fingers for a few minutes sends extra blood to the scalp tissues. This helps increase the flow of nutrients, oxygen and hormones to the hair follicles and keeps them healthy, says Kingsley.

• Don't comb your hair with a bristle brush when wet. This tugs at the hair and causes it to fall out more quickly. Use a wide-toothed comb or plastic brush with soft, widely spaced bristles instead.

• Stay away from greasy gels. Gels make your hair clump together, exposing more of your scalp. Light hairspray is a better option for men who are starting to look a little light-headed.

Working Out with a Cold

Q I've heard that exercising while you have a cold is fine, as long as there's no fever or soreness. Is this true?

—_R. C., Austin, Texas_

A The best answer for a bout with the common cold is a dose of common sense. Exercising while under the weather won't hurt you so long as you're not planning to run a marathon or set a new bench-pressing record. "If you have just a cold—runny nose, sore throat, the usual—then it's okay to engage in moderate activity," says David Nieman, Dr.P.H., professor of health promotion at Appalachian State University in Boone, North Carolina. Breaking a sweat might even help lift your spirits and make you feel better.

On the other hand, a bad case of the flu is a different story altogether. If your lungs are congested, you're running a fever or you experience aches throughout your body, head for bed. Extreme exertion at a time like this won't do you any good and could make you a good deal sicker.

The Effect of Smoke on Sperm

Q My wife and I have decided to start a family, but I'm a little concerned. I gave up smoking about six months ago, but before that I smoked more than a pack a day for 12 years. Now I read that smoking can damage a man's sperm. Since I've quit, am I safe? Or is the damage permanent?

—E. W., Sheridan, Oregon

A Lucky for you, the male body is a veritable gamete Kmart, moving stock off the shelves and out the door faster than you can say "blue-light special." The sperm you produced when you were smoking is long gone, replaced by healthy, toxin-free wrigglers ready for action. "Once a man has ceased smoking and gone through one full cycle of sperm production, roughly two months, the newly developed sperm should be free of chemicals," says Donald Mattison, M.D., dean of the School of Public Health at the University of Pittsburgh. As long as you stay away from cigarettes from now on, you're in the clear.

That's good news, especially in light of what smoking can do, not only to a man's health but to that of his kids as well. Some studies indicate that men who smoke double their chances of having offspring with certain birth defects such as hydrocephalus (a potentially fatal buildup of fluid in the brain).

Their children are also at increased risk of developing certain cancers such as lymphoma and leukemia. On top of that is the fact that smokers expose their children and pregnant spouses to toxic secondhand smoke. Bottom line: If you're planning to be a dad, don't be a drag.

Maintaining Healthy Fat Intake

QMagazines say that a healthy diet should get no more than 30 percent of calories from fat. Does that mean I should never touch foods that go over the limit?

—I. W., Red Bank, New Jersey

AAbsolutely not. What they're referring to is an across-the-board average. Say you're eating 2,500 calories a day, about average for an active 175-pound man. That means no more than about 800 calories, or 89 grams' worth, should come from fat. Now, you can keep to this limit by following either of two different routes: (1) Eat nothing that's above 30 percent fat all day long, which isn't practical. (A typical cut of steak gets 40 percent of its calories from fat.) (2) Eat whatever you want as long as you eat less than 89 grams of fat each day. For example, you could conceivably blow nearly half your daily fat allotment at a single sitting by consuming a cheeseburger or two slices of Supreme Pan Pizza from Pizza Hut, and then still keep your day's total to less than 89 grams of fat by sticking to low-fat fare for the rest of your meals.

Importantly, though, even if every morsel you bring to your lips is less than 30 percent fat, you can still eat too much. Calories count, too: "A lot of people will eat a whole box of fat-free cookies, but what they don't realize is there's still a ton of calories in there," says Georgia Kostas, R.D., director of nutrition at the Cooper Clinic in Dallas and author of *The Balancing Act Nutrition and Weight Guide.* "Eventually, those excess calories turn to fat."

Choosing Your Child's Gender

QMy wife and I have two beautiful daughters and will be trying for a third child soon. What can we do to increase our chances of having a boy?

—R. S., Wayne, New Jersey

A few centuries ago, heirless French noblemen sacrificed their left testicles to have a boy, the idea being that the left begot girls. (It didn't.) Since then, couples have concocted any number of home remedies, everything from making love under a full moon to calling football audibles during ejaculation. All harmless and equally ineffective. Basically, you have two options. First, you could let nature take its course—which, by the way, is not a bad idea, since your chances of having a boy naturally are 52 percent. Or you can enlist the aid of fertility specialists.

Here's what happens: You donate some sperm. They put it in a test tube filled with a dense liquid. The semen floats on top of the liquid, but some of the sperm—predominantly the male-bearing sperm—are strong enough to penetrate the liquid and reach the bottom of the tube. After a period of time, the semen on top is discarded and the remaining sperm are about 75 percent male. Your wife can then be artificially inseminated with this male-dominant group, which results in a 75 to 80 percent chance of her bearing a boy—that is, if she conceives at all.

And that's a big if. Many perfectly fertile couples fail to conceive a child until the second or third time with artificial insemination. At $600 to $800 per throw, this genealogical roulette game can get expensive. And in the end, you still might get a girl—not to mention that there's no actual sex involved in this whole procedure.

The Truth about the Male G-spot

Q Lately, I've heard that some men might have a G-spot similar to women's. I wouldn't mind knowing if I'm one of them. What's up with this?

—G. N., Dallas

A This whole fascination with the G-spot has its roots, as far as we can tell, in the fact that some women (some, not all) have a hard time reaching orgasm, so any help is usually welcome. The G-spot actually gets its name from Ernst Grafenberg, a German gynecologist who claimed there was a secret erotic hot spot on the "roof" of the vagina, about three to five inches in. He argued that this region was so erotically charged that pressing on it could produce orgasm completely independent of clitoral stimulation.

Is there a male equivalent? Actually, yes. Not just one, but two. (If women can have them, why can't we?) For educational purposes only, we turned to Dr. Seifer. The hottest spot of all, you probably won't be surprised to know, is the frenulum, that little ridge of skin running down the underside of the penis, just below the head. Here's why: This region contains bundles of sensitive nerve endings, more nerve endings per inch than any other area.

The other supersensitive spot is less obvious. In fact, it's not even on the penis. Instead, it's a small, soft dimple, about the size of a dime, tucked just underneath the scrotum. An adventurous partner can find the spot pretty easily, and should gently press on it or stroke it in an upward motion. "There are a series of muscle fibers and ligaments from the buttocks and the base of the pelvis that come together there, along with plenty of blood vessels and nerve endings that heighten sexual pleasure," says Dr. Seifer.

Fighting Acne after Adolescence

Q I am 32 and recently developed a bad case of acne that seems to get worse each time I wash my face. It dries out immediately afterward, then becomes more oily than before. I'm trying to cut down on fatty foods, but that doesn't seem to help. What can I do?

—*B. K., Northridge, California*

A That really stinks—a guy of your age getting acne. Just be glad your voice isn't cracking, too. Fatty, oily foods probably aren't your problem, says Joseph Bark, M.D., chief of dermatology at St. Joseph Hospital in Lexington, Kentucky. Instead, it has to do with genetics. "Acne tends to run in families," says Dr. Bark. "It's an inherited defect of the pores."

So, you probably have a tendency to sprout zits, but in male adult acne, there's often a hormonal trigger as well. In the thirties, men produce a higher level of a natural male hormone. This hormone has the side effect of stimulating the oil glands. Some guys weather this with no problem. Others break out.

As for foods: Fatty snacks and chocolate, or any of that other stuff your high-school buddies warned you about, won't cause a breakout. On the other hand, there is some evidence that iodine-rich foods—such as beef liver, clams, crabs and other shellfish— may aggravate acne, but you'd have to eat them in pretty large quantities to see any difference, Dr. Bark says.

Another likely culprit is stress, but taking a vacation won't solve your problem. It turns out that a blemish on your skin takes up to four weeks to form, so the problems with your mug today could be a reflection of last month's troubles.

How to handle the situation? Gently, says Dr. Bark. Use a mild soap. Special acne soaps may be too harsh and can irritate blemishes. Similarly, scrubbing too hard can stimulate oil production— which you need like Senator Packwood needs another sexual harassment charge. Once the skin is clean, follow up with an over-the-counter medication containing benzoyl peroxide (Oxy-5, Oxy-10). (Yeah, that stuff really does work.)

Spotting a Broken Finger

Q A few months ago I ran into a wall playing racquetball and hurt my finger. It's healed since then, but it still bothers me occasionally. I'm wondering if I broke it. My friend says if that were the case I wouldn't be able to move it. Is that true?

—*H. E., Colorado Springs, Colorado*

A Hardly. "That's been a misconception for hundreds of years," says Allan Levy, M.D., team physician for the National Football League New York Giants and author of the *Sports Injury Handbook.* "We see people come in all the time with what they think is a sprained ankle but what turns out to be a bad break." In fact, you can move all kinds of broken bones, especially if the two broken ends are jammed together. This creates what's called an impacted fracture, which stabilizes the bones while still allowing you to move them.

Although you might be able to notice a slight bend in your finger between the joints, the only way really to tell if you've broken a bone is to get an x-ray, something we highly urge, especially if you're still playing racquetball. Though it may be well enough to leave alone, if it has fused itself together improperly—that is, if it's twisted and can't straighten or bend properly—it may require that the doc rebreak and reset it. That's not a lot of fun.

Eating Late and Gaining Weight

Q I've gained 14 pounds in the last three years, and I suspect that part of the problem is that I'm eating so late. I generally get home from the office around 7:30 P.M. By the time I have a beer and rustle up something to eat, it's 8:30 or later. Are these late dinners the problem? And since my boss wouldn't approve of my cutting back my work hours, is there anything I can do to offset my late eating?

—*T. E., Montville, New Jersey*

A Those late meals may indeed be partly responsible for your weight gain. Studies of obese people show that most get more than half of their calories after 6:00 in the evening. The problem is that if you eat late, you're stockpiling fuel for the least active part of your day, the hours that you sleep. "Instead of being burned up as fuel, the food you eat before bed has more of a chance of going into storage," explains James O. Hill, Ph.D., an obesity researcher at the University of Colorado's Center for Human Nutrition in Denver.

If you exercise frequently or have a high-revving metabolism, nocturnal noshing isn't that big a deal. But if you spend most of your day at a desk only to come home and ride the couch, you may need to do a few of the following things to get rid of that paunch.

• Schedule snack times throughout the day. Eating a big dinner causes the body to produce excess insulin, a hormone that helps transport energy into storage (read: fat). But consuming a series of smaller meals—say, four or five throughout the day—keeps insulin levels low, meaning you'll burn calories more efficiently, even at night. And a hearty 5:00 snack will mean you'll have less of an appetite at dinnertime.

• Eat your bigger meals in the morning and afternoon. By consuming most of your calories before 2:00 P.M., you'll be fueling yourself for the most active part of the day.

• Get active before you eat dinner. Take a few minutes out for a light jog, a series of jumping jacks or some push-ups and stomach crunches. Research indicates that exercise suppresses the appetite, so you'll be less likely to pig out. Bonus: It increases the rate at which your body burns calories, even after you're done exercising.

Defining Extra-Lean Meat

Q My local supermarket carries various grades of ground meat, including one that's marked "extra lean." Sounds good. Is it?
—_T. M., Kent, Washington_

A Not nearly as good as it seems. "Even 'extra-lean' beef is pretty fat-laden," says Helen Seagle, R.D., research dietitian at the University of Colorado's Center for Human Nutrition. To be called extra-lean, ground meats can't contain more than 15 percent fat. Trouble is, that's fat by weight. The more useful way to measure food is by the percentage of calories contributed by fat. When calculated this way, that extra-lean beef gets about 53 percent of its calories from fat—well over the average of 30 percent recommended by the American Heart Association.

Most red meat, even the lean stuff, will come in over this amount. That's okay, say the experts, if you keep portions reasonable. Six ounces of red meat a day is acceptable as long as your overall food intake includes plenty of fruits, vegetables and grains. The association's recommendation is an average, so you can go below it and above it throughout the day.

Aspirin and Heart Attacks

Q If taking aspirin is good at preventing heart attacks, would I get the same clot-busting benefits from ibuprofen?
—_P. M., Beverly Hills, California_

A No, you wouldn't. As similar as aspirin and ibuprofen are when it comes to pain relief, aspirin is a much more effective blood thinner, and that's a key matter in heart health, explains Dan Fintel, M.D., chief of the coronary care unit at Northwestern Memorial Hospital in Chicago. This thinning of the blood is good for your heart because thicker blood is more likely to clot in your arteries—essentially, it'll gum up the works. Studies have shown that taking low-dose aspirin (81 to 160 milligrams) every day can provide you with long-term heart protection should your doctor decide that you're a proper candidate. Also, chewing one or two tablets at the first signs of a heart attack can cut the risks of a clot forming by half—and double your chances of surviving.

Since ibuprofen has shorter-term anti-clotting effects, it offers fewer of those heart benefits—though, don't mistake us, it's perfectly good as a pain reliever. Now, with all that said, if you discovered you were having a heart attack, and you could find no aspirin, taking ibuprofen is better than doing nothing, says Dr. Fintel. Then, don't delay. Get to a hospital.

Protecting Suit Jacket Pockets

Q Why do suit jackets and sport coats come with their pockets sewn shut?

—*R. K., New York City*

A To make the jacket look better until it finds a good home. "Imagine hundreds of men trying on the same jacket and all shoving their hands in the pockets," says New York City clothing expert Warren Christopher, style adviser for *Men's Health* magazine. "Stretches the material. Spoils the shape."

Christopher suggests you keep your hands out of suit jackets, even if you own them. "The best way to remember this is to leave the pockets sewn shut," says Christopher. Sewn-up pockets will discourage you from using your jacket as a storage bin for keys, matches, wallets and other bulky items. Instead of making your jacket function as a backpack, carry your essentials in a briefcase, exchange your wallet for a billfold or just try to travel a bit lighter.

The Mystery of Yogurt

Q Why is yogurt so nutritious? Also, why do some yogurts have a clear liquid on top? Does this mean it's going bad? And what are "live active yogurt cultures"?

—*T. G., Beacon Falls, Connecticut*

A Yogurt really is a big, mushy mystery, isn't it? First, let's start with the one question you didn't ask: Just what is yogurt, anyway? Basically, it's milk that has been curdled and fermented using two special bacteria. It's then warmed in an incubator for several hours, where it thickens and takes on its tart flavor.

The bacteria in yogurt aid digestion and may correct some common causes of diarrhea. Unfortunately, not all the cultures survive the heat pasteurization process that many companies put yogurt through. That brings us to your question about "live active yogurt cultures," one of the ingredients often found on the container's label. This means the above-described cultures are added again after pasteurization.

Even without the additional cultures, yogurt has plenty of other benefits. It's high in protein, calcium and vitamin B_{12}, while delivering little or no fat—if you go with the 1 percent or nonfat varieties—or cholesterol.

That liquid on top is just the watery part of milk that separates from the curd during the fermentation process. Mix it back in: It's high in minerals and vitamins.

Stretching before a Workout

Q I know I should stretch before my workout, but I only have an hour to get to the club, exercise, shower, dress and get back to work. Are there one or two basic stretches I can do to cover myself?

—*R. C., New Orleans*

A A little stretching is better than none. The exercise physiologists we spoke with agreed that if you have limited time to limber up, you should go for what's known as the figure four stretch. It'll work your calf muscles, hamstrings, hips, back and shoulders—all in one shot. Here's how to do it.

Sit on the floor with your right leg straight in front of you, toes pointing up. Bend your left knee to place your left heel against the inside of your right thigh, near your groin; keep your left knee almost touching the floor. Now reach out slowly with your right arm and touch your right toe. If you can't do it, try grabbing your ankle. Hold the position for 30 seconds, return to the start, then stretch toward your right toe for another 30 seconds. Repeat the stretch twice on the other leg.

If you have two more minutes to spare, toss in a lying side stretch. It's great for loosening the lower back, hips, hamstrings and obliques (the muscles that run down the sides of your torso). Lie on your back with your feet together and your arms straight out to the sides. Keeping your left leg fully extended on the floor, slowly lift your right leg until it's straight in the air; then, without bending your knee, rotate your right hip and try to touch your right foot to your left hand. Keep both hands on the floor. Hold this position for 30 seconds, return to the start, then repeat. Do the exercise again with the other leg.

CREDITS

The graph in "The Fat Index: How Much Is Lean, How Much Is Lard?" on page 71 is from *Sensible Fitness* (p. 30) by Jack H. Wilmore, Champaign, IL: Human Kinetics Publishers. Copyright © 1986 by Jack H. Wilmore. Reprinted by permission.

"Race, Health and You" on page 104 is adapted from "Your Heritage, Your Health" by Russell Wild. Copyright © 1995 by Russell Wild. Reprinted by permission.

"Basic Training for the Mating Game" on page 129 is adapted from "The Good Sex Workout" by Mark Roman. Copyright © 1994 by Mark Roman. Reprinted by permission.

"Sex Education from a Lady" on page 145 is adapted from "What Women Wish Men Knew about Sex" by Jen Sacks. Copyright © 1995 by Jen Sacks. Reprinted by permission.

"Smooth Operator" on page 159 is adapted from "Give Me Some Skin" by Guy Martin. Copyright © 1994 by Guy Martin. Reprinted by permission.

"Talking to Dad" on page 181 is adapted from "Pop Psychology" by Denis Boyles. Copyright © 1994 by Denis Boyles. Reprinted by permission.

"Sexual Harassment" on page 215 is adapted from "Work Ethics" by Chris Byron. Copyright © 1994 by Chris Byron. Reprinted by permission.

"Success in the Sales Game" on page 222 is adapted from "Birth of a Salesman" by Denis Boyles. Copyright © 1994 by Denis Boyles. Reprinted by permission.

"Ten Deadliest Office Sins" on page 228 is adapted from *Never Read a Newspaper at Your Desk* by Richard Stiegele. Copyright © 1994 by Richard Stiegele. Published by arrangement with Carol Publishing Group. A Citadel Press Book.

Index

Note: <u>Underscored</u> page references indicate boxed text. **Boldface** references indicate tables.